A River Of Memories From The Mountains And The 50's

Jack Burris

A River Of Memories From The Mountains And The 50's

Jack Burris

A very special thanks to all my friends and classmates at Pisgah Elementary and Erwin High. Especially Donna Worley for your incessant encouragement to publish a book. Thanks for the special memories of growing up with you all.

The folk written about in this memoir are real. Many of which are deceased. All that I mention have given permission to tell their stories. I thank each one for their input and friendship with all my heart.

The Biblical illustrations are my own thoughts and paraphrases.

For Mom and Dad who set the example for life,

And always kept the porch light on. For
  Laura who gave much. For Jeffrey, Gregory, Micheal
James and Lisa.   And for my kinfolk from
Shelton Laurel, The Chandleys and the Sheltons.
For my people from Marshall NC and South Ga.
For Jesse, Ashley, Sarah, Rachel, and Vince. For
 Jock and Karry , special friends. For Peggy who
 loved me. And for Gerri, who loves me now
 and saved my life.

I have traveled some of lifes many paths
I have walked many a mile with Miss Pleasure
She and I have talked and sung all the way
But being with Miss Pleasure has not made me any smarter
For all that she had to say...

But I have also walked and ran many a mile with Miss Sorrow
And Miss Sorrow has never said a word to me
Nor has she ever sung a song to me
But O Lordy the things I have learned from her
All the times when Miss Sorrow walked with me....

CONTENTS

Old Barns

The old barn has a story. I closed my eyes and could feel the barn 'talking' to me. It seemed to say: I knew some of your kin. They came across these hills and settled in here. They built shelters and church-schoolhouses and then they built barns like me. I'm just old and useless now. I can't even perk up for a picture, but I remember well when my owner began felling these trees around here. He squared them up and notched the ends. It was backbreaking work but he got enough for a start and some of your kin and others came and helped set my foundation strong and stacked the logs. Then, he cut more trees and drug them down the creek to the only sawmill in the entire county. He traded two hogs and a cow for sawmill work. When he hauled the lumber home on the old sled, folk came from everywhere to help. He got nails and hinges from the old fella that was a blacksmith. He traded a good Hawkins 50 caliber rifle for that stuff. The walls and stalls were built well. Oh I was a pretty old barn. Next he made shingles from white oak wood. Later on about 50 years, I got a tin roof. I thought I looked better with shingles.

I loved my owner. All these long hours of work to shelter his animals and store his tobacco said volumes about his character. My upper tiers used to be full of tobacco. There were hay and corn shocks in here. The mule harnesses and gear always made me smell like leather…Oh I was a proud old barn. I helped my folk make it. I was a necessary part of this family.

Folk would say 'looks like you got yourself a good barn there.' 'yep, couldn't do without my barn' was my owners response each time.

There used to be a shingle come off or a board come loose, why in no time at all it would be fixed. I wish I were tall and strong again. I wish I was full of tobacco, to hear the rustle of tobacco leaves being 'handed' again, he musty smells, the small talk, and yes the laughter, even occasionally the youngans playing in the loft, and the sound of rain on the roof. I wish the mules were in their stalls crunching an ear of corn—nary a kernel got left. Oh I was something a long time ago. Oh I was needed back then, I was young and strong, a safe place—warm in winter and cool in summer; but, look at me now. Things changed. They say progress, but I beg to differ.

First, automobiles and jobs, then those awful tractors came along. The mules got sold, but mostly my people got old. They couldn't farm like they used to. The young ones left when they were old enough, and there was no one to fix me then. So, I got old and unused, and things just went south from there. I got some wood rot in my joints and nails worked out here and there and my rear end sagged. One night I just gave up the fight, heading back to the dust I came out of, useless, worn out, and neglected. Why you want to take my picture son? Oh, you think you know some things about life back then, do you? Son, you don't know what work and love for this country is...

The last time I saw my builder was early one morning he came out on the porch with his cane and turned his old straight-backed chair toward me and sat down. He looked my way for a long, long time and I am sure he heard the mules, cows, and chickens that used to be here, and could smell me; then, he began to cry. This hard working, God loving mountain man cried for me, and a time passing us both by. A lifetime of memories ran down his wrinkled, furrowed cheeks...And he said goodbye old friend, and that was enough.

Jack Burris

Just Work

     I am constantly in amazement at the amount of work, hard work that mountain folk had to put out just to have shelter and food. Tobacco, corn, taters, beans, hogs, milk cows, chickens, and a horse or mule were some of the things that were absolutely necessary to 'make it'...Hand me downs were handed down till they were finally cut up for quilts. Clothes and such were made from flour sacks and perhaps a bolt of cloth when the terbaccy was sold. Shoes were bought then and the 'company store' was paid. It was a good year if there was a smidgeon of cash money left. So many incredibly gifted folk never got to utilize those gifts because everyone had to work, and school was on the back burner a lot of the time.Do I love the hills because of the solitude I have found deep in the coves and hollers when I traipsed around sang hunting?? Why do I smile and get a warm feeling every single time I drive up 40 and finally see them in the distance??? Every time and I have made that journey a lot of times. Why in the world should I still feel homesick for my childhood in Hominy Valley; dreaming about those times of cowboys and indians, marbles, bean shooters, jacks, stick pickups, the swimming hold, the creek, rabbit tobacco and corn silk and pin hook fishing. About falling in love with those gorgeous South Hominy girls and picking zinnias and daisies and picking the petals, 'she loves me, she loves me not'. And as Alan said, I can still hear the barking of my dog pals long since dead and gone—but I can

Jack Burris

still hear Butch's bark sometimes it seems like.

Funny Books

A special memory was trading comic books and devouring every word including the Grits ads over and over. The Lone Ranger, and Tonto, Archie, Hopalong Cassidy and Superman—able to leap over tall buildings in a single bound. I used a towel for my cape, as I jumped off of 'banks' in pursuit of 'bad guys'...Why do I want to tell all that stuff or write it down, I have it in my memories and how many really care about a time so long ago?? It doesn't seem so long ago to me. I can close my eyes and see myself in the tobacco field with Hollis Roberson carrying all the water I could to put in his tobacco setter—and mom coming across the field with that look because I came home early with the pink eyes and didn't tell her where I was at. Well she wasn't home, and Hollis needed me (or so I thought). I remember the switch I cut that day. Are these memories why I love the mountains? Was it the freedom of those times when you could go anywhere and stay all day, and folk didn't have to worry where you were? How much did going to church and memorizing Bible verses have to do with it?? I can still quote most of them and every time I need encouragement one will pop up. Was church the reason I love the mountains? I loved to go, mostly to trade something or flirt with the girls and kick the ground or cause I didn't have a choice about going or not going—we were going period. It's an amazing thing how much God taught me then, and I didn't even know it.

Seems like back in those coves or in my grandpa's barn

with the soft patter of rain either on the leaves, or on the tin roof had a permanent effect on me. Lying on my back in one of the coves and hearing the smattering of drops and feeling them on my face is a memory I cherish. I laid down on the pool deck when it was raining the other day and traveled back up on Pisgah in the rain. You oughta try it...I don't know about you but those were the golden years for me. I did not know it then, but I know it now. I can still recall like it was at dark last night, coming by Con Davis's fence in the dusky dark time and his whiteface bull (which I teased relentlessly til I would get scared) suddenly bellowed and pawed the ground right beside me. That was as far as I know the only time hair on my neck and back of my legs (if I had any) stood up. As far as I can tell I ran the 100-yard dash in a second and a half; but, you know what? I think that old bull liked me and them cows giggled for hours I'm sure; but, I did get even with my red rag the next day, waving it and yelling at him til I got scared and ran home...

Glady School, Stony Fork School, Pisgah Elementary, Enka High and finally Erwin High, all hold sweet times for me... Friends and classmates, that's it isn't it? Why do I love the hills so much and why do I feel sad cause I'm getting old and some of my dreams probably ain't gonna happen? Love and a sense of sadness all rolled up together. You can't beat that. I guess I just told you some of the reasons I love the hills and you. I doubt I ever stop getting in my old canoe and float-ing down the rivers of my memories to see who shows up. I hope some of you will enjoy the ride today—well I best get ready, tomorrow is Monday and Mom's wash-day. Lord I hope it rains. I have to pump all that water and wipe the clothesline and hang out and take in. Enough to make a boy sick to his stomach. Besides, Connin wants to go fishing tomorrow and I seen a big hogsucker from down on the bridge today, but if it rains it will wash my dam out and I'll have to rebuild it. Oh well. You be blessed this day and every day, you hear me???

I Can't Get Back

Sometimes I have to just sit back with a good cup of coffee and relax and get into my old reddish wore out canoe and push out from shore just to see where my lil mind will take me. How can you discover new rivers of memories without pushing out from the shore and away from land? Sometimes just a tiny thread of thought or picture will flash through and it will seem like yesterday, or at least not 65 years ago. This is not original and I may not say it exactly but it is how I feel about this: One of the top five things our parents could give us when we grew up in the mountains was when we were poor, we didn't know it. We were not poor as doing without, but we were blessed cause Dad had a job at the Enka Plant. We didn't have a lot of bubblegum either or extras and I had no clue where we stood on the society scale of life. I knew there were a couple who wore hand-me-downs and seldom had a decent lunch to eat. It bothered me at an early age and it still bothers me now.

Not every canoe trip is pleasant. Nothing wrong with hand-me-downs cause I woulda wore them had I had a brother close in age. Maybe that is one reason young couples have so much of a challenge keeping families together; both have to work, and stress and such are always around. It was and is so much fun to travel in time by reading, it carried me to places I had no idea existed. The dog stories centered around Big Red by Jim Kjeelgaard took me to the Maine woods, dog shows, hunting, danger, and heroes. I didn't realize it then, but I was writing my own book of life in the hills. I was doing things I still wanted to do, like damming up the creek, fishing off the old oak bridge with worms in a Prince Albert can, a home-made pole and pin hook, and running the ridges searching for that perfect slingshot, hunting ginseng on a misty day, falling in love over and over, going to the prom and always that first kiss...time stood still then—for a long time...going on that first squirrel hunt and on and on we go...Now I put the iPod or XM Radio on and go back there and escape with the greatest pleasure, time. The trouble is, I can tell time, but it don't listen—I've always dreamed of going back to the hills, but it isn't going to happen.

I'm not going to get back...time has taken that away... When we were 10, 12 or so we dreamed of being older, and now that is reversed isn't it? I dream of old times just like a kid. I don't dream or even wish I was younger. I've had my time, I didn't use what I had very well at times, but I could have. I read where someone said writing made you feel time, it's more like getting out of a car after riding several hours or maybe just getting out of bed sometimes. I feel time all the time somewhere, don't you? I poured an 18-yard (two truck) driveway Thursday. It was hot here and it was a special mix that dried pretty quickly—I felt time in a big way when I broomed the last yard; so, I thought, "Boy, I'll lay around tomorrow." Then, Friday morning a "friend" called at 6:30 and said, "Would you pour a ditch for me?"

I went and it was a full load of a ditch two feet wide down an asphalt parking lot. I didn't take knee-pads or most of my tools to pour a "ditch". Two and a half hours later on top of Friday I felt time in a big way. Time is not my friend as far as old goes. Each day adds another something I won't get to do unless I take "time" I don't use the phrase "killing a little time" anymore. Oh well, what a ride this Sunday, no great story line here---remember it is better to be an hour early than a minute late......And if you want to get mad, consider this: Liberal judges expect us to stand when they come into the room, forget the flag...Be blessed and for goodness sake, save some time.

Nobody Like Him

Everything we see, from the large to the small,

Everything we have to love, God made them all.

The beautiful colors of flowers that burst forth in the spring,

From the red of the cardinal, to the humming birds tiny wings;

From the blues of the Smoky Mountains, to the rivers running by,

To the many hues of pinks and reds that light up the morning sky,

From the snow and cold of winter, after fall slips away,

To the new life of spring and the warmth of those days.

We have eyes to see the beauty, and ears to hear the songs of life so very well,

And lips that of His goodness, we must; we must always tell.

JB-As the old preacher said, "there ain't nobody like him"

Skipping Rocks

I have been in the old canoe today off and on; just cruising down the rivers of my memories going no where in particular. I was in East Tenn talking to my Uncle Bud about his childhood and sitting at his dinner table (noon) and him sharing pickled beans with me. I knew he liked me cause he was real fond of them beans...I miss him too along with all the others who have gone on.

My lil mind wandered to the Davis Creek and the fun we had in and around it. One thing us boys did, and a lot of girls too, was skip rocks. I never knew too many boys who could get around a nice still pool and not look for a nice flat rock. Five skips is my limit; I got five a lot of times, but never could skip one six times. I threw enough rocks to cover a large building too. I loved one about the size of a silver dollar or just slightly larger. There was something about skipping rocks that makes me still do it when I see a flat rock and water. You are also aware that a stream of water that you can jump or step across is a branch. It can only be a creek if it's too wide to step or jump across. I remember going up branches and catching black spring lizards for fishing. You raise up rocks and they will shoot off and you have to be quick and they are slick. I tried it two years ago when I climbed up on Chester sang hunting; I almost drowned in 5 inches of water. I could not hold them when I was lucky enough to touch one. That would have been a sight for sure, my britches legs were soaked but I was so stubborn it took a while to sink in, "You can't catch them very well any more Jack." So, I finally quit and had a good laugh.

Some of that mountain water eased my thirst many times, getting down on your knees and drinking like an animal. One of my sweetest memories was looking up with water dripping down my chin and on the other side of the branch was a few bunches off ginseng, the bright red berries looking right at me, it almost took my breath. I looked away for a spell and eased my eyes back around to get that feeling again…same result…I left several bunches because of the beauty but I never could get back there. I hope it's still there and some dad takes his little boy and he sees what I saw.

Water coming down off the hills is cold, so cold, and I've always been amazed that it keeps coming year, after year, after year. Think about how much water runs by every hour on the French Broad…and it keeps coming…We have to have it for drinking to live, we eat the fish it raises, we boil our eggs in it, we swim and play, we dam it up, and it can flood and destroy us…Now floating around on the river today, I am in no danger except my ole canoe leaks a bit, and when we go, we go. ---But skipping rocks is sorta like standing in the road and hitting rocks for hours with tobacco sticks. I would pretend to be Mickey Mantle and winning the game with a home run. I never tired of this or playing baseball in the cow pasture… Lordy that was soo much fun. Then, along came the Schwinn that gave me wings; I felt like I was free on that bike. I could be at the swimming hole on Hominy Creek in a flash, or to the book mobile at Clay London's store….

There wasn't much traffic, so we would get at the top of the hill and say, "ready, set, go." We would pedal 3 times as hard as we possibly could and see who could coast the furthest, over and over again. Just distant memories now, but I wish kids today could go up the branch, catch some lizards, hunt some sang, play ball in the cow pasture, go skinny dipping praying for the girls to come, and hit some rocks with backer sticks, and coast down a hill—with the wind in their face and a smile on their lips—I just wish....

Empty Barns of Yesterday

I love these relics of a time fast getting away. Old barns were a necessary part of a family. They were maintained and cared for with love. If you could of been in this old barn with me you would know I'm telling you the truth. They had 'souls' and so many are still upright and strong, just waiting to be filled with backer, animals and tools. Listen, I felt like this old barn was talking to me. Nostalgia washed over me and it felt like something broke loose inside and was running.

I could feel those strong mountain men who gave us a heritage like no other, putting the harness on the mule, or the horse, and sometimes a steer or an ox. They were a team; they knew Gee (right) and Haw (left) and exactly when it was time for dinner, and corn to eat for fuel. They truly were a team. Sometimes from sunup to sundown, both sweating and give out at the end of the day. You can bet your bottom dollar they were taken care of before ary a bite did he eat. The old mule and horse my grandfather had stepped up the pace heading to the barn, a place of rest and food, a safe place. It's no wonder the thought came to me in the other story about this barn, that the old man said goodbye with tears in his eyes. He knew... Gosh, I would give anything to climb up in my grandfather's barn and play in the hay, just lie on my back and listen to the rain. I felt like the old barn asked me why I wanted to take pictures of it, what with falling down and almost gone. I know how much the old barns were really worth. I know most of the folk who read this stuff remember some of the things that went on in these old barns...I have no clue who owned this barn in the picture, but I don't mind telling you my old eyes leaked a bit just thinking about what the barn would tell me if it could talk...And maybe it did, at least it felt that way.

You know it's no wonder folk want the wood for their homes. You can't buy paint that will make a piece of wood look like an old barn plank; weathered, battered and neglected. Sorta sounds like some old folk I've heard of. You and me are mostly gray and worn. You and me, we have given of ourself, our time, resources, and work to make a better life for ours. After visiting some of these old barns, I'm not sure we have done them any favors. Pride in work well done, independence, helping others, your word your bond, a love for God and country, maybe these are what really matters. I felt like this old barn told me to 'come back now and then when you can', 'but you best hurry son, I'm about gone.'.

Another barn is just across the mountain from Big Laurel going to Shelton Laurel. It is one of my favorites. I have never stopped and talked to the folk who live there, but I might next time. Old hand hewn logs combined with sawmill lumber. It could be anywhere from 200 years old, to a hundred years old, but Lordy the stories it could tell. Nowadays the old barns are full of junk, a place to toss stuff and forget about it. They are full of wasper nests cause no one keeps them up anymore. Oh there are some barns still being used-mostly as shelter for horses, or infrequent use by cows or goats. Those barns have no stories to tell...No matter where you are from if you get the chance to go to some old barns, just go inside and find you a safe place to sit a spell. Close your eyes and listen; you may be surprised what comes up.

Jack Burris

The stories we could hear if the walls could talk

Silence

The peaceful, sweet

Sweet, calming, caressing,

Wonderful sounds of solitude...

Sitting by a trout stream,

or in a old barn

Close your eyes and hear it......

Mule Collar

I was over on Laurel a long time ago and we were going to help Chauncy Fender get a sled load of rocks off his backer patch-an every year job. It was good mountain ground and grew lots of rocks. We were in the barn and I told Chauncy I would gear his mule up; Then, I did the dumbest thing that still comes up in conversations sometimes. I heard Chauncy 'giggling'- "Hee hee, hee hee, son, you got the collar upside down." I think even the old mule laughed. I know the barn stored that up cause every time I see that barn, that image pops up. One thing I learned early on, you did not want those old farmers to get anything over on you, cause they never forget and delight in telling it over and over. I loves them folk and these old barns, ginseng and babies, sweet tea and memories— so many good memories…

Beagles and Bassets

Well I got in my old canoe and on the rivers of my memories and run into two old friends. The best beagle I ever had is on the left, her name was Bisquit, and she could almost invent a rabbit. I let her run loose most of the time because we lived at the end of a dirt road and had plenty of room to run. She would never give up. I think her and some of her rabbit friends had an understanding, the rabbits said, and I quote, " As long as you don't let the old man come out of the house with a gun, we will let you chase us every other day-You must promise not to go so fast that you catch us though. We will have some fun" Biscuit replies, "I agree-the old man is contrary at times, but he is really a pushover; but, you have to promise not to go to ground for at least two hours." Brer Rabbit and Bisquit shook on it. That's about the way it went for a couple years.

The other friend was Detour. A complete joy and 100-percent Basset-and he sure smelled like one, but I loved that rascal. He would lay in the dirt road in the middle of course, and I would have to stop until he made the laborious effort of moving. He would slowly lift his head and put those sad eyes on me and say 'you again, I'm getting tired of this.' Then, he would slowly get up on his front feet and pause for a minute as if to rest, then he would make it all the way standing up. He'd shake the dirt off of course, then have to make the most major decision on which side of the road to go; Sometimes, he changed his mind—get almost out of the way just to turn and sloowlly go to the other side. I know he planned this stuff. It was a circle drive and he knew which way I would come in. No need to hurry, just squeeze the steering wheel and sing 'Goodness gracious, great balls of fire' and mutter. He would put those sad eyes on me as I drove past and wag his tail, like he was thinking 'I win again, old man.' I would feed him and pet him and 'like' him; but you know what really endeared this old Bassett hound to me? He would be lying in the road, 'just to aggravate me' and Bisquit could bark one time on a rabbit trail, and that old Detour would jump up in a flash and take off at a dead run. He would run rabbits as long as Bisquit did. Now, I've seen him at least a hundred yards behind and he never could catch up; but, he would run with his head up and bay like a treeing coon dog, and every now and then he would trip on a log or a limb or a rock and plow dirt and leaves up his nose. My, my it was a sight, and such a blessing.

You couldn't look at these two buddies without laughing. I figure anything that will make you laugh is worth having, don't you? Some of you all say, yeah my husband or my wife makes me laugh. Well, like most animal stories, there are sad endings. I do think at times we forget they are animals with short lifespans, and that God gave us them to enjoy. Someone stole Bisquit and Detour. I had heard them running down in the woods that day, and they just never came home. I searched and searched but never had any luck. But you know, its been pretty nice to revisit them this day, and I can hear them running in my mind. I am especially thankful for Bisquit, Detour, Tippy, Butch, Bandit, Sue, Little Bit and others I have known. Their cold noses and loyalty is cherished this day. They're still around; they'll always be around.

The wind comes to me and brings the barking of   dogs of long ago

And some yelps and barks of not so long ago

I hear among them the barking and yelps of childhood friends

And I can hear their growls of warning and their yelps of fear

As they warn of danger those they hold dear...

The wind shapes the broomsage and grass and the trees

into shapes and images of dogs known

Laughing faces, wagging tails, loving eyes, pointy ears, and cold noses

How could we suspose these clear vivid images of dogs we have known are not real....

Hurry back my friends to the rivers of my memory Into the canoe we will go sailing down the summers of life gone by

We will play in the creek and we will chase sticks and balls all day long

And I will love and miss you all over again

Some of the woods have been cut down

and some of the dirt roads have been paved

But you are still around, You will always be around.....

The Master Builder

Soft soothing rain, October is here. Another fall, an array of colors that still takes my breath at times; like the Harvest moon, huge and bright, a sun by day and a moon by night. The seasons come quickly nowadays. Seems we just had Thanksgiving not long ago. Well, it really wasn't long ago. Sometimes I really believe time speeds up the older you get; or it could be we appreciate time a bit more. Those long hazy summer days were long ago. I have seen the morning sun many times but the red hues of brilliance still makes me marvel sometimes. Everyone has a picture of the sun coming up over the ocean.

This world is beautiful in what the Master designed. What is ugly is man made. Man has a tendency to destroy or use up with no thought of consequences sometimes. I truly love nature, the intricacies, balance and brilliance. Everything is fed and cared for. Man upsets the chain at times and wreaks havoc; and don't care if a dollar is involved. Plastic lasts several lifetimes; but it isn't regulated or outlawed because of the huge profits and payouts involved. There could well be a cure for cancer already out there, hidden. Look at Congress. Money is the operating force. There will always be the rich and the poor, the free and the slave, Muslims versus the world, old and new. Did you know that the same amount of water that was created is still here? Oh we pollute it, but water can't be destroyed.

The Master's creation lacked nothing, should the earth shift just a few degrees we would either freeze, or burn up. Some say it just evolved that way...Oh well, Ill just look at the colors of fall and enjoy the beauty of our land, and I will acknowledge where I think they come from...It's way too perfect for me not to have to take a deep breath and give thanks— To the Master Builder.

Switch Or Paddle

I didn't say you was guilty, I said I was blaming you. Go ahead and climb all you want, but if you fall out and break a leg, don't come running to me!!! Mom would say something like, 'You get grass and dirt stains on them britches, I'm going to wear you out, and you can write that down in your day-book.' Shoot, I didn't even have a daybook and couldn't write real well...getting wore out to a frazzle was a dreaded occurrence. Tizzies and conniption fits were things to avoid causing. If I made Mom mad enough to have a tizzy fit, I was going to have to cut big switches.

One thing for sure, when most of us went to school and misbehaved, we were going to get punished. I know this is hard to believe but the principal bent me over a desk and got my back pocket and pulled it up tight and wore my innocent little butt out. The paddle was about 6 inches wide and had holes drilled in it for punctuation. Now honey-child you didn't want but one time with that thing. To make it worse, Mom wore me out after I got home. Right on top of them pretty red welts already there. The shrinks say It could have turned me into a psychopath, a loner, mean, hateful, scarred for life, bitter, unfriendly, suicidal, I spit on people, I let my underarms stink, wore saggy pants, started smoking and drinking moonshine, plotted ways to get revenge, declared my innocence over and over. It was awful. It was so heart-wrenching that I avoided the principal's office like the plague. All the other "good" youngans crowded around and asked questions. I was a celebrity for a spell. I had no qualms about dropping my pants and showing the wounds of war. Girls like bad boys I learned at an early age. Never did know what to do with that information...the teachers rap with a ruler when I would put a bobby pin in the desk and twang it like a guitar string was worth the risk. The boys laughed and the girls looked sideways at me. Oh, I was the life of the rulers.

After a spell it wore out. I finally learned you could get sugar with honey. A whole lot sweeter and those "S's" for conduct was good for my homelife with Mom. She had trained me to be a professional woodcutter. It all evolved from switch cutting. Bless her heart. I said all this stuff, because I wish teachers could discipline and get control of classrooms. A lot of little boys need a good attitude adjustment. I know a lot of kids have tender spirits and other family issues and should never ever be physically disciplined. But some boys just need it from what I see. Feeding them pills to calm them down is worse than a hanging. I've seen some act like zombies, spirit broken.

The teacher's hands are tied and the parents won't get Johnny under control. They been watching too much TV about how whipping or spanking or slapping their hand with a ruler is cruel and unusual punishment. The teacher is almost forced to report how little Johnny is fidgety, aggravates the girls, daydreams, talks too much, etc... and then the docs tell us Johnny will never learn without Ritalin or some other drug that is making people who care less, rich...What options does the teacher have? Time out? Notes home? Pills? They spend all their time trying to get the kids to pass some stupid test and trying to keep a classroom in some kind of order, with little help. I would never make it as a teacher; the first time I got sassed, spit on, or cussed I would be fired. I reckon I'm old school and I may be outdated. Maybe I'm wrong but I know a ton of really fine folk that grew up with a leather strap hanging out in the barn, and it wasn't just for the mule either. We all knowed it. Oh well, you pray for me, and I will pray for you, just like I used to pray Dad would have to work overtime at Enka, cause I had heard Mom say, "just you wait till Charlie gets home"...Be Blessed, cause you are.

Kindling and A Axe

We were living in Hollis Robertson's house right at the foot of a mountain that had a large white flint rock up at the top. Mount Pisgah was just to our right. They were, or already had put up the first "TV" tower. WLOS channel 13 I think, if you had a TV, which we didn't. Our neighbor Con Davis had one while we were living there. The picture is Stony Fork School in the 40's and early 50's. I went there for a spell.

Anyways, we had a wood cook stove, and a warm morning heater in the living room. The bedroom doors stayed closed in the winter so you needed lots of Mom's wonderful hand-stitched quilts on the bed. The windows would frost up on the inside at times. One of my chores, or jobs, or privileges was keeping the wood boxes filled. After one or two times of not meeting my obligations and an attitude adjustment, mountain style, I never neglected my duties again. Some of them switchings were akin to a hanging to me. Anyway, Dad would buy a load of sawmill slats for kindling and wood. We would saw them and split them. Quite a few were split into kindling to start the fires with. I remember cutting kindling with a double bitted ax at an early age. It was just something you did. It was fun for a spell, I was told and showed by example how to do it, and that was that.

At that time there were skeletons of chestnut trees all over the hills. A lot were on the ground and there were a lot still standing. The blight that decimated them came along in the late 20's. Folk used the chestnuts to eat and for feed. Hogs especially loved them. There was a market for them for a few cash dollars. The wood didn't rot for a very long time and it was light gray and light. It was the best kindling outside of 'rich pine' or 'fat lighter' in Georgia. It was so easy to split in slender sticks. I loved splitting it. We would go up on the mountain and drag it out by hand. Downhill and steep so you could get some pretty good-sized stuff, so it lasted for a long spell.

I loved going up on the mountain with Dad. It was a couple years before I got nerve enough to go to the top by myself. After all, there were Panthers, huge black panthers with yellow eyes, and bears as big as a car, or so I had been told. After I started ginseng hunting and was older, whenever I came across a chestnut log, sometimes covered with moss, I would usually sit down for a while and think about how it used to be. I loved jumping up on one and there would be ginseng looking for me from the forest floor. Those old chestnut logs were part of another time—sorta like barns, and tobacco warehouses, and credit at the country store.

We had a small gray kerosene can. When school was out and Dad had to catch the Enka Bus at 6AM, He would beat on the wall beside the bed. It meant, hit the floor Jack and get the fire going. Cold? Ha...if it still had coals I would throw some kindling and a couple pieces of firewood along with a dash of kerosene and I would be in business. If no coals, I would put paper in there, then the kindling, and a double dose of kerosene. Strike one of those big wooden matches from the box on the wall and whoosh, a fire. Put some more wood in it then turn my backside to it, and back to the front, then run and jump back in bed before I froze. One of the most dreaded sounds to me as a little boy was when Dad hit that wall. But my goodness, I'd like to do that again.

Wood heat is wonderful and it will warm you several times, cutting it, hauling it, splitting it, carrying it, and cleaning up after it... Not to mention a chain saw, a truck to haul it, a wood splitter to keep up, a wood stove and fireplace or pipe vented. But I loves that wood heat, I shorley does.... I had on my bed a string run from the bedpost to the bare light bulb, so you could turn the light off or on before getting up, or after laying down. I also had on that bedpost at various times bubblegum. I would chew that stuff till it would be hard. Sometimes put some sugar on it for taste. It didn't matter if I forgot to get it, I could always get it the next day or two, or more.

We had a well pump outside the back door; it wasn't hard to pump except on wash day. Mom was one of the "cleanest" persons I have ever known. So wasn't any shortcuts around there. Pump, pump, pump, then pump some more. I wish I could pump her a tub full again, Just one more time. I was up there a while back when the house was empty. It wasn't much different except a bathroom and indoor plumbing. The basement was still dirt. The front porch was about 10 feet up a set of steps. After I went into the woods where the hog pen and outhouse was, I came back out to where the chicken house and lot was, and looked over the remains of the smokehouse.

In the back of the house was a poplar tree that had been there in the 40's. About the size of a soccer ball back then. I just shook my head and laughed out loud when I saw that tree. I had cut numerous hickory saplings and made me bows with them. I would put them behind the cook stove to cure. Anyway, they bought me one of them store bought bows with three real arrows. I would lay in the hayfield and shoot them straight up, and marvel at how high they would go, never a though that they might come down in the top of my empty head. Anyway, I leaned that bow up against that poplar tree and commenced to climb it. I put my bare foot without realizing it on top of the bow, and it broke. You might as well have shot me. I knew the value of money so I never let on. I cried over that deal.

Then I went to the front porch and climbed the steps a lot slower than I did way back then. I put my back against the wall and just slid down. For a long time, I had read funny books over and over on that porch. I read about Mother West Wind on that porch. I could see the old oak bridge and the creek in places from the porch. I found some sang at 8 years old over in the hollow. I killed my first squirrel with Bill's 22. Mom cooked it for me. Dad ate it with biscuits and gravy. I never could eat them...but I kept dad supplied. I haven't even touched on over half the things that went on over in the house in the woods. One thing that went on was it filled me with something you can't get in a store. The memories have given to me a place of rest from this journey that has been brutal at times, and even when the tears were streaming, and nausea gripped me, there was a place of rest for me.

He said in the ancient scrolls that there is a place of rest; Bethel for Abraham, Curled up in the bottom of a boat was Jesus, A good book for some, A movie, A night out with the kids at home, Church, A camping trip, sitting on the porch —one of my favorites—flowers, gardening, working, for some, building something, or playing golf. Whatever and wherever that place is, I think we need to go there often. Think I'll go cut some kindling and I ain't even got a stove—where is your place of rest? We have daily bread in the oven. If we don't get it daily it gets scattered in the yard----and we don't smile near as much----you be blessed, you hear me???

Lowes Blessing

Well, I was in Lowe's Today and looking at a roll of black plastic for a 30 by 30 pad I was getting ready to pour. This gentleman was standing there looking at some ladders, he was scratching his head and looked a bit confused. I said, " how you doin', my friend?" (A stranger may be a friend you haven't met yet) He turned and looked at me and said, "I'm doin' ok." I said something like, 'well I hope you had a great Christmas.' His eyes welled up, and he said it was good. He said now it's back to work, and of course I asked what he did and he said water treatment plants and sewer systems. He said I've waded water colder than today is, and folk ask me, "Charlie, why don't you retire?" He said, "I could retire, but I love what I do, and I'm only 72." I said, "Well, I'm 74 and going to pour a 30 by 30 floor as soon as I get it graded and formed, I like what I do too."

Then, his eyes welled up again and he said my wife is a worker too. She has worked all her life and she retired at 68 a couple months ago… She was diagnosed with cancer two weeks ago and she may see Easter, or may not. I come in here for a stepladder and can't even keep my mind focused enough to choose one. For 55 years this woman has loved me and I her —I don't know what to do now…His voice shook with emotion and my heart went out to him. So I said this: "I went through what you are facing and one thing I know for sure, she needs you to be her strength, she needs you now more than she ever has." I said, "if you concentrate on how she feels and try to forget yourself, you will be more satisfied after it's all over. Give 100 percent and you will not second guess or question yourself and I guarantee you God will help you." I said, "I was feeling sorry for what I was losing until I finally realized just what she was loosing."

He was looking at the floor and he looked up and said, " My neighbor and friend for 40 years lost his wife over a year ago, and every time we look at each other, we start crying. I'm doing just what you said—feeling sorry for myself and what am I going to do instead of putting her on my shoulders." He said, "I gotta go put in a new valve over at the water plant, but I am going home with a different attitude...I'm going to help her forget about being sick......I'm Charlie Tipton and I wanna thank you for what you have reminded me of..."

I told him who I was, and we neck hugged and he started up the aisle, and when he got about halfway I said, "Charlie--" He turned around and I said, " Charlie, if I don't see you again, I'll see you across the river won't I?" He said, "I'll be there, we settled that a long time ago, I just been distracted..." He pointed his finger at me and said—I'll be there......

I got my plastic and sat in my truck with my head on the steering wheel and had to give thanks. I end almost every prayer with this statement—and finally Lord, give me the opportunity to say or do something for someone else...and He does...and lots of times unexpectedly. The reason I was at this Lowes, is because of divine intervention. I was across town and planned to stop at the Lowes on I-77 toward Mooresville. My son James was getting an infusion at the hospital and he called and said, "Brenda was out here waiting on me and she left the lights on and our battery is dead." I thought, now I got to go get cables go do this and I'll be late. He said, "she has cables in the car." So I said I'll be right there. So the car started instantly and Lowes was a mile or so away and so that's where I went—and also why I went there...You say just coincidence?? Don't you believe it.

217 Ways To Starve

217 ways to starve or stink. I decided I wanted some honey-nut cheerios. So I went grocery shopping. Did you know that there is an entire aisle dedicated to starvation? An entire aisle with nothing but cereal. Not only did I find cheerios, but I found 12 different kinds of cheerios. By the time I read each box it was lunchtime. Then I happened to see Kellogg's. I thought oh boy, just corn flakes. My gosh-with strawberries? Blueberries? Nuts? Crunchy? Banana? Original? Nothing is original; but by then, it was suppertime.

Then I noticed oatmeal, pretty simple huh? Stone ground or not? Maple? Blueberries? Strawberries? Instant? And on and on, I just couldn't decide. Well, I missed supper and I had only looked at three cereals. I glanced back up the aisle and every color in the crayon box jumped out at me. Athletes said this was protein filled. Pretty ladies said this was energy filled. Doctors said theirs would cure illness, one said lose weight and eat all you want. Good for your heart, may reduce cholesterol. My head was spinning by then. I was shaking from hunger and dehydration. By now, it was after midnight.

So, I decided to go get some milk first. Uh-oh. One percent, two percent, three percent=whole? Skim or goat? Half and half? Half of what? Milk and coke? Milk and water? Low gluten? Isn't that some kind of glue?? I decided it was between chocolate, white missed, whole white, or out of a quart you could use 2 percent. I guess throw the rest away.

By now, my stomach was upset and I headed for that

bathroom. I accidentally went by the toilet paper section. I couldn't believe it! Soft, super soft, super soft and strong— doubled or single? 14 different kinds, and all promised a fine wiping. Absorbent. By now it was after 1 and I had wet my pants a tiny bit and I was feeling a bit weak...Sure enough I went into the bathroom and the paper was rough and turned the wrong way. It's a good place to pray cause no one else is around or won't be around long.

So I tried to bribe God. I said if you will help me walk to the front door without looking right or left, I won't ever come in here again, and He did. So in my weakened condition I stopped at Burger King. Oh Lordy, Single, double, one-third pounder, one-quarter pounder, regular or thick burger, or 4 different chicken sandwiches, not to mention strips and nugget...lettuce? Tomato? You ever drive in a drive thru then just pull out and leave? So I prayed again, Let me keep my eyes ahead; so, I pulled into McDonalds and said, " just give me a burger and some fries and a small coke"—while looking straight ahead. And you know what that shameless hussy said? What kind and what size burger would you like? I said forget it —it's time for breakfast anyway. I'm going to go get me some honey-nut cheerios......and off I went...

Outhouse After Dark?

The garden was down the hill in front of the house. But for me, at 6 or so years old, the creek was down the hill in front of the house. To me, that was a whole lot more satisfying than the garden; but I did learn how to plant beans, chop weeds, and 'smell' for copperheads. Old timers said you could smell them. I found some babies one time and thought they were worms at first but at least I had sense enough to see the colors and knew what they were. They didn't live long around our house.

The outhouse was in the woods. Now you can see why I never made it all the way to the outhouse after dark. The hog pen was out in the woods to the left and lots of time I carried "slop" to them after supper. It would be getting dusky dark. Sometimes, a bobcat would squawl or a coon dog would sound off with mountain music and ole Jack would leave the hog pen faster than he went to it. See the front porch about 10 feet off the ground. I read funny books I 'borrowed, traded' for and anything from grits to sears catalogues on that porch sitting leaned back in a cane bottomed chair.

That's why when I went back a few years ago and no one was there and the house was empty, I went up on the porch and just slid down the wall for an hour or so. Took a great ride in my old canoe down the rivers of my memories then, as I am doing now. When we were there the well and pump was out the back door on the left. It was good water and running water in that you had to run and get it. An enemy on washday when Mama always had to rinse everything twice and the water had to be pumped. For the life of me I cannot get a clear image of either one of my older sisters ever touching that pump handle. I know they never washed the clothesline..twice..as per Mama's instructions...The woods in back was full of fishing poles and bows and arrows and slingshots...bean shooters to us. Over in the hollow on the left was some ginseng that Bill West showed me. I was hooked then...and have since enjoyed a lifetime of fun in the woods.

Con David lived across the hill on the right. I was scared of him, he was big and strong and didn't say much—but it didn't stop me from playing mind games with his bull or rocking his two cocker spaniels or whipping his boy once in a while (I was older and bigger). But I found out later when we were moving, that he liked me and knew about everything going on.. I visited him after I was grown and cherish that time sitting in his yard.

The creek was full of fish. There were horny heads, suckers, chubs, water dogs, water snakes, turtles, and some trout. The water was and is cold coming off Mount Pisgah and Chester. I tried to dam that creek up 16, 780 times or thereabouts and about calf high is tops... But it was fun trying. The few times my bare feet were really clean, in spite of Mama's warning about "wash them rusty feet before you get in that clean bed...." Gosh Mama loved cleanliness, enough to make a little boy sick...

One time Dad and I were going up the trail behind the house to get some chestnut for kindling when my dog Butch who had went on ahead come barreling down and went between dad's legs in a dead run with the hair sticking up on his back. Dad said it must be a bear or panther up ahead, and just kept going. Now the hair on my neck was standing up... It took a long time for me to go back up on the mountain by myself after that...

One chimney—on the backside was the kitchen and cook stove and the living room on the left front with the warm morning heater. The bedrooms were not heated. So like most of you, you backed your butt up to the heater and turned around and ran and jumped in bed. There was a string tied to the bedpost to turn on or turn off the light. Enough of Mama's quilts piled on to keep us warm. Can you imagine having to get up in the middle of the night in this house in the dead of winter and having to go pee? The outhouse was across the yard on the left and up a little incline into the woods. Close your eyes and see if you can picture me or you going all the way at night???

Well, I have enjoyed my little trip today; I hope some of you went back in time with me...the girl?? In the picture has nothing on me—I made all my fishing stuff and I did use bailing string some—Mama's sowing thread doubled and tripled was better...Course I wouldn't have used a pole as sorry as she has, I cut long slender saplings and used rocks or iron nuts for sinkers and made pin hooks. I remember my first ever real fish hook that dad brought me from the Enka Plant, he told me one of his buddies about my fishing and he gave dad some fish hooks for me. Somehow for me the pin hooks I made fit into my canoe trips better. I loves the old times, I surely does... Remember to look for a chance to say or do something nice for someone—cause you are blessed and you know you are— wouldn't be fair not to share...

Ginseng at 74

Well boys and girls, I got sanging off me a bit today...I got up early and drove to South Hominy. I had this incredible urge to drink from a mountain brook and take a close up of Pisgah while being high up on a mountain right across from it. I had this incredible urge to hunt some ginseng with red berries on it so I could replant the berries. May I submit that the incredible urges was fulfilled to a t...

I stopped at the store where Clay London's used to be and got me some crackers and a can of viennas and a musketeer...The store is just below Glady "church" school—the one room school house where I started the first grade—before moving to Stony Fork school...I passed by Pisgah Elementary where so many wonderful memories were made.... I get a bit homesick when I go up that way. Of course I looked at the Sams store and the Lige Pressley's store and I looked to see if Patsy H was outside today. Then I saw the new construction at the intersection of Davis Creek-complete with red light. Then I looked across the way at the Hollis Robertson house where I spent many many wonderful days growing up. The mountain still comes all the way down to the house from every side except the front...I almost had to stop and just look cause my little mind gets in high gear and nostalgia overtakes me. I loves the old days, I shorley does...

Wish Ma and Pa was over there today and I Could ask some questions I failed to ask; and of course say "I love you and thanks for all you did for me." I didn't say it enough. Anyone out there still got one or both of your folks, you best be asking and telling...Then you won't have to wish you had one more day like most of us—Well I pulled into Pisgah Ranch and parked like I had good sense and was supposed to be there... There is more to it than that, but anyway I put my boots on and an old green T shirt and took off up the logging trails... I crossed a couple trails and ridges and found a bit of sang— at least there is small stuff left to replenish for the little ones who may be fortunate enough to get to go. Finally, I reached the branch running down the mountain. I followed it up and traveled from side to side and found some pretty good stuff. Finally I lay down across a rock and drank deeply from the cold clear mountain stream. I turned over several rocks before I found a black spring lizard. Yes, he got away, I ain't as good as I once was, and I don't think I'm as good once as I ever was.

That water was soooo good. Memories of days gone on flooded me and I sat a spell. It never was about the quantity or money. Its always just been the woods and the sounds and the brooks, the old growth timber, and the blue of the sky and the rain showers falling gently through the trees. Of course Sang was the lure that got you in there, then the rest of it just gets inside of you... Anyway, I took my time, sat and ate a cracker and such, and of course the musketeer. Bears had been digging in two yellow jacket nests and had tore up a couple logs looking for grubs. I heard turkeys and of course there was deer sign and I noticed one red tail high overhead. I left almost all of the ginseng in the woods and I took the berries off and replanted them. I have good woods sense, I went around the mountain on an old logging trail and when I reached a place I thought it was time to go down the mountain, I went.

I came out within 50 yards of where I started. It was a good day. A day of thankfulness. There has been sorrow around this year, and some other situations are not where we wish they were—but these age old mountains has a way of putting my mind at ease and giving me a "peace that passeth understanding"...I appreciate Him giving me another year, and letting me go back one more time and drink from a branch and find some four prongs with ripe red berries to re-plant...I thought of my people who have gone on while on the mountain...I miss them all...But I love and am thankful for the sweet memories...You all be blessed this day and every day, you hear me? You know you are...

The Most Beautiful Plant-American Wild Ginseng on A Mountain in Western North Carolina. Mount Pisgah.

Jack Burris

Moonshine, Hornets and Cleo

Cleo Owens was a friend from Brevard, NC. I lived in Brevard for 3 years or so. I ran a Smile Service Station and worked for the telephone company. This was about '67 thru '70, or thereabouts...Anyways, Cleo had a huge hornet nest on the eave of his garage and he wanted it down. So at that time, being Saturday, we had opened a quart of Carolina koolaide and we devised a scheme to take the nest down. We were going to take a stepladder and double two grocery bags—they were paper pokes at that time—and put the bags up over the nest and squeeze the top shut, and bingo—hornets and entire nest was trapped and would suffocate quickly and we would then go fishing with the larva. Wonderful plan of attack in our somewhat confused minds, after dark of course.

Well the plan went okay for getting the stepladder and setting it up, and the bag part went well. Leaving the house porch light on wasn't part of our plan, but it should have been cut off. The plan went okay with me holding the ladder and Cleo eased the bag up over the hornet nest. In our confused state of mind we never considered what with the nest as big as the bag opening, that it would be virtually impossible to squeeze those stiff bags around that nest without some gaps appearing. In our plan, and bags...gaps appeared. Upshot of this magical adventure—I abandoned the ladder, Cleo fell sideways with a handful of hornets who hadn't had any koolaide and were slightly angry about getting woke up —if they were ever asleep—I ran toward the house and the lit

porch light and Cleo screamed and followed dragging his left
ankle. The light on was a huge mistake. The hornets had a tar-
get lit up for them. I almost tore the screen door off and didn't
bother hold it for Cleo cause I took a few hornets in with me.
The kids and womenfolk locked the kitchen door on us...Cleo
finally made it and finally thru the koolaid haze, realized he
had a piece of the nest in his hand and threw it out...It was a
very exciting time on the back porch, locked out of the house
with some mad hornets in there with us. I had 8 stings—and
black hornets know how to inflict injury—3 on my face, one
eye swelled almost shut and pain everywhere. If Cleo had been
allergic he would have died. His whole head swelled up and
being crippled from the fall slowed him down some and then I
held the screen door and wouldn't let him in, out of fear for my
life for a minute or two and that increased the potential for
further damage...I don't think he has ever fully forgiven me
for that...But hay, it was his nest and mostly his plan, so risks
were there...

We did not share this story at work for fear of getting
in fights when they laughed at us. Neither one could see well
enough to fight. We threatened the women and children but
it leaked out anyway...This was a blessing though, because I
think it was the first real step in never drinking mountain
koolaide again...This is an absolutely true story, as dumb as it
sounds...It's amazing what I have learned after I knew everything. In a few days, as soon as Cleo could see well enough he
rolled some bags and newspaper up in a tight ball around a
mop handle and dipped it in kerosene and burned the nest...
and almost caught his garage on fire...Oh well, he said it would
have been worth it. By the way, he didn't ask me to help.....
Cleo died a few years ago and all the family knew about our
little adventure, he said it always came up at family get togethers and he told them I was the reason it didn't work...

Trying to hold them hornets in, is like trying to hold
my thoughts and sadness under control in this time of ex-

treme sorrow for our families. As most know, my friend and cousin, Boyd, is under hospice care. Thank the Lord he is communicating some still and knows his family. I just can't get my head around him leaving us—It's always been a comfort to know that Boyd and Rena are over there, and that I was always welcome…Please continue to pray for him and his family. The better person you are, the more you will be missed—he will be greatly missed for sure when the Lord comes for him…Thanks

Love Well

I remember that my dad and I loved each other so very much, but we did not love each other so very well. And the same thing with my oldest son Jeffrey William. We loved each other so very much, but not so very well. Does that make sense? Let me try to explain.

I have no problem now baring my inner soul to others. I can say to anyone 'I love you'. Can I do something for you? I have missed you so much while you were away! You are so kind! Or I am equally at ease telling others my troubles and my many shortcomings. As I've gotten older I have come to the conclusion that relationships are vital. And it is certainly not what we take with us, but what we leave behind that really matters.

But it has not always been this way. There were so many things left unsaid when I was young and I thought I knew everything. It is truly amazing how much I have learned since I thought I knew everything.

Dad was a kind, gentle man of strong faith and tremendous work ethics. We never spent much time doing anything but chores and such together. I played ball and he never got to see me play. I did not have a problem with that at all, but we just never talked—and there is a sadness about that.

My firstborn son had tremendous work ethics and was blessed with intelligence; except in his social life. He became an alcoholic and used drugs for his escape route from responsibility. He gave me two great grandchildren that he would not take care of. So we had no meaningful conversations for the last few years of his life. I should of asked more questions. But we drifted as far apart as strangers—and therein lies the sadness.

Dad is gone now for several years and my firstborn died last year on someone's front porch all alone. There are so many things I wish I had said, and so much more I wish I had done. People we love very rarely leave this life with all disputes settled, and every important message delivered, every need of forgiveness asked for or received, or all words said that needed to be said. Dad and Jeff left this world before the conversation was said! —And there is always unfinished business.

The pain and grief never goes completely away. Do you think God understands all this? Certainly. Do you think God understands our need for reconciliation? Certainly. I have been gently reminded that He turned His back on His Son at Calvary...He understands our needs for sure.

But what can we do about that if it's too late??? Do you believe in Heaven? I believe in Heaven and that there all our mistakes; all our shortcomings in this life will be forgiven. But I have wondered 'is there a corner reserved for me and Dad and Jeff to sit down and finally have that conversation?'

I do not know. But if there is, it will be by God's Amazing Grace. If there isn't a quiet corner somewhere, it will be because Heaven is so full of God's Glory that heartaches and sorrows are washed white as new fallen snow, and tossed into God's sea of forgetfulness, to be remembered no more. I know one thing for sure; I'm a winner either way. And it all is hinged on a profession of faith in God's darling Son, Our Lord Jesus Christ.

So, if you love someone so very much, make sure you love them so very well also. There is a difference...isn't there.

Jack Burris

My Dad, 1948, South Hominy NC. He taught me how to be a man by example. I miss my Dad.

Green to Gold

Another time, another vital way of life for mountain folk. Green gold. You were allotted how much tobacco you could raise according to the size of your farm. Some raised as little as 2 tenths of an acre. For someone to have over an acre was unusual in those days. This crop would buy clothes, shoes, seed and fertilizer, Christmas, and the necessities that they couldn't raise. Baccer money was almost a must have to lots of folk.

What they did was buy seed and prepare beds and sow the seed and cover the beds with white canvas. Gas the beds and when the plants were large enough and the signs were right, plants were pulled ad set. The ground would be plowed and disked and ready with straight rows. Most mountaineers had to have straight rows. They made for a pretty field and also easier to plow with the mule or horse. Back in the day of backer the men used a setter. You dropped one plant at a time into the setter and there was maybe 3 gallons of water in one side of the setter. They stuck the setter into the ground and squeezed the handle and set the plant and watered it at the same time. You needed a strong grip and a stout arm to run a setter for an entire patch.

One day when I was about 7 years old I got sent home with the pink eyes. I saw Hollis Robertson setting backer and I figured he needed help. So, I put my books in a chair and took off across the fields to help him, about a quarter mile. Well I carried water for Hollis and time eased on. Hollis said, "Uh-oh son." I looked and mom was striding toward me. Now there is a difference in walking normal and striding. I was in trouble cause she saw my books and I wasn't there. So I cut her a nice switch. I guess Hollis was able to finish without me.

My friend Jock had a couple tenths and he got sick and I handed and tied part of it for him. It was cold and some wind blown snow outside the little shack I was in. I remember it distinctly because Jim Reeves song, "He'll Have to go" was playing on the radio. I had fell in and out of love over a thousand times by then so I related to the song.

Anyway, as the tobacco grew it tousled and suckers came out on the stalks. So, if it was mature you topped it and cut the suckers out. Usually had to sucker it more than once. When the tobacco ripened they drove tobacco sticks into the ground, set a spud on top of the stick and cut the stalk off near the ground and jammed it down over the spud and down the stick. 5 or 6 stalks was pretty normal. Let it set in the field for a day or two and then pick it up on a sled or truck and haul it to the barn. Boys and men would climb up into the barn and spread their legs from tier pole to tier pole and the backer was passed up to the top and the tiers were filled up. Waspers and bumblebees were to be avoided, if possible. The tobacco was cured and at the right time when it came in "case"...Enough moisture to work easily without crumbing...Then the process was reversed and the sticks were taken down and the tobacco taken off the sticks and the leaves were graded into usually 4 cases. Lugs on the bottom, reds next, bright red next, and the tips. Graded onto a board divided into 4 sections.

Then, someone begins tying the leaves into hands. Put as many leaves as you could hold in your hand and you made the leaves even, then you take a nice leaf and fold it and tie the hand, go around and around and bring the end down and up thru the middle. Then the hands are put in 4-foot baskets and ready for market. This is a simple and not very complete piece on tobacco. One thing it does not do is let the reader smell the musty smell of a tobacco barn. It does not let you feel the 'family' time that was a part of working the backer. There could be five or six in the barn and the only sound was the whisper of the leaves as they were stripped and graded. No subject was off limits and there was always many things discussed, and mountaineer humor was always in play. Ma would leave the barn in time to fix dinner and as soon as she put stuff away, back to the barn she would go.

Most children did not go to school when it was time to work the backer. Most boys didn't care either. One thing they all cared about was the cash money the tobacco companies paid. Year after year, depending on the weather, praying for a good season. No hail or high winds...The old timers took great pride in their tobacco patches. They plowed and hoed the patches until the backer got up high enough. Just like white lightning tobacco was a critical commodity up until even the 1960's.

Then, the way of life in the hills began to fade into the fogs of time. Men and women began to go to work. Big companies began to grow and raise their own tobacco. Then they finally realized the tar and nicotine could kill you; so the local demand slumped. I know some of you all either helped raise or work the old style Burley tobacco. I wish I could go into an old barn and get the walls to talk to me. Can you imagine what you could hear... The laughter, the silence and throw in the musty smells...A piece of our past is gone. The barns sit empty with stories to tell.. A product of the mountain man's dream, made from wood, love, sweat, and dreams. A little piece of land, some shelter a few animals, a good barn, and a backer allotment...Christmas for the kids...Oh my I loves the old ways, I shorley does...Tobacco, ginseng, and moonshine... all had vital roles in mountain livelihood.

Tobacco--Cash money for Christmas and seed for next year. Green Gold for mountain folk many years ago.

When The Kids Get Gone

Everyday will be so good when the kids get gone. The garage will not have bikes and toys and skateboards all over the place. Maybe then I can find my saw and do some wood-work. When they get grown. Everyday will be better when the kids get grown. The wet towels strewed in the bathroom, hair curlers everywhere. Can't ever get in either one seems like. All those papers and notes on the fridge will finally come off when the kids are grown. Baseball gloves and bat left outside again, don't know where the ball is. Boy, wait till the kids are grown and gone. You can't even get a chicken leg around our table. There is never enough milk for my cereal seems like. I would love to see our kitchen neat and clean for a change. You just wait till the kids are grown and gone. I'll bet you I have a cup of coffee and my newspaper with no interruptions then...I can't wait. We can vacuum and mop and dust and see furniture we haven't seen in a while. When the kids are grown and gone. No more running to soccer or baseball games, no more school meetings or pajama parties. Mom will have time for long hot baths with no fusses, and she can do her nails and go shopping for herself. No more to the dentist, to the store, to the school, to the vet, to the recital when the kids are grown and gone... the sink won't be full of dirty dishes or the mustard jar lid won't be gone and jelly prints won't be on the door when the kids are gone. I'll see the back seat of the van...fingerprints, tongue licks, and dog tracks won't be on my windows when the kids are gone. No more fist beating the bathroom door. I won't hear the wazzup, or gross or yuk when the kids are gone.

I won't be hunting toilet paper or a dry washcloth or shutting the front door while yelling over and over 'was you raised in a barn?'

Yep, one day when the kids are gone, things will be in order. The place will get cleaned up and maybe look elegant a bit. The clink of china will be heard occasionally. Yep, the house will be clean, and calm, and quiet and empty; and we find ourselves not thinking about everyday, but thinking about yesterday's memories, and trying to figure out how we can get the grandkids over here and get a little life in this ole house...

RCs and Moon Pies

Davis Store just before Stony Fork School. I sat on that porch with my bare feet hanging down many time with my friend Walker Hinson. Walker had grandchildren but for some reason they didn't like to go with him to cut, rake, and bale hay. Walker took a liking to me. He always stopped here whenever we went that way—always a moon pie and an ice cold RC. That was the best times. I chased rabbits and helped him fix the twine and such. I could catch the small rabbits, and I turned them loose of course. It was great fun for a little boy. I did small chores for Lois, Walker's wife. She was a good cook who made cookies on a regular basis. So I went up there on a regular basis. One time, he had a huge whiteface bull. He was so gentle and Walker led him to water or a different pasture on occasion, and I rode on his back—to me it seemed like his back was an 'ax handle wide' A little scary but I didn't let on.

I remember holding or helping hold calves for him when they were sick or had the 'scours'. He would pour coffee down their throat and they usually got better. I don't remember why, but he had a bag of arsenic and I was playing in the barn and knocked it off the shelf and one of his calves got into it and died. I won't tell you whether I confessed or not; but, really I think he probably knew. Lesson learned. He had a show bull, I guess for 4H and I led him to the creek for water every evening, or most of the time…that was scary too but I never let on.

It's good to take a ride in that old canoe on the river of

66

so many good memories this morning. I wish I could run up to Walkers, barefooted, and get a saucer with 2 cookies and a glass of milk this morning. Or hear that old ford trucks horn blow and Walker say, "Come on boy, let's go to the store." You be blessed this day for sure, you hear me??

Sunday Dinner and Decoration Day

The cemetery was up on a hill there in Shelton Laurel. Most burial grounds were in places not really suitable for gardens or crops. On a hillside or at the crest of a hill, and usually they were fenced in with barbed wire cause they were part of a pasture. Some places made it hard on pallbearers cause you couldn't get very close to the graves. One good part of that was that the preacher would be winded from climbing up there and so he would be "short-winded."

The main reason was, they went to folks houses on Sunday and was fed good southern fried chicken and taters. While you and I had to settle for the back if it was left. I still resent the dratted ole preacher coming for Sunday dinner. Sometimes we would wring the pullets neck and then chop its head off and sometimes just lay its head on a chopping block and let her bleed boys. Now some of you all don't appreciate that I know, but I bet you like Bojangles or KFC. They make a living chopping chickens heads off...it's like shooting that hog you raised from a cute little pig.

You made do then, now you buy it prepackaged. Same difference except them fresh tenderloins and biscuits was the best eating around. Plus, there was a feeling of family when those get togethers came around. Folk would help each other. Just keep that chicken loving preacher away, I say. When Berry Watts brought them two boys of his and Ruby there wasn't much left for ole Jack.

Then the men folk would go sit on the porch and smoke or chew. Us youngans would run the woods or go down to the creek. I kept my homemade fishing pole(s) hid in the woods near the creek. I didn't want them rascals messing up my fishing hole. Oh well, we never had too many visits cause we needed our chickens for eggs and such.

Anyway, back to the cemetery business, every year usually around Memorial Day, folks had a "decoration day" Lots of times men folk would go to the cemetery on Saturday or so and clean up the cemetery; cut weeds, and remove limbs, fix the fence, and cut the grass. Great pride was in place to make the cemetery neat and cleaned up. Now decoration means just that. Folk come and bring flowers and memories and they visit and talk and remember loved ones gone on. There is a lot of laughter and a lot of tears. Usually there are some baby graces. Lots of babies died at childbirth or shortly there after because of lack of medical knowledge and the in home deliveries. My mother Annie Burris was a mid wife, and I've often wondered how many babies she saved and how many died. Doctors were in short supply and most couldn't afford one anyway. Anyways, after the decorations were done, usually some one led in singing some old time gospel songs —always "Amazing Grace" and "Shall We Gather at the River". Then usually a preacher but not always, would preach. If no preacher was there someone would always speak. It was family time and a mountain tradition that still goes on today, though not near as much.

Everyone had their own memories or heartaches to reminisce about. My Mom had her own memories that were kept pretty much inside for 80 years. She was put out of the home when just a little girl because of the size of the family or because of the demands of a new woman in her dad's life. There simply was not enough room, so the story goes. Anyways, for Mom it was forgiveness and reconciliation even though he was long dead. We went up the hill while she sat in a chair and talked to him, then she got down on her knees and cleaned up the grave and put flowers on it. Then she was ready to go-either home or to Heaven.

The old cemeteries can be a place of remembrance and healing. How do we forget those who have given us so many good reasons to remember them?? I wish my Mom had made that trip to Shelton Laurel many years earlier. Surely keeping feelings of hurt inside takes a huge toll. I usually carry a grudge for a while. I want to get even. But one thing about dropping dead in your back yard can do, is help change attitudes about some things. I said to myself, Lord, I don't know why my heart started beating again, but I reckon you ain't through with me; and I don't know what you want from me, but I made a change to be more loving to all people, to try and let go of "grudges" if I was wronged, to look daily for ways to help someone else. All three happen, not every day, but the chances and reasons come.

I love my Mama who died not long after letting go of those feelings—she was a mountain woman and knew what switches was for...and used them with gusto—but she loved me and I cried when I saw her on her knees talking to her dad in that cemetery. We don't do Decoration Day here in Statesville; but I take flowers occasionally and put them on my first wife's grave, and on my two sons graves. I know I shoulda been a better man, and a better husband, and a better father. I am always saddened for a spell, and then I think of the good years and there were so many and I am blessed. Maybe he left me here to put flowers on those graves...Man I wish I could go back to that other time when Mom insisted I be cleaned up and my hair all combed in place and we were on the hilltop singing Amazing Grace. Remembering and respecting those who have paid their dues and gone on.... Decoration Day...

The Old Man and Me

The old man and me met on a dirt road. He got out of his old Ford truck slowly and deliberately. He sized me up without seeming to, the mountain way. He nodded and I explained who I was and who I knew and where I was heading. I knew if we were going to talk he had to know those things. He lived there so he had no need to tell me anything. I was an outsider to him; and that is one thing I love about mountain folk.

He said it takes all kind of folk to make up this world and some we could do without. I knew then and there we were going to be friends. He said too many changes heading south. Too much government. He said, when I growed up you did stuff for yoreself or you did without...and at suppertime you had two choices: take it or leave it...Used to be everybody helped everybody else...to build their houses, to raise their barns, shuck their corn, split their rails, build their fences, string their beans, kill their hogs, make molasses-or just get together with a friend or two and go hunt some sang—nowadays if you run out of gas you best start walking.

The old man and me, we set the echoes flying from out of the past, and really stirred up the whispers of yesteryear. He shivered and pulled his coat a bit tighter and said, Ma used to say winter thinned yore blood, and it does; but no one makes sulpher and molasses for a spring tonic to lift the spirits and cure the blood anymore. They used to make cherry bark and whiskey mix for a tonic...now the menfolk liked that one. He said I could use one of them now. He said, now who'de you say you was kin to? I knew he heard me but it was my time to talk...

I mentioned that I missed the slow ticking clocks and the cry of the whippoorwill, the long lazy days of summer of bare feet and the woods and creeks of a time gone away, where dirt roads and paths meandered into hidden coves and valleys and homes hidden in the woods. He said, hear that? A chainsaw was running in the distance...used to be a silence, a brooding kind of quietness in these hills, and the ring of an ax or the yelling at a stubborn old mule to 'gee' or 'haw', along with the bray of the mule was common sounds. Now, it's tractors and four wheelers and chainsaws and a good peaceful, quiet time on the front porch is hard to come by. He said, do you like porches? Boy, that was right up my road. I said I love porches, I love to drive along and see folk sitting out on their porches. I said, but I really love to see a light on a porch at nighttime. I really like just a single naked bulb hanging down with a string attached to turn it off and on. It says things to me, like you're welcome here, or a light for the prodigal to come home...Now in the summer they draw bugs to the porch, but nevertheless someone turned the light on, on purpose, and someone has to go out with the bugs, or cold and turn it off. I loves porches and lights, I shorely.

Then, he paid me one of the best compliments I have ever received. He said, I live just up the holler and I got a nice wide porch, next time you come this way, stop and sit a spell. He said, I'll show you some spoons and buttons made from cow horns that my dad made and we used. He said, I've also got a beegum made from a hollow white oak that he made—that's why I said you made do or you did without...I haven't been back yet to sit on the porch, and I hope I make it in his time; but it took me back to laying in the hayfield and looking up at the Carolina blue sky and the peaceful silence and the slow ticking clock...Maybe the mournful bay of a hound off in the distance; 60 plus years ago when I was going to live forever, with not a care in the world. I love these old time mountain folk, ain't nobody no better...

Con Davis

Con Davis worked for the state, I think. I know he could run equipment. He drove a pick-up truck and he smoked Lucky Strike cigarettes. I know cause Connie Gene would get us one or some every once in a while. Boys in the late 40's and 50's were apt to smoke because many adults did-even between SS and preaching the preacher ad men would go out and smoke. Sometimes during altar call the men would come back to the pews and tell you that you was hell bound and needed to get saved; between onions and cigarette breath in your face you figured it was a good time to go, so I went several times. I never did get "it" but got away from those who really meant well.

I thought Con was so cool with his arm out the window all muscled up and a Lucky in his mouth. I was scared of him. He had that look. Now he never gave me reason to be, but he never put his arm around my shoulders either. Besides that, I teased his whiteface bull till that ole bull would paw the ground when he seen me. He would come towards me from the other end of the pasture when he saw me coming down the dirt road. About the time he got halfway ole Jack would kick it in overdrive and set the 100 yard dash record for little boys under 10.

Anyway, Con made cash money and he bought a TV. Black and white, test pattern, warm up and outside antenna. That was my first time seeing a TV. Imagine that; been listening to the radio and "Inner Sanctum" and "Grand Ole Opry" and here was a picture—moving and talking. Ole Ed Sullivan. How many saw Elvis in black and white. I do not recall when Ole Yeller came out in living color; but that was the best. You had to cry when he had to shoot that ole yeller dog.

Con let me come over and watch TV with Connie. I have always been grateful. I went to see him a long time ago and told them how grateful I was; and I told him about the bull. He couldn't say much because he was on his gray horse and he had his shotgun chasing that old bull. It was whispered that he was drinking a bit. Him and Dad killed a deer that wandered through and when mom cooked it, he told me it was rooster meat. I think they were out of season.

Anyway one sound that I liked to hear was that old oak bridge flooring rattling when a car or truck come across it. If it was Saturday night, it meant Con was home and Ed was coming on TV. I wish I had talked to him; but his big old strong mountain men looked huge from way down to my size, up to his...I think I practiced the saying-"speak when you're spoken to, come when you are called, and if you are not spoken to, don't come at all." I have knowed some men and women that I should have known better...Con was one, and lordy he had a TV, he musta been rich...

PS-I got sidetracked on a rabbit trail—us boys smoked oak leaves, dried corn silk which had a sweet taste, grapevine, and most anything else that would light. One of the worst whippings from my dad was over me and Connie sitting on top of the hog pen in the very dry woods smoking oak leaves rolled up in a brown paper from a poke...We coulda burned the mountain down—that was one I really earned—All the other switchings—not guilty of course—Mom could hear me sneaking a match out of the matchbox up on the wall from out of the outhouse out in the woods—Them moms, they are something else—be blessed this day and every day—she woke me up early, she is good to our dog, she has a green thumb, and we don't smoke or chew or kiss people who do.

Mom and Dad

I remember my dad always worked. He worked in the AC dept at American Enka. He retired there. At South Hominy we lived about a quarter mile from the road, and I remember running over to the road to meet him. The Enka Bus ran everywhere we lived and picked Pop up. A Ramsey fella from Marshall drove it. It was like a school bus painted blue and white. I used to follow behind Pop sometimes and try to step in his tracks. It has been a good reminder to me that someone is always watching and may well be trying to be 'like' you. Don't underestimate these young kids—they see and hear more than you think.

Pop was a good man who loved the Lord and provided for his family. I did not talk in depth to him like I should have. I miss him, and I let time slip away. Maybe somewhere there will be a corner in Heaven and we can sit down and have that conversation. Things you do not do in this life of time can hurt too; like a low blow to the belly, just a feeling of "regret"....

How many times have I seen Mom over a sink doing dishes?? It always meant she had been preparing something to eat. She had thought about what was for dinner and supper before breakfast was over. A cook extraordinaire; and as my Mom got older, seeing her bent over a stove or a sink doing dishes did something inside of me. She was a homemaker until I got gone, then she went to work as a maid in a motel. The extra money was a real blessing for her and allowed her to do and buy some things she needed and some things she wanted.

She never drove a car. She rode the town bus from Woodfin to work and back; but she still fixed all the meals. My dad washed the dishes lots of times in the later years, but I cannot ever remember going home without one of them asking me if I was hungry.

To me, the second best thing I ever accomplished was when I went "home". Really went home and was a son that they were pleased with. Isn't it wonderful when He gives us that kind of opportunity to undo and repair things that just need "fixing"...When my Mom was on her 'sickbed' I could still see her eyes light up when I went into the room; and I really realized that no one ever loves you like your mother—except the Lord—no matter what.

I could sit in there with her and never have to say a word. I looked at her hands so many times. So many thought of her 'washing' my face with her thumb, I can see her breaking beans, using the corner of her apron to twist a jar lid off, I can see her finger pointing at me and shaking her head, I remember her filing and working on her nails, but mostly I recall those hands rolling dough for biscuits, or cornbread, or stirring a pot of homemade soup. Sometimes I can see her bent over a sink wringing out a dishrag. She feels good then because she has fed whoever is there...And I've talked about the preacher getting all the chicken, but I remember Mom always making sure her baby boy Jack got a piece of chicken—even though she did not—but that is what Moms do isn't it?? They will give up their own dreams to make ours come true...I miss my folks. Good honest mountain folk who made do.

Christmas Goodies

Well, it's nearing Christmas, and are you ready? Is it the popcorn strings on the tree? And the tinsel? Did you go all out into the fields and woods and search so long and hard for the right tree; joking and laughing and studying each tree so carefully? You knew there was something good on the old woodstove for when you dragged the tree back for mom's inspection.

It's kinda funny, I remember hunting for a tree, and cutting one, and dragging it hoe, but I don't remember decorating it. Perhaps my dear sisters ran me out of the house, and maybe the woods called to me. Sometimes we cut a cedar, and sometimes a pine tree. There was one thing that was about always the same though. There wasn't a lot of presents under the tree. At the most two, and usually only one; but the stocking was a treat. What was in yours???

Probably about the same as mine; an apple, an orange, some nuts and hard candy. It was so hard to go easy on that stuff and make it last. I tried, I guess. Some. I do remember 'stealing' some of Leta's candy once. Once was enough. I didn't consider it stealing; I figured she owed it to me because of all the junk I had to put up with. Two sisters at home, and both older than me. You talk about living 'careful'. I was an agitator; and I was gifted at it. I was probably the only professional switch cutter on South Hominy.

Dad didn't have much education but he had a deep and profound love for the Lord. I remember going to church so much. I remember those brown paper pokes with the same things in it as my stocking...I don't remember a Christmas play, or any service; but I remember those pokes for sure...And one thing that has always made me swallow slow and feel so blessed is the tender heart my father had. He could get blessed at the drop of a hat, and he carried a hat to drop. Tears came easily and unashamedly. I must tell you this to ease my feelings—I didn't think much of it when I was young and knew everything; and I didn't do for my dad like I could have. As I got older I realized what a gift it is to have a tender heart. I know I have one. I can cry at TV weddings, and the movie "The Notebook", a basket case. I always want boy to get girl.

Dad's love for God Almighty was his joy. A good song, a verse of scripture would set him off. Dad was a Pentecostal and we didn't agree on denominations and such but we didn't argue either...my regret?? I didn't realize how much he really meant to me until after he died; at Christmas I always get in my old canoe and float down the rivers of my memories in hopes he comes along—and he always does.

Lordy, don't be like me and miss someone after they are gone. Don't buy me no stupid flowers after I'm dead. Say it now while you can. Maybe it's a brother or sister or a parent or that black sheep in the family. It's Christmas time...Christ is coming in the Old Testament, He has come in the New Testament, and He is coming again.....Shoot, Lets go hunt a tree and throw this man made gorgeous tree out in the yard—Well maybe not, dad isn't here to chop it down---I wish he was--

A Time To Remember

It's pointless to write with a broken pencil...Did you know bicycles can't stand up because they are two tired? I am still perplexed about two and three seater outhouses. Sitting beside your best friend in an outhouse? Gas and all? Looking at pictures in a Sears Roebuck catalogue, grunting and making noises? Not me, sounds like carpenters showing off....and by the way, I used to be an avid hunter. I have never killed or wounded one. My friend's son is an avid hunter. He killed a nice 8-point while avid hunting. No luck on avids though, just a buck. Them avids has got to be slyer than a coyote, slicker than a whistle, and elusive as fog. I'm glad I quit avid hunting...

I also found out another great truth in 2017...You do not need a parachute to sky dive. That's right, only if you sky-dive twice...and by the way, why was there those two vent pipes in the outhouses? Or even one? Surely they didn't really believe the odor would just float out did they? It's truly a mystery that has bothered me ever since the Sears started closing...Sears is responsible for cleaning up a lot of mess, I say give them some sort of congressional medal...Another dele-mon: my buddy is an avid fisherman, with no luck...but I was deciphering that and could be when I been avid hunting they are hiding in the water; so maybe I should get my avid killer off the wall and go hunting avids when he is fishing for one.

I miss the old outhouse with the rich smells. I miss the

corn silk cigarettes, I miss the paths up into the woods where the hickory trees drawed the squirrels when I was avid hunting and I settled for them. I really miss walking out of a night and hearing a coonhound after some critter...like a lonesome train whistle. I miss the fog and eerie look of Mount Pisgah at night that made shivers, I miss my Mama quilting and cooking and washing and canning and all that stuff that went with the 50's and those golden years of yesterday. I miss them man, I don't wish to go back cause I have lived and cried and bled and wept many many times—there are lots I would do different and there in lies the sad part, but I have lived and loved and had several good dogs. Shoot man, I have even died, ain't many can say that right there. I've felt like dying when I've buried friends and family, and I feel like living when I see a baby or hear one cry...

I see these kids in foster care and I wish they had a trail up into the woods, or kindling to split and wood to carry. I wish they had somebody to show them something real. That's why we do this. I can't take them back there to shoot marbles for keeps, or make a beanshooter, or dam the creek—but we can take them to church and show them by example there is a better way to live; we can give them things to do so they will feel involved in family...and we pray for them...

I was playing basketball with a 12-year-old boy we have yesterday. We was playing horse. You get a letter for each shot you miss that the other made; first to spell horse, missing, loses. I did a fancy dribble in front of the basket and was in the process of doing a spin move for a lay up...Instead, I found myself on the concrete with a skint knee and a sore hip. My feet got behind in what my brain told them to do. I swanney, I didn't know old age was going to be like this...But, like the lady said, "I'm just so proud to be here"...I lost the horse game...First one I've lost all year.

I don't care who you are; dark times come along sooner or later. Illness, deaths, job losses, fires, floods, accidents, tornadoes, and the list goes on. Sooner or later. Better later huh? You and I know that no matter how many clouds get in the way, the sun keeps shining. No matter if the warm rays are blocked from our view, the sun will reappear and shine just as brightly as ever......Sometimes it takes a lot of strength and determination to make it past those dark times that show up, sometimes suddenly—but patience and our love for life, family, friends, and God Almighty...will pay off eventually, because love and the sun have a lot in common with each other... they will shine no matter what----sooner or later....Musings of an old man with one foot in a canoe and the other in a parking lot at a doctor's office waiting on my son James...Little cloudy here, but we will make do, and make "it"...

Old Friends

If you don't get together with friends occasionally, you should. I'm setting up a catered meal and we are going to really decorate the tables with red and hearts the Sunday before Valentines—a gift for each one. Us men are going to wear our black slacks and white shirts with red tie or bowtie. We are going to celebrate the ladies of our church. We will be the waiters and have some old time 50's and 60's music after the meal......

I mentioned this before and only do it again to encourage some of you fellows to maybe treat the ladies at your church. They are the glue and how boring would we be with just a bunch of old men trying to sing. I'm thinking of getting a white wig and a dress, and doing a skit if I can recruit someone to wear it or help. This should really be a fun time. I loves the wimmens, I shorely does—quote out of Jerimiah Johnson— my sentiments exactly...I did have pintos, turnip greens, cabbage, and of course cornbread—with a slice of onion. Irons out the roof now.

Well, it's 2018 already. Yesterday it was 1954. I have no clue about the brevity of life. At some point in time, long ago, the summer days seemed to stretch out. Lazy days of summer. Boy I had fun those days; but like everything else they came to an end in August, back to school with excitement; Old friends, new ones, and good-looking South Hominy girls to look at sideways and dream. We always hoped some would show up at the swimming hole in the clear cold-cold water and go skinny-dipping with us. Never did happen, but some dreams have come true....

The Rock Gardens

So like you, today begins the rest of the story. Autumn time for sure. I went over to the cemetery for a visit. It reminded me of a rock garden. The granite is polished and shines —laid out in neat rows. In a selected and special hill the rock garden has been planted. In the spring, trees bloom and grass appears. Some of the polished rocks have moss and black seams on them...I give thanks to God for these here, many fateful to the Church nearby, others from various walks of life, memories loved and cherished. My mind wanders to the ancestors and Indians...They too buried their dead and archeologists tell us there is evidence of love and loss in the artifacts buried with the dead...Now, visiting here I realize we bury our loved ones and make these rock gardens to remember them and cherish their memory—and also to remind us how much we wish they were still here—to talk to and to hug one more time.... Perhaps even to say I'm sorry...

The polished surface of each rock in this Rock Garden is chiseled with names and dates and we remember the love relationships of the past and now we have a place where we are reminded of that love...The Rock Garden is a special place blessed by the beauty of nature. Each polished rock offers a deposit for love and other memories...All together they remind me of the labors of others who have entered into a Haven of rest from their labors. This old cemetery is where yesterday, today and tomorrow come together...it is for me, where the joys of yesterday, the sorrows of today, and the hopes of tomorrow mix and mingle to challenge us to press on toward tomorrow...

This canoe trip may not be the best way to start off another year, or another day, or maybe even another hour—but the visit certainly impressed on me how blessed I am—and how much I have lost...I went over to Shane's grave—A preacher friend of mine's son...He was 18 and he was troubled with being a teenager and not yet a man and took his life on the back porch one night while his dad was teaching The Book...They came home and found him...He asked me to do the graveside part of the service—now I ask you—what do you say to a Mom and Dad who are broken??? Paul's prayer in Ephesians was all I had—Now unto Him who is able to do—That's all I had—but it was and is enough—Happy New Year—take time to reflect on those who are gone home..

Home For Christmas

I'll be home for Christmas, you can plan on me. Please have snow and mistletoe, and presents under the tree. Christmas Eve will find me where the love light gleams, I'll be home for Christmas, if only in my dreams. Maybe kids get too much junk nowadays. I can recall the joy of expecting something under the tree on Christmas day. I recall the brown paper pokes we got at Church with much happiness. They always had the same thing year after year seems like; but the anticipation didn't diminish. An apple, an orange, a few nuts, and of course the old time hard candy. What a treat. Give this to kids nowadays, and it would be left to spoil. I tell you this; it didn't spoil at my house. One time at Open Bible, they had too many and I got 2 pokes. Now honey child that was it. They lasted a whole day.

Can you recall the fun times at Christmas those many years ago? The trip through the woods searching for that 'one' tree? Then cutting it down, and putting it in a bucket with rocks and water? Popcorn strings and silver tinsels. Paper cut outs hung with care; and of course a star, to honor the birth of the baby that changed everything. We hung socks on the mantle or behind the warm morning wood heater on the wall. Oh it was family time and great fun. Yes, I believe in Santa Claus still. I couldn't figure out how when our roof was steep and the chimney was so small, how that fat man came down the chimney...

A sock hung with care would have in it much the same as our 'church pokes'. Seems like I remember getting bubble-gum in mine. Maybe I just dreamed that, or wanted it so bad that it seems true. One year I got a billfold. One time, a real bonafide set of six shooters with holsters, and once, a real bow with arrows. Usually the sock full and a gift under the tree was Christmas; but there was love to fill the gaps—and it's funny, but I never remember Mom or Dad having presents until I took them when I went home for Christmas, but that's what moms and dads did back then. We inched up to Christmas back then, we counted the days and watched the sky for snow clouds, and we couldn't wait, for a paper poke full of goodies, and maybe one present under the tree....

The fireplace with its bright red coals sent out a warmth to me in the house that I built by my hands in the woods in the early 90's. I had an open fireplace just for sitting in front of it and thinking with my heart and not my head. I remember Sarah, Jesse, and Ashley stamping their feet on the porch getting the snow off, then coming in and gathering up close to the fireplace with frozen fingers and feet and the steam rising from the gloves and shoes; but I remember most the laughter and joy they had running through the snow... Cause I guess it took me back to the late 40's and 50's when I anticipated Christmas with that same joy.

That's why the lock is not locked on the door—I say come on in my friend, whether it's family or kinfolk, or a friend. Come sit a spell, I'll stir up the fire and never a word to be said, we will be deep in though with our hearts and not our heads—for the Christ Child is coming, the stable is ready —Christmas is here...Lets warm up our souls and wait for our children to stomp the snow off and come by the fire. Maybe I'll tell them the old, old story and about Rudolph and about the brown paper pokes and the Present under the tree—that meant so much.... I love the music of Christmas, and I love thinking with my heart this time of year, I love our candlelight service at Church with communion, and I really love how I personally saw the star and went to the stable one Easter Sunday morning and met the baby who changed everything... I'll be back there for Christmas, if only in my mind...Merry Christmas to all...

The Wise Shepherds

There's a new kid I town, and He's lying in a manger down the road—Friday I had the privilege to sit in a rocking chair at our live nativity and tell the old, old story. It touched me when I was a player I the plays we put on in church in the 40's and 50's, and it really touches me today. The Wise men were wise; they sought the Master. The Shepherds were wise cause they put seeing Him first. You and I are wise if we saw the star and found the stone to be rolled away. A baby changed everything, forever, in a cow and sheep stall. A Virgin and a husband who stuck around. Don't forget Joseph, that was a miracle too in that time.

The sad thing is, our country has had influences that have gradually, quietly taken our faith and slid it to the back burner. Simple moves like soccer on Sundays, Blue laws erased, liberal teachers and professors who believe only on their own intelligence, or lack of it. News media and Hollywood with brainwashing tactics. Slowly and consistently. Most of the younger generation care less, and know even less about our History. Technology has taken away conversations face to face—family time—just plain thinking—why think of solutions when you have Google. What made us great at one time??? It started on a night in a stable—and I have a hunch it could end from the stable.

You Can't Forget

I'm in the 3rd grade riding down the rivers of my memories in my old wore out canoe that leaks a bit. I've used it thousands of times, but I have really used it when trouble has come around. At times, trouble came pretty often; having a place of refuge is such a blessing. A lot of old time classmates have ridden with me, and they didn't even know it. Folk who have made a difference in my life are regular riders. Family is always around. I have an intense desire to understand how the mountain folk in my family tree acted and reacted to life in general. I mean nostalgia sweeps over me sometimes and almost sits me down. It might be a song from the 50's, or maybe just see a tricycle in a yard, or a '50 Ford or a '57 Chevy. I used to visit my cousin Danny Windsor in Marshall on Bull Run and he had a tricycle. I couldn't keep my hands off it. I thought Dan must be rich to buy him a tricycle. Little things like that light up my life.

I poured 1 (one) yard of concrete today inside a building for an AC pad. Wheel barrowed it in and I was tired; and nostalgia hit me and I realized I ain't ever going to do what I have done again. It's going to get "worse". I though the other week if I was just young enough I would go to Houston or Florida and help...I thought of chinquapins a while ago. Little nuts encased in a burr of spines much like a chestnut. They tasted so good in a classroom. George Austin and Hugh Watts and others would bring them to school and we would trade. Marbles, pennies, or about anything else including bean shooters (slingshots). I mean this was a big deal. I would get hazel nuts off Davis Creek and take them to school; while they were pretty good, they had a hard shell you had to crack. Hard to even give them away. What good was something you couldn't sneak and eat in the classroom? I always look for them when I go sang digging, which has decreased dramatically the last few years; but I can go in my old canoe.

I can hear the soft rain through the leaves of the huge old growth trees, I can see the red tail high overhead on his way to Pisgah, shoot it would take me a day to get there, and he's already there. See, it's easy to remember and still throw in dreams of doing it again. Then nostalgia sets in. I was just reminded of Mom looking at me from her bed with the sunlight on her coming through the window. I have that picture ad I know she loved me cause its right there. She showed me because I let her know without saying a word how much she meant to me. The note she left comes along to my mind when se said, "you won't forget me will you?" and it sorta haunts me that she would dare think I would ever forget her. She raised me right, how do you forget someone that raises you right?

We played marbles in the red dirt at Stony Fork School in the 2nd and 3rd grade. It was serious business. Us boys craved good agates for shooters. Many a shoulder fight broke out over marbles. Mom said the Book said, "Marble not" and don't play for keeps. I found out later, it was "Marvel not"...I love for Mom to show up in my thoughts. I know where she came from and the struggles she had. My Dad shows up at times ad I always wish I had asked him so many more questions. He raised me right too. I just messed up on my own.

My sister Laura shows up sometimes and she is a giver and a helper. She is a quilter and a doer. She set aside her personal life to care for Mom and Dad. I smile when I think about her being back in Georgia with her family. My cousins in East

Tenn are part of the trips. Most of my first cousins have gone on, and there are not too many of us left. I lost my friend and mentor a while back and it was difficult on all of us. He was the patriarch of the family I thought. Rest my friend Boyd; you are one of the very best.......

Wade When You Can

I've always tried to ride around in those good times of youth. I have tons of stuff about love and courting and marriage and work and life after the service. I wrote some stuff one time and a couple of 'friends' told my bride I was living in the past. That's funny, but I just quit writing about those things. Now, I want to, so I am. You talk about folk and the Good Lord helping a man-child, boy they saved my life...and I let them ride with me sometimes.

I am a hospice volunteer, I love to work at my pace and choice, I paint at watercolor, I love music and all kinds, but back then mostly. I teach SS and have conducted services and "preached" filled in several times; I am a mountain man at heart, though I live in the Piedmont. My canoe is docked on Davis Creek, I hunt arrowheads and golf and fish. My life is full, but at the same time I feel a longing for the old days. Maybe, just maybe I coulda lived way back yonder. While I'm at it, I never liked Roy Rogers or Gene Autry—whoever heard of a singing cowboy??? Enough to make a boy sick. Oh well, the water is shallow and I think I'm going to wade in the creek, (something I do every time I've been to Cades Cove or Pisgah Forest). I'll see you on the river—Be blessed cause you are, you hear me?

The Button Trip

I got out an old work shirt that looks like it needs replacing, but you know how some things are too good to get rid of. They are like old friends. I've worn the old stone washed canvas shirt for a lot of winters, through snow and rain and sunshine. How can I discard an old friend, I ask you. I bet every one of you have some wore out on the outside stuff that you can't let go. Well a button was missing and I went in the bedroom closet and got a needle and some miscolored thread and got my readers and threaded the needle. I evened up the ends and around my finger and rolled it and made the knot, and it came to me.

So, I jumped into my old canoe and took a little trip down the river. I'm getting too old and lazy to paddle upstream...and Mom showed up. The thought came to me—Mom showed me how to make a knot in thread when I was very small. It had to do with making fishing line and doubling the thread; and not only how to make a knot, but when to double the thread and when to use one line. She showed me by example how to sew on a button. Crisscross and do it enough so it won't come off again. I watched her make small neat stitches on the many quilts she made. She used a thimble and told me why. I thought goodness; most of the stuff I know was taught or showed to me when I was just a small boy.

I knew how to wash clothes and run tem through the wringer...pumping the water for the wash wasn't stuff I really needed to know. I watched mom cook and she wore an apron and she would use a corner to twist off the lids off of those half runners, or the peaches, or the canned sausage. I watched her make biscuits and knead the dough and have flour a plenty to roll them in so they wouldn't stick to her hands. So many things I never really though about; like keeping my mouth shut unless spoken to, the importance of being quiet in Church, combing my hair, being clean, and I sure knew when not to sass my folks.

I was going to be clean inside and out and my hair was going to be combed when I left for the school bus. It was around a quarter mile to the stop and there was rocks to throw and a creek to cross and my dog tagged along. Momma got unusually irritated when I got grass stains and red dirt stains on my jeans...and the toes of our shoes would get wore out from shooting marbles...I cut more switches from those two things than all the rest combined. I couldn't pass a game up, and I got pretty good too. I hid my winnings from Mom along with me and Connie's occasional Lucky Strike he would sneak from his dad, under the old oak bridge at the creek. Oh I was slick I thought.

I have loved sewing that button on today. I can see my Mom bent over a stove or washing dishes I a dishpan or washing clothes outside in the summer or when it was warm. I can see the struggle in her eyes over part of her childhood... I can see the hurt when I didn't call or come around when she needed me and wanted to see us. She showed and taught me so much and I'm not real sure I ever told her how grateful I am for all she did for me when I didn't even realize she was doing it. Maybe next time, I will tell about my dad, but today I wasn't cutting wood or working on a lawnmower; I was sewing on a button—I never saw dad sew one on...But I watched my Mama —and I wish I could see her quilting those tight little stitches again, while I played under the quilting frame...She didn't always know I was watching...

Kraut and Church

Sometimes the most unusual thoughts come along at the oddest times. Sitting in Church trying to be my very best and be attentive and spiritual I thought about kraut. You know about kraut, don't you? Made from cabbage and used in various and sundry places. Sour kraut? Reubens? I thought of making kraut. When I was a boy, once upon a long time ago, we made kraut every year. Something about the kind of cabbage was called Dutch. Perhaps the kind of cabbage Dad planted. Long rows, big, round, hard heads, sorta flat like tightly wound. Do you have any idea how much little boys with slingshots, wagons, six shooters with rolls of caps, home-made fishing poles and bows and arrows, and with a creek nearby—enjoyed helping with kraut??

It was cruel in the first degree. If you think breaking half runners all day was pure torture, try chopping cabbage and getting the pieces all the same size (Mama's desire). It was tedious and awful sitting at a table with those huge heads of cabbage all around with no end in sight. I was so aggravated I wouldn't even eat any for a couple hours. It didn't do any good to nick your finger and squeeze blood out; Mama just wrapped it a bit and stuck that dratted ole knife back in my hand. Didn't even have duct tape either. Thoughts of running away entered my mind. Throwing up wouldn't work either, and too much sass would get labor stripes on my legs, and I had to go cut the switch unless she used one of the dozen or so on top of the cabinet. Oh it was painful chop, chop, chop for hours.

Cutting cabbage was not easy; then, when it was cut to her specs she rinsed it, and packed it in crocks and let it rot, or stink, or both. She packed it in there too, and raw cabbage became kraut; like most mountain and farm raised women, she could fix kraut in several ways and much to my disgust; I loved them all. Particularly with pork chops cooked in it, or hot dogs, or sausages. I still like the sour stuff; but I will never forget or forgive for those hot summer days or cool fall days, or any other day when I had to "help" make kraut, that I pretended to not even like.

You know what—I might would trade a few of my tomorrows for another day under Mom's penetrating look, swelled up like a poisoned puppy, resentful, pouting, fearful that the creek would run dry without me in it—chopping cabbage—just one more time...And where were my two sisters in these thoughts? I never see them doing one thing—nothing—I had it all to do......Oh well, I just heard the benediction and it was about—uh let me see—uh he said something about uh, uh "cabbage"????

Mistletoe-Love Has Many Faces

Here at Christmas, love is pretty easy to show. There is a mistletoe and hugs and kisses and laughter and good feelings all around. As long as everyone has a job and the health is good and there are presents under the tree and the fridge is full and the kids and grandkids are on the way. It's easy to smile and love 'everybody'; even that bad waitress you grouched about. You may have not known that her husband had walked out and left her with 2 young kids, or that her car had tore up, or her Mama was sick. Or when the HP pulled you over and wrote a ticket for 12 over the limit; boy, easy to cuss him out in your rear view. Could it possibly be that the drunk drier coming your way had finally gotten off the road just when the HP let you go?? Or how about those leaves and limbs falling in your yard and it ain't even your tree? You can't even talk to him without feeling like telling him off about his tree. Could it possibly be that his wife is not well, or that he has to take medicine that is so high he skips every other day just to get by?? He has nothing to offer about his tree. Of course he won't ask you for help, he senses the anger over a few leaves. Or how about that worthless couple that invaded your stable and run two of your goats out then she had a baby and they stayed in there for a couple of days. Of all the nerve, people like that just need to find a job you say....

I have often wondered what my folks said about me when I didn't show up for Christmas or Thanksgiving. I have long suspected that for a few times they made excuses for me.

I wonder did they finally say something like "he just doesn't care enough about us to come"?? The truth of the matter was; I was ashamed of myself and the lifestyle I was living at that time. I lived in a beautiful place (Asheville) but I had an ugly problem. I simply drank too much. The car probably needed tires and I know the boys needed things. Why would you want to go around folk that love you deeply and you wonder if they want you around anyways. Oh I was a real bonafide prodigal. Through and through, and I had love, but I lacked the kind of love that said, "I love you more than me and my problem."

My story has a good ending, no a great ending. When and after coming into contact with that baby, that changed everything, everything changed. I suddenly had an intense desire to provide and be a better everything. Instead of dodging family get togethers, I planned them. I became a son and husband that I was supposed to be...In my new ways I made real mistakes though, I tried to make up to my boys what I had taken away, and I overdid it. Why am I painting such a dark picture here at Christmas? I need to remind me that you never kick a man when he is down, to remind myself that it is so easy to say a word of encouragement to that waitress who spilled a little tea, than to swell up like a toad and keep her tip.

Love has many faces, kindness is easy, and Lordy the importance of a strong handshake and a neck hug. Look at this picture and tell me my Mom don't think I can walk on water. The agape Love of God allowed me to make up for those 5 or so years of foolishness. When I feel a little cocky?? I can glance up at this picture and see me coming up that dusty road with no shoes on and clothes in rags and sick and skinny, but I know that just up the road is home. I am praying the porch light is on and the yellow ribbons are on the tree. I don't have nowhere else to go.....

If the porch light hadn't of been on I probably wouldn't have been in this picture—and this picture always reminds me of the line she put in a note to me that I didn't read for a year until I found it in a doll box I had given her—First it started out with this line, and it put me on my knees in the closet —"To my darling son"—and she said, "You won't forget me will you?"

How do you forget someone who gives us so many reasons to remember—and besides—she didn't forget me— They were standing in the middle of that dusty road and wouldn't let me go.... no farther.... Merry Christmas

An Axe and A Rifle

Our forefathers settled this country with an axe and a long-rifle. They came from all over the world and all nationalities. They had a dream of a better life, independence and fierce pride. They would help each other relentlessly. Usually shelter for the family, then, they would build a church/school. They chopped and sawed logs day after day to build their one-room log cabins. Chimneys of fieldstone, chinked with mud, and the fireplace was for heating and cooking.

A mountain heritage we inherited. There are no more loyal, fierce, proud, honest, loving folk in the world than were the mountain men and women who settled the valleys and scratched out a living out of the earth. Did you ever think what they ate until crops were made? The mountain men hunted for food. It was not easy. When we see an old barn, or the remains of a log cabin we smile and take pictures, and we should; but sometimes we overlook the work and hardship it took to survive.

These people came over these ridges and looked to settle down, with their tools and dreams and always with an old KJB or English version of the Bible. They had a tremendous faith and exercised it openly and often. Sunday was rest day unless your ox was in a ditch; and if he got in a ditch often, you sold him. My grandfather was a mountain man. He was lanky and dark and had Indian blood along with Scotch-Irish and German and others according to family tree searching. I remember a little log cabin beside a trout stream in Shelton

Laurel with the mountains rising up all around it.

In my imagination I can see one of these old pioneers coming up on top of a ridge with rifle in hand and supper in the pouch of a hunting jacket; and looking down in the valley below, see the warmth of smoke rising from his stone chimney. A hint of fog coming off the creek. The mule standing in the opening of the barn, perhaps wondering if plowing was on the agenda or was it Sunday, he hoped. I can see him standing there looking at his work; looking at his oldest son milking over by the gate; Another one is letting the chickens out and checking for eggs, though it is early in the day; And there is his woman, one reason for all his hard work.

She is sweeping off the porch with an old birch broom. As he listens, he can faintly hear her humming and singing. The sound is so sweet to him, and he weeps—the words he hears??? "Amazing Grace, how sweet the sound"; and he heads down the ridge to go to work, yet another day.

I said many times that our people came across these hills from every conceivable walk of life. They had a dream: find a spot of good land and build a home, be a free man, to be fiercely independent. They had the rifle in one hand and the ax in the other and a Book under their arm. They would find a holler that had water and a place to raise a garden and wood for building and heating. They would claim it. The more affluent ones had mules, horses or oxen. The first unwritten 'rule' of mountain folk was you helped your neighbor; so if one of my folk had a mule, you had access to the mule. They took those axes ad a strong back and cut trees and hewed logs and built a shelter; first for them, then for their animals and chickens. They would help each other from daylight till dark every day except Sunday.

After the cabins and barns were built, they always built a place to worship. This cabin served as a schoolhouse as well. Cause one thing was for sure, there was going to be lots of chil-

Jack Burris

dren. One thing they needed hands to help farm and work and log. The womenfolk needed girls to help with the gardens and milking and washing and canning and sewing. So much work to do, all day, every day, except Sunday; which brings me to my thoughts for today: Worship.

Lots of communities did not have a preacher, and when one wasn't around they read scripture and sang shape note music. Now there were circuit-riding preachers who would travel from church to church and preach. He might get there at daylight so the 'church bell' would be rung and folk would come hear the preacher. Then he would go on down the road, usually on horseback, to another community; and as long as his voice held out, he would repeat this process all day. He was not limited to only Sunday's. Whenever he came the bell would be rung and the folk would gather. These men would be paid rarely in cash money. I've often wondered how they carried eggs and butter and food, because one thing was sure, the people appreciated the parson and they took care of him.

I remember 50 years ago going to a little church on Laurel and hearing shape note style music. The preacher got up, a tall lanky mountaineer, and opened the Book. I sat there in awe. Whenever he finished reading scripture he commenced preaching. He never stopped for half an hour, and he was a 'hacker'. The only breath he took was between sentences. He was loud and I did not understand very many words he said. No notes, just preached. I didn't know what he said, but afterward the people hugged him and thanked him and said, "great sermon". He was soaked. That impressed me.

The Presbyterians build churches and hospitals around and were a major influence in Shelton Laurel. The folk there had more access to education and the communities were so much better off because of the help the Presbyterians brought to the table. My mom got me to go to the 8th grade even though she did not get to stay with her brothers and sisters and her dad. On the other side of the county my dad only got to go to the 3rd grade partly because of less opportunity and also the need for hands to work the hardscrabble farm he grew up on.

One circuit rider preacher came across the mountain every week to Shelton Laurel and one week he was late. Story goes, they asked him what happened and he said his horse got sick. Well you're riding him, so what did you do? He said I laid hands on him and prayed for him. One fellow said you mean you prayed for your horse? The old preacher said, "Son, I wouldn't serve a God who couldn't heal a horse." And that was why they did what they did. For little or no reward. They still worked and farmed just like everyone else, but there was a fire n their bones and they had to go tell the old old story of how a Savior came from Glory.

Some of the churches/schoolhouses had fireplaces in them, and some in later years had a wood stove in the middle of the room. You might as well hug a firebug up by his legs for all the good it did. So it was very common for folk to either leave a quilt there or bring quilts with them to every service in wintertime. Look at those homemade benches in the picture and you can see why no one went to sleep. Course the preacher woke the dead preaching Hell hot, and Heaven sweet. They usually baptized in the summer time unless someone was on their deathbed then there was an urgency to get er done...I suspect that frigid mountain water had something to do with sprinkling as opposed to immersion. There were tremendous revivals where whole communities were revived and the lost were saved and folk would be plowing and God would hit them and they would fall on their knees and get saved. Same thing happened all over the world, in England, and the great Wales revival. God Himself was in these mountains and He was ever present because he was exalted and honored by the God fearing men and women who lived here.

Our religious heritage is one reason mountain folk are

the salt of this old world, which has turned away from God. It is another heritage that is fading into the fogs of time. In just a few years the worship and fear of love of God has slowly faded into the background. A lot of our old time churches are social gatherings now.

$\mathcal{KJV}$

They came across these hills from everywhere. Scott-Irish, German, and European and all parts in between. They saw these beautiful mountains and valleys and sank deep roots into the soil. They worked from light to dark, grubbing, chopping, sawing and building. They came across the hills with a broadaxe, a horse or mule, a few tools, and a deep need for freedom. They mostly all had an old KJV Bible in these. They used it for worship, for their guide to life.

They first helped each other build a cabin for shelter and a shed for livestock. They had to get a crop in the ground for wintertime. They had to make corn crops, and hay. They used every part of their corn: the ears for food…Hominy, corn-meal, mush, and to kick-start their work animals. My grand-father would plow the hillsides so steep if you had a tractor you couldn't use it, and the old mule Fred and him would stop at dinner and he would give Fred an ear of corn-for reloading he said. It was enough that the old mule would work day to dark. Sweat, stink, and fart…

The smell of sweat and leather is unforgettable…Those old barns smelled like work. They used the stalks for feed and the shucks sometimes were dipped a bit n coal oil and used for light—we get the phrase 'light a shuck', going home in the dark or to the barn or outhouse maybe—Anyway, after the cabins were built, next came the school-churchhouses. Though our ancestors had little or any education, they still realized the importance and most wanted it for their children. Most had large families for lack of birth control but also for help on the farms. Everyone worked...Large families meant more preparation for winter, more food to can and store in the root cellars. Our ancestors were independently fierce and proud people. They would probably disown our great country if they were aware of the mess we are in now.

There was very little cash money. Did you know that one source of cash money was wild American ginseng? I've heard that Daniel Boone had Indians digging for him. I don't know about that but I do know that history teaches that it was valued hundreds of years ago, and it is still here. Poachers and fools have practically eliminated it in lots of places but it's still here. I can see my grandfather with a little sack made out of a feed sack tied to his waist with a biscuit or some such in it for food. He had a sang stick 6 ft long probably and he kept it sharpened for balance as well as for digging. Heading off up a holler for higher ground and "cash money".

Can you imagine, you've just had a brutal summer making sure you had firewood for cooking and for heat for winter; you've canned and stored food for winter as well as food everyday. The hogs are getting fat, fences are repaired, harnesses are repaired and oiled, roofs constantly fixed, hay has been cut and stumps are burning on that new ground. You get to go to the woods and hunt for the most beautiful plant in all the world. I think it would be like a vacation, better than a vacation. I suspect lots of old timers put some things off just to get in the woods. I would have...

Think of that great heritage we come from boys and girls. Next time you look across a holler and there on the other side a long way off you catch a flash of red, and you feel that surge of 'joy', 'excitement'—think about your ancestors feelings those many years ago...They almost had to find that gold. I live on sweet memories a lot at my age, and my hope is you make yourself some memories worth keeping this season..... Leave some in the ground—they did...you be blessed, you hear?? As David says—grow, grow, grow.

Military and Beer and Good Music

I served in the USAF. I was in Okinawa, Turkey, and Spain, Fla. and NC and Texas. I was a crew chief on a fighter aircraft—the first was the F-102 and the last was the F-105. While in Turkey and Spain I was on the alert pad most of the time. The birds were equipped with nuclear weapons then, in 1963 and 64. We had drills and could get them on the runway in minutes. We had our own sleeping quarters and kitchen—on alert 24-7. I suspect they still are. We have soldiers all around this world today; and weapons armed and dangerous.

While I am thankful that I served, and I do realize how much the air force means to war. The real heroes are the men and boys and women and girls whoa re 'ground' soldiers. The realization that somebody is trying to kill you and bullets are flying must be devastating. It is no wonder so many come home wounded with no scars on the outside. I cannot imagine storming Normandy, or crawling though the jungles of Viet Nam. I wonder how I would have reacted. It is so sad that so many are in such need and pain, both mentally and physically.

I came home after 4 years unscathed except a taste for alcohol which was abundant and cheap. The fighting men and women come home with that problem and a lot of times with mental anguish that takes years to overcome if they ever do. You want heroes??? Look at the war vets. Support them in their quest for help from our Government.

I wish we would just take care of our own country. We have enough problems with a Gov. who it seems like is out to destroy us. No wonder some don't vote—seems like no matter who is elected they go brain dead and are bought off by lobby-ists. I told about the veteran on a Harley I met on the Parkway. He had terminal cancer and was riding around the U.S. Liter-ally all the way around and back home to Maine. He was rough looking and I spoke to him anyway and we began talking. His wife encouraged him to do this ride, so e was. He was a ground force fighter in Nam. He said, "I hope I make it back to her, I need to hug her a few more times before I die." He said I may not make it all the way, but that's alright. This rough touch old bearded soldier teared up (me too), and he said this—If the Good Lord wants me before I make it, well that's alright—But if He don't, I've asked Him to help me get back home to her. I think about this now and then, and I wonder if he made it home; but I am happy that I know he either made it home here, or went home with the Lord...we meet 'angels unaware' every once in a while don't we??? You be blessed this day and every day in Him—You hear me??

How about this from an old old hymn?? 'In my hand no price I bring, simply to the cross I cling?'...Or 'There is a river' or 'there is a fountain' or 'why me Lord', or if I go or if I stay, I'm on the winning side'. —This last song was my first wife.

Peggy's anthem near the end of her battle. She sang it and recorded it on a cassette and they played it at church. To say it was special is an understatement. It was blessed to the nth degree...There has to be a song doesn't there? I don't care what type of music you like, but there has to be a song...At certain emotional trips I love "Go Rest High on That Moun-tain". Tomorrow might be Elvis only the next day country and Dolly singing 'I will always love you' or bluegrass for days 'Vincent black lightning' by Del McCurry and of course good southern gospel with Gaither...

I couldn't make it without a song and music, could you?? Now don't be so self-righteous and beat your chest and say, "I don't listen to nothing but gospel". Don't be so rigid that you can't live in the real world; besides, you will miss some great songs and music about life and love. As Johnny Cash said, " Could be the Lord likes a little picking and grinning too." I don't know about that but I do know laughter and music and shagging are good for the soul.

How many of you have listened to music today??? Maybe even beautiful Christmas music. My wife likes 'I want a hippopotamus for Christmas' She's only 70 and still relates to a children's song. See what I mean?? It sticks to you like oatmeal, and brings back wonderful memories like the song "Love Me Tender" or 'Pretty Woman' or "The way we were"— I bet all of you have a special place in your heart for certain songs. Maybe the song you danced to at the prom or one you and your soul mate really liked, and claimed it for your own... I guess one of my all time favorites is "A Summer Place". It stirs something way down every time I hear it. Memories of love and tragedy and laughter and life all bundled up in the music. No words are needed for me in this song. Sit back, close your eyes, and hum something—You will feel better, I guarantee it!!!

Mary Gave All

She broke the box over His head, holding nothing back and giving all she had—to the One who walks wherever He chooses-even on water and even into our hearts and souls- Its very difficult to give all, keeping nothing back—sometimes especially those of us who have endured intense grief and hurt in our lives—we just do not know how much more we can stand, so we are afraid to be so vulnerable as to give 'all'. I am convinced that when we find that 'place' of rest in Him, then we can give our loves and even friends a part of ourselves knowing that 'even though we might could of held back and missed the pain, the dance is worth it'. The truth should be said, even if it hurts; and there is relief, unbelievable, when we tear down the walls...Break the box, pour it out, tear them walls down—or at least tear them down a little at a time—You will be surprised how good it is to be free—and for goodness sakes don't forget to smell the alabaster perfume—He still had that sweet smell 3 days later when they crucified Him. Mary slept well, for she gave all—

God Has Blessed Us

I was a 17-year-old just finished high school when I went into the Air Force—4 years active and two reserve—I had no delusions of grandeur for much of anything else except seeing something different—Asheville was the only city I had been to and I wanted to see other places—I spent time in Texas, 18 months in Okinawa, 3 months in Spain, 3 months in Turkey, 3 or 4 in Florida, and the rest in Goldsboro, NC. I briefly visited Guam, Japan, and Hawaii, and Newfoundland; but you know what, now I want to be in the mountains of home.

At 70, my mind is on those days of growing up in the hills of South Hominy—there is no place I've ever been-including the West, the Rockies, Alaska, Yellowstone—Custer's last stupid stand that gets to you and in your very soul like the Appalachian Mountains. I would have, and still would give my life to defend not only America, but our right of free speech and choice of worship and the right to bear arms—If you want to rob me, go ahead but I am armed and dangerous—might be a little crazy too—

I say God bless all Americans-those who served and those who would have if called—and the women folk who held it all together—I wish we could be what we once were —God be with those families whose young men and women have died in lands of no consequence and wars with no ends —as Christians we believe God is in total control and so we have been silent, waiting on Him to "fix" everything—but you know what—when you get a headache do you sit around and wait for him to heal you?? Or do you go get a couple Advils and go on? I think He is "disappointed" in us, maybe—Written in 2013 but still applies—Is the world better now than 2013?? I don't think so—perilous times are here, for sure...

Brown Paper Pokes

One thing of importance to me even after 60 plus years, was the brown paper pokes that we kids (and grownups) got at

Christmas at the Open Bible Church on Davis Creek in Hominy Valley; an orange, an apple, some hard candy, and usually nuts (English walnuts usually). Now this was a treat sometimes almost duplicated in the socks hung up on the mantle at home... and these treats along with a little something on Christmas morning was Christmas for us kids...But you know what, we were so full of anticipation and the spirit of the Season that I was never disappointed. I loved hunting a tree and putting popcorn strands and angel hair on the tree. I do not recall being overly religious at the time although I know we were very aware of the Reason for Christmas. I wish we could have Christmases like those again—this commercial stuff is way off base—give me a paper poke again——

Now, it's 2015 and the memories of Hominy Valley and Christmas are fresh anew this morning. I woke up remembering the brown paper poke full of goodies many times and usually there wasn't much left. But the sock was usually loaded with the same stuff; and a present of some sort, but the joy of the season is still fresh. The beautiful music, The Babe in the manger, (there's a new kid in town), The dawn of Grace, A life of Faith, new beginnings and hope for all people. To the lowly shepherds first, then to me. I must confess that for a period of my life, I wasn't very nice. I came out of the air force with a drinking problem.

Any of you who had those problems yourself or in your family know about the mental abuse to those who love you —and those you love; but one thing that kept me 'together' was home. The Homeplace. For me one was the rented house of Hollis Robertson's on South Hominy, and the house on Curtis Creek. My grandfather's place in Madison County. Finally, the home dad bought in Woodfin. All homeplaces of my heart. I think that is one reason they all mean so much to me—the memories of a wonderful time to grow up. Those things and a family ho loved me helped me to get up one morning with a pint of liquor beside the bed in a 3 room apartment and say to my soul—there is more to life than this—I walked to the sink in the bathroom and poured it down the drain.

I was 28 years old and now during this wonderful Christmas season I am a blessed 72, and I have never tasted another drop of alcohol. Don't misunderstand, it wasn't me with the strength altogether—The Baby n the manger was the real strength for me; and I didn't even realize that for a spell. Listen children, leave the porch light on, light the tree in the yard—that prodigal may be coming today—and he may want to use your sink—I love you all for your blessed friendship—be blessed, you hear me? God spared me this year when death was 92 percent certain-what do they know-He is Christmas—love each other this year like you may not be here next year—and be blessed...

Mr Boone and the Cemetery

I stopped near Laurel Branch Baptist Church to take a picture. Outside of Marshall near Bull Run where my Father was born and raised. A ton farm truck eased up beside me and didn't stop, but looked me over with great intensity to see if I was up to no good. I thought, "Now there is an old timer that I might like to meet." So he drove on off slowly and after I was through I followed him. I was going to Laurel Branch Cemetery where my family is buried. Well I went around the curve and there in the road up to where the cemetery was, sat his truck with the old man looking in his rearview mirror, at me.

Well, I pulled up beside him and rolled the window down and sorta pretended I didn't know where the cemetery was. He said, " why you looking for the cemetery?" I said my family is there. He said, " Who is your family?" I told him and he said follow me, and I'll show you the turn off. So I did and when we got to the turn I stopped and got out. I told him who I was and my family and he said I know all of them. I said who are you and he said C? Boone. I said my first cousin is married to Earnest Boone. He said that's my brother. Over an hour later I got invited to dinner, invited to come see him and 'sit a spell' any time I could.

He was, is 87 years old, a Korean War veteran, has worked his entire life and lives off SS. He said this; "If I couldn't get my prescriptions through the VA I would have to choose between medicine or food every month. He draws 780.00; and I thought, what a disgrace. This stupid government and so called president give illegals and immigrants 1800.00 and our veterans and old folk who founded our country and worked their entire lives in fear and broke. No wonder we are in such a mess...I would not take nothing for these mountain folk and country folk I am blessed to run into.

There is no better people, they don't want handouts... and I'm reminded of what the Book says—take care of your widows and orphans—I would add also take care of your old folk. Mr. Boone was a delight, a highlight of the week. I will go 'sit a spell'. I went on up to the graveyard that is very difficult to get to and climbed the hill and sat a sell with Mom and Dad and family. I'm not much on cemeteries but it was a special time to get into the old wore out canoe that leaks a bit and travel down the rivers of my memories for a spell. Up on that hill under the shade of an old oak tree I shed a tear or two for those gone on, but also for my new friend. It's almost like meeting angels unaware...With that 45 he had I coulda been an angel if I had been up to no good...Thank you Lord for good people.... You be blessed this day and every day, you hear me???

I Think Myself Happy

Paul said to Agrippa, " I think myself happy"...I love this statement. Whenever I'm on one of my pity parties, if and when I think of this, I must smile. What in the world did this old preacher have to be happy about??? He had something wrong with him that God would not fix. He had a horrible past. Stood by and watched Christians being persecuted and even killed. Surely his past would plague him. He had to be on daily guilt trips, after all these folk he was trying to preach to knew all about him.

Some of my past bothers me and I wasn't near as bad as Paul—at least not on paper; but then again, he said guilty of the least, guilty of all. That's a sobering thought.....Agrippa probably looked at Paul cockeyed and thought the same thing I was thinking. He was being run out of towns, due to appear in court, plus his past, and He thinks he's happy??? How could he be happy? I think most of you know why he could say this. His past was forgiven. God had promised him Grace to bear his physical problems. He had delivered him from his enemies time and again...but I think mostly he was happy that his sins were forgiven, and God had taught him for a few years so he could go and preach to you and I and pen I think 15 books of the NT.

Just think, chosen, groomed, and sent personally to preach..I think myself happy that through the pen of Paul, the Holy Spirit wrote us a love letter. But that's just like Him—

choose folk you would never think had a chance and use them out of the mire into the choir...My mindset is just like Paul's— I think myself happy...And if I die today or next week or when I'm 90—I am a winner either way—How about you and I? Can we get out of bed and set the tone for the day?—and say to the world, "I think myself happy."—Amazing what attitude can do isn't it...

Love is Forever

I have had the unwanted task of burying a spouse of 38 years, two sons, and an infant daughter who got the cord around her neck two weeks away from due date. I have helped bury Mom and Dad, two brothers and uncles and aunts, all of whom I loved deeply and forever. Don't let anyone tell you that you get 'ready' for death to come to someone you love… you help, you comfort, you make jokes, you cry inside, and scream in side, so loud you should be able to her it a half mile. You put on a face of encouragement…and you cry, and your insides are shaky—and all sorts of questions come to mind—you plan for the event—the funeral home—the church—the pastor —you do all you can—you thank everyone for the food, for the visit, for caring, for giving—but still at times you want to just be quiet—and just think about your loved one who is leaving you and just remember some good times—and maybe smile along with the tears…

But you hide the tears when you can, and if someone says I know how you feel, you somehow don't scream at them and say, " Oh no, you don't"—but at the same time there are others who love us too, and they need to say goodbye—and you ant them to—it is such a load to bear—and after—after is when you need a hug and a phone call—Let's don't forget that in the coming weeks—Love is forever—and folk need it most when they are lonely and tired and heartbroken…Please continue to pray for my Tenn. family—thanks.

I dreamed of yesterday
In the corner of my mind
A time of sweet sensation
A time of peaceful, warm summertime
Hand in hand we walked
Through the meadows of life
The fragrance of the flowers
Ever gentle on my senses
And I knew that you were going
To be around a long, long time
But you went away on my birthday
And I think of you
Ever gentle on my mind

Tent Meetings

How many of you ever went to a tent meeting? Complete with sawdust shavings and 100 watt bulbs strung from post to post all the way around the canvas cathedral—now on hot summer nights fans would be waving......those meetings were hot on the devil too-he can dish it out but good old mountain preaching put him on the run...my dad had one tent meeting one time...seems like it was in a field across from the two stores before you get to Stony Fork School. My sister probably knows exactly where...but we mostly went to meetings-

I remember Preacher Hall, and R Conners and Bentley and some others...they mostly scared me some what with all the "unknown stuff'—and usually most nights revelation that "there's someone here with stomach problems, or with headaches". You get 20 people together and somebody has one or both of those. Pretty sure prophecy I'd say...And so that time came to an end—the methods of preaching Christ has changed dramatically in my lifetime—but the message of John 3:16 has never changed—

So after I grew up I went to a couple of tent meetings— the best mountain preacher I ever heard was Ralph Sexton Sr. No frills or empty promise, just Christ, crucified, and most importantly, Risen. Ralph got arrested in Weaverville for preaching from a car with loudspeakers. When they went before the judge, he asked: guilty or not guilty? He said, "Since God saved me, I'm not guilty." They took them to Asheville and locked them up for preaching the gospel...charged them with disturbing the peace. Ralph said he knew that was a lie because the book said 'the wicked have no peace'. But they kept preaching.

Ralph went to school with no money and they let him in and he milked the cows...he said that northeast wind blew thru that old barn and the devil would say, why don't you give up and go home and be the life of the party. He said he would start milking with both hands and start singing and that old barn would come alive...Holy Ghost would show up, devil would have to go, and he would have church in that old barn —to the point the dean told him that they appreciated him loving God, but he was waking people up at 4 in the morning...Ralph said that was the best time because that's where he really went to school..

Ralph knew mountain folk cause he 'were one'. I suspect Trinity has some tapes and I know some books he wrote. God delivered hi and cleared the way for him so many times... and he put it down on tape and called it Hands Full of Honey... and that's why I know he was without a doubt, God's called man...He simply had a heart for people—his son had a tent out towards Hendersonville in about '91, it ran 6 weeks and maybe more he had a tent meeting in Wash DC...Them Sextons can preach.... oh by the way, Ralph had a tent in Sylva that was not going so well—and 4 high school boys came and sang for him, the meeting went 6 weeks + ad so the Inspirations were born—Time to get out of this old canoe, I could go awhile about one of God's gifts to the mountain folk—Ralph Sexton Sr.

Tater Sallit and Nanner Puddin

One thing I have learned over the years is how to make friends. I've found that if you meet someone who seems reserved and hard to get to know, that if you will invite them out to eat and buy them a bowl of pintos with some turnip greens and cornbread and a slice of onion on the side, you will have a friend for life; kinda like petting a stray cat.

There is a saying about us reformed Presbyterians, we are the frozen chosen. That's not quite accurate, we are the friendliest folk around when we are meeting and eating. I used to love homecomings at the old time Baptist Churches. Mountain women just know how to make tater salit and nanner puddin. I remember sitting in Open Bible Church on upper South Hominy on Homecoming day and thinking, " I wish Preacher Watts would shut up and lets get on with the chocolate pie." I still think that way when we have events planned at church. Just hush, for goodness sake—I mean everybody is thinking about that pot roast and strawberry shortcake anyway. Nobody wants to get saved on Homecoming day anyway, they just came cause we tell them about all the great cooks we have… 'If you ain't eating, you ain't meeting' is our slogan.

I've been thinking about Peter having enough faith to get out of the boat; and the one conclusion I've come to is that Peter was not a Baptist. He was a Presbyterian. He was not a Baptist because the Book says, 'beginning to sink, He asked for help.' Baptist don't do that, they wait till they are purt near drowned before they will ask for help...or directions...

I have a confession, I was a Baptist by choice cause I tried them all, and I married a Presbyterian so you know the rest of the story. Three pre-nups—I had to like children, I had to like animals, and I had to go to church with her.... So there you go. A Baptist by birth, and a Presbyterian by marriage...

Preachers are the hard headedest people I know. You cannot convince them that about 20 minutes preaching is all most folk can absorb. The great old time mountain preacher who founded the Tennessee Bible College, Lee Robinson, would stand beside the pulpit and have your total attention without yelling, stomping, or jumping up and down. He always, always preached almost exactly 20 minutes. I always left refreshed and not exhausted worrying about the pot roast getting cold. Take a kid fishing this Sunday—after Church —You will be double blessed. Let's see now, let me check the paper and see if anyone is having Homecoming—there is something about tater salit and nanner pudding that gets me feeling religious—

The Shadow of Craggy Prison

I woke up this beautiful June morning and put the water in the Bunn and in minutes had a hot cup of coffee. It's humid this day, but a sunrise means another day to help or say a word to help someone along this journey.

I was thinking back a few years when I was at Pisgah View Ranch just lollygagging around and we were sitting down near the lake and enjoying the view of Pisgah and the lake with the ducks in attendance. We weren't checked in as paying guest, we just went to enjoy the atmosphere and beauty and probably lunch. It seems like the shadow of Pisgah came over that place in the evening; and the tranquility and serenity then came with the ending of another day in the mountains is almost undescribable. The softness of the shadows of twilight can be as refreshing as the newness of early morning with the accompanying chorus of our birds singing the Glory of God to us. Couple that with a good up of coffee and memories—

Another 'shadow' came to mind this morning. A somber and bring you down to earth shadow of thoughts. One that I really don't like to think too much about, but I suspect God is behind this particular memory of another time and place. I won't name his name but I had a friend in Asheville who helped us finish concrete. He was a lot older than me and he had a wife and a home; but he also had a bad weekend drinking wine problem. He had been arrested for public drunkenness numerous times. Back in those days it was a misdemeanor to be in public drinking. Nowadays, half the people on Friday and Saturday night would get arrested...

Anyway, he was serving jail time in Craggy prison on the river, during the weekends. Of course he was an alcoholic and would drink thru the week and sometimes he would report on Friday evening lit up; and they would add to his sentence. He was a good man, with a drinking problem and I loved him in spite of that and so did the Lord; but I took him sometimes to report in by 5 on Fridays, and I remember very distinctly one particular Friday when I pulled up to the entrance the shadow of the prison was about half over my truck, and as I sat there it moved all the way over it...That shadow... And as he walked into the gate and was frisked and checked out, the thought came to me—But for the Grace of God, that could be me......Sitting there under that shadow caused tears of thankfulness for myself and tears of sorrow for him, walking with his slumped shoulders and with the pain in his eyes. Sitting in that shadow of the prison has helped me thru the years to be very careful about judging and condemning others too quickly. But for the Grace of God——

I much prefer the shadow of Pisgah and the newness of mornings—but when I need a come uppance that memory comes long—You may ask what about my friend?? God Almighty loved him just as much-no more-no less-than any of his children. Drinking was his outward problem—what was or is yours and mine??? Better be very careful passing judgment on good folk.... Some more rambling that may not say a lot to you, but means a great deal to me—you be blessed this day, you hear me??

Our Bolonga Sandwich

I hope we all realize where our thanksgiving should be directed, not only on this day, but each day we are able to draw a breath, close our eyes and relive some of those best times—we came through the bad and really bad, scarred and beat up, but stronger—and some with a renewed desire to help those we know get through tragedies of this fleeting life—God alone has a way of taking a half dozen and making a dozen out of it...

We came to the picnic table with our little bologna sandwich and mustard, and someone is always there with fried chicken and potato salad and sweet tea, and German chocolate cake, and we get invited to eat with them. They always say 'oh we like bologna sandwiches too, so lets share' and there we sit—we came like a pauper and ate like a king—and that my friends is the way our relationship with god is—we come with nothing and he gives us everything—everything—everything—it's not that he needs our bologna sandwiches, fact is we need His Chicken...You be blessed this day as you give thanks—and I hope with those you love—

Backseat-51 Chevy

I was in the back seat of a '51 Chevy that belonged to Jock Fender from Laurel. I had attended a Sunrise Service because of pressure from family and friends...I did not want to be there—It was Mt. Bethel Church in Jupiter, NC. The sun had risen beautifully. When Bob Ballard said the stone was rolled away, something broke inside and tears came. I eased over behind Peggy and tried to hide—Bob knew—and so did a lot of others that the Holy Spirit was on that hill...when he said Amen, I went to Jock's car and got in the back seat. I didn't know what was happening to me but I couldn't stop crying—Bob walked by the car and stopped and came back—he leaned in the window and in his deep gravelly voice said four words that changed my life—"Son, you need Jesus."

--1973—Have I been a good boy all the time; Certainly not. Am I a good man now all the time; Heaven's no (knows), but He chose at that point of time to forgive every sin I had ever committed and not only that, but to forgive every sin I would ever commit...That's Grace—Now I didn't say fellowship wasn't broken and I know repentance is a must, but he always has, and always will forgive me—and you—now you know one reason I like '51 Chevy's and mountaintop churches —Ain't nobody like HIM!

Good Smells

Do you remember the musty smell of tobacco in the barn? What about the silent fellowship of friends and family grading and tying tobacco? No words are needed. Do you have friends you can sit with or ride with and never have to say a word? The smooth worn woodcutter at that old store with the mixed smells that hit you when you walked in? The mixed smell of candy, onions, cloth and kerosene? The soft patter of the rain on that old barn roof where you played in the hay? Or your mom and dad always asking if you were hungry? But we were young then and didn't pay much attention—now we are asking our grandchildren if they are hungry…It's funny isn't it how much we learn after we know everything? The mournful cry of a dove, or the whistle of the Bobwhite- (almost gone) The sound of a coon hound treed, or beagles hot after that cottontail—awww poetry—doesn't rhyme, but has a reason to make you smile or cry-----

I've never been a fan of cussing (there have been times if you had written some choice words down I would have signed them)—I see friends and hear friends use bad language and at times I cringe—we are judged by our conversation you know— I've always felt I was smart enough to express how I feel without the usual cusswords—does that make me better? Or do I look down on my nose at you and think, "I'm smarter?" No of course it doesn't—but my conversation may cause someone (Just one is enough) to turn to Christ for life's answers…when and if I cussed it would simply say I'm just another one of the good old boys who sit in the pew but doesn't represent Him very well—I've always said if you make a statement you will get a chance to prove it—how's your mouth today--

A Jesus Man?

16 degrees here this morning. Winter. Some see the bleakness and gray of winter. And it is definitely bleak and gray—at times; but we have Thanksgiving Christmas, and Easter during "winter". All are times to gather together as families and friends and reflect on the goodness of the One in whom we have believed. I do not care how much you or I have suffered or experienced in the last year, there has also been goodness and blessings. Sometimes we overlook the little 'miracles' that we experience. One time a foster child we had, he was 7 years old, said to me after I said grace at breakfast, "Are you a Jesus man?"

I hung my head a moment and finally said, "I wish I was." Then I tried to explain to him that, yes, I was a believer in Jesus Christ, and I was a Jesus 'man', but not a very good one. I said it meant far more than giving grace, it meant being kind and good to all people and I wasn't always that way. I said you talked mean to me last night when we were trying to get you to do your homework. Was that fair and kind? So being nice and good to folk who you meet is the Jesus way. He never said no more, but for a couple days we got his homework done without any problems...

Winter for me always makes me think sooner or later about Paul in the Mamertine prison. Cold, dark, lonesome, was the great old last apostle of Christ. He wrote his young preacher friend Timothy, 'come before winter'. And bring my cloak, and don't forget the papers. Come before winter. I need you. Please come see me and comfort me. Your warmth and the cloak will keep me warm. This dungeon is damp, cold and lonely. This winter there are many in our community who are alone, cold, and hungry. Put a five in the Salvation Army pot. At least it will be used for the people...

Come before winter was the plea. I have fought a good fight he said. He was a Jesus man. We don't know if Timothy made it or not before they took the old Jesus man out in the dusty street and beheaded him. He gave all I give some...Hope you do too...Merry Christmas

Where Have The Days Gone

Where did they go?? Those days that marked the beginnings and ending to periods of our lives, marked by events like graduations, weddings and Christmases. I had hardly learned to say the '70's when it was the '90's...decades gone like a whisper in the wind.

Some of that lost time was marked in feet and inches on the doorjamb or wall in the hallway. We measured our children because they wanted to grow up so fast. Now they are there and wondering where the time has gone. Where did it go??? We changed diapers and blinked and they were gone. And now? Time has made us short of breath and energy. And winters coming—mark my word—winter's coming like a freight train running free.

Where did the days and months and decades go??? To ballgames, camping trips, schools, church, PTA meetings, vacations, state parks, and home again, and parties, and malls, and hospitals, and yes to funeral homes and funerals—and always to work and home and work—over and over—Even if we could find those days we could not bring them back. They have disappeared into the morning fog with blinding speed.

But where are they, you must ask?? The days, months, and decades that have gone by so quickly...They are on the back-roads and rivers of our memory. Some really good and some we want to forget, but there are treasures there in our memories that turn up at the oddest times and bring great joy, and much needed joy to me and you, I'm sure.

One that is so wonderful is that Easter sunrise service in the back seat of a '51 Chevy, I had got in the car to sort out these feelings I had and to figure out why I was crying after I heard the old time mountain preacher say 'the stone was rolled away'......That old time bearer of Good News came by and saw me and stuck his head in the window and said in his rough, gravelly, sweet voice, "Son, you need the Lord, don't you?"—And right then, in that moment in time God showed up and it felt like something broke and ran inside of me....

The days, months, and decades have faded into the fog and I know not where they have gone—but I can assure you of this—time has left me old, and tired at times; but God?? I've tried many times to ignore Him, and not go to church, and do things my way—but He won't leave me alone...I can't get by with anything. He's always got me o the potters wheel or in the blacksmith shop. And I love Him.

Time?? Ain't no friend of mine—but I do thank God so much for the time he has given me, and I pray that I've pleased him at times with the way I have used the gift of 'Time'. You all be blessed this day—you hear me???

Christ and Easter

The reason Easter Sunday mornings usually cause some tears to seep out of my hard head is that on such a morning in 1973 He shoed me that the stone was indeed rolled away. High on a hill in Jupiter at Mt. Bethel Church. I remember Bob Ballard in his deep preachers voice declared 'the stone was rolled away—not for Him to get out—but to let us enter in—' I was hiding behind my wife and Jock Fender and the emotions running through me were overwhelming. There was a large crowd there but I felt exactly like everyone was well aware of me. It was a funny feeling for sure—it was like I was exposed for what I was, and of course conviction does that—causes you to see yourself much like Isaiah did—Woe is me for I am undone—Lordy I wanted to get away from there.....

Do you remember the times in church or campmeetings when someone came out who was lost or under conviction, everyone knew and would pray without being told? Seemed like the place would get smoky like and heavy with the presence of God. Back then when He was preeminent in our lives and in our county the churches across America were full and the moral standards were high. Stories of great revivals and of men being in the field plowing and the power of God hit them and put them on their knees, and great stories of town drunks and evil men and women going from the 'mire to the choir'. It happened all across America.

Those days are long gone—when was the last time you sensed the Holy Spirit moving to and fro in your church??

When was the last great revival where many would turn to Christ?? I am so sad for our once great country. Internal moral decay has been the onset of collapse of all great nations of history. There is no fear of a Holy God anymore. We have taken the Burger King motto—have it your way—and we are self-destructing from the inside out.

Anyway on that Easter Sunday morning when Bob said "Amen", I took off around that building and got into the back seat of Jock's '51 Chevy. Now there's a lot of things you could do in the back seat of a '51 Chevy, but on this day a young man with no hope was brought to repentance by the High Sheriff of Heaven. That old mountain preacher walked by and saw me crying—he stuck his head in the window and in his raspy, guttural voice said these words that helped me so much that morning, "Son, you need Jesus."-And there began a wonderful relationship that has sustained me through good times and through hell. Up and down like a roller coaster for me. In and out. Good and bad. But one thing has always been the same. Him.

Our relationship has been like us when we were teenagers and so in love. We would ride in a car and she would almost always be sitting in my lap, you all remember that... sit as close as possible. Share an apple and such. Then get married and after a while she is all the way over against the door and wouldn't eat an apple after you anymore, and she says, "What's happened to us, we used to sit so close and all.."—And he says, "I haven't moved, I'm still here under the steering wheel, see, I haven't went anywhere." There it is.... He is still driving and in control but we ride with something else occasionally and we drift apart. The good news is, This Easter, there is no stone between us and the driver. You be blessed, you hear me??

Two Day Old Easter Eggs

I was alone in my memories this morning. What a wonderful place to reflect on life and events that impacted everything I had ever done. I mean everything. Sometimes when I am here or up on Pisgah or running through the hay fields of yesterday I am saddened by some things I let get out of hand throughout this life he has blessed me with. I do not know if tomorrow will come, and neither do you. Then why don't we live like that? Well for one thing it probably wouldn't take too many carefree days to go broke. And then if God spared us a long life, most of us don't have Ma and Pa to move in with. But there is a time of year that I find a quiet place and just reflect on and enjoy with so much thankfulness—and that time is here—Easter.

Do you remember running around crazy like hunting Easter eggs? Whether at church or home? We hid the eggs over and over and they were not plastic either. I remember every once in a while getting hungry and eating one. I also remember finding a stray one a day or two later and eating them too. They would get cracked and dirty but that was not a deterrent for great fun. I not know where the egg deal originated from, but it was fun then. I still enjoy hiding them and for a while we had anywhere from 10 to 30 kids over for a hunt. It was a lot of fun to watch the intensity and joy at finding plastic eggs with treats inside. I like the real egg deal better.

Anyway, that was part of Easter growing up. But that's not the part that I reflect, rely and am so very thankful for.

I have told this before and will continue telling it forever. I was on the outside looking in. Going nowhere with a family. Drinking on the weekends, and being stupid was 'normal'. Well my friend and wife were on to me about coming to Weaverville where he lived and going to a sunrise service with them. I had no desire to go cause I knew where I was and I knew where I needed to be. Anyway, I went up there and the morning about 5:30 when we got up I was as nervous as a cat in a room full of rocking chairs. Raised in church and I knew the talk, I had been to he altar many times, I learned many verses in SS and I dreaded going up on top of that hill at Mt. Bethel and watching the sun come up.

We got there and I felt as out of place as a cat in a room full of German shepherds. Bob Ballard, in his deep raspy voice began to speak. I got behind my friend and my wife and tried to get where he couldn't see me. Cause I was afraid he knew about me (he didn't) but he was talking to me—if you understand what I mean. I could not for the life of me stop tears from leaking out. My throat felt swelled up and I swear my heart would explode if it ran today like it was that morning. At least that is how it felt. You know it's a funny thing, even after all these years, I still can't stop the leakage just thinking and writing about that day. I do not remember a word said except 5 words.

Five words changed my life forever that morning. Somewhere during his talk he said, "The stone was rolled away." That's all I heard and it kept roaring thru my mind —rolled away. Rolled away. I was a wreck. Really. When he said amen I was near the corner and around the corner and into Jock's '51 Chevy, in the back seat I went. They said they didn't tell him, I don't know, but that dratted old preacher came around the building and was passing the car and saw me. Preachers who are for real are like bloodhounds, they won't give up and they have a sense about the lost, or at least that was how the Holy Spirit used to operate. Whole churches would just know who needed what and when. Somehow we have gotten in the wrong gear in most of our churches...

Anyway, he stuck his nosy old nose in the window and said this, "Son, looks like you need Jesus"...You might as well throwed a bomb in the car, cause I went to pieces—And that my friends is where the rest of my life changed. I have not the slightest doubt that I would not be here to this day if that decision had not been made. Make no mistake, I did not go to Him, He came where I was—and because He lives, I can live through the pain and hard places that have been many. So you see, He really does "Roll the stone away". It allowed you and I to enter into the very presence of God...I don't understand all of it, and I don't know what tomorrow holds, but I like the song, I know who holds tomorrow. Happy Easter and be blessed this day and all your days—

Spit on the Worms

I remember 60 plus years ago hearing lots of old timers, when they testified, would say something like this—I want to go on Home to be with the Lord, or Lord please come today and take me Home, I'm ready to go." As an energetic young boy, I couldn't understand that reasoning. The swimming hole was open all the time; there was always a good marble game somewhere at recess, Christine Burnettes' red hair always turned my head and created dreams. Walker Hinson had a barn full of baccer sticks to hit rocks with, and besides Dad really overdid it when he bought me my first bike, a Schwinn, red, black, and chrome fenders with a horn, and you throw in a couple clothes pins and cardboard and it was a real Harley. The suckers and horny heads were always hungry and my pin hooks and sewing thread and sapling pole was a deadly combo, particularly the red worms in the Prince Albert can were unbeatable when I spit on the worms for luck. So you see, I could not understand those old saints wanting to go home so bad. I later found out maybe they didn't either, cause when they got a little sick, they run to the doctor in an intense hurry. Now as I've gotten old, I know somewhat how they felt. Life was had then in the mountains. There was work to do all the time, and some would grow weary.

Kids, farming, school, church, counting pennies, and saving green stamps, it wore you down…Feed sacks, quilting, sewing, plowing, and cutting wood all the time. Some young folk would leave as soon as possible—I joined the Air Force the day after graduation. Dad worked at Enka so he didn't need me so I left to see the world at 17. Okinawa, Spain, Turkey, Texas, Florida, stops in Hawaii and Guam and Japan and finally NC, Seymour Johnson AFB in Goldsboro.

I do not want to 'go home today'. I am ready and have no fear of the grim reaper. But, I'm not that tired yet despite all the tragedy and hurt that our family has endured; but I love those old saints of God, who lived by a handshake and would pull their shirt off for you. Workers and friends, we need that today. I looked at them and listened to their testimonies then with some disbelief; Now, I realize how much Heaven or the mere thought of Heaven meant to them. "I go to prepare a place for you, and if I go I will come again and receive you unto myself, in my Father's house are many mansions, if it were not so, I would have told you."

He showed me in those old time testimonies what the blessed hope is—and for that reason one day I made a decision to ask forgiveness and ask Him to be the Lord of my life —And you know what, I look at the immorality and evil I our own America, and I say with the old timers—even so come quickly—and by the way, I've been all over this country, and those blue ridges and smoky mountains? Unbeatable—Why you think Jesus went upon Pisgah (Jack's theology) to pray??? Hay, someday I'll see you at the 'House'.

Just about Living Life

Well, another cold spell coming on…some say Easter squall, Blackberry squall, and a couple more squalls. I always heard spells. Little cold spells; just long enough to make you dig out a coat or long sleeved shirt that you thought was put away for good. I took a ride own the rivers of my memories again today. The old wore out canoe appears to leak worse and hopefully it will hold up as long as I do. I really don't know where I would be without that escape hatch.

Most of you have been so blessed except for losing you folks or grandparents; and a lot of you have been blessed with soul mates for life. Others are not so fortunate. So, not all rides are fun down the old man river. When you bury your children there are always good memories from the baby bed till bad things happen. So, I focus on the good times; and he blesses me. But broken dreams and death even getting old and not doing half the things you want to do wears on me—and you. Time will not wait will it?? It is no friend of mine. It used to seem like forever till payday, and then when I became the payer, it came around every 2 days it seemed like.

Today and this little cold snap took me back to spring time n the mountains. It was so wonderful to take them dratted old shoes off and run through the hay field. I felt like I could fly. Me and that old dog of mine would run and run and run some more. Mama said she never saw me walk till I was 12. Did you ever just run through the woods and climb a long tall sapling and ride it down to the ground?? Or did you ever roam the hills looking for that perfect bean shooter (slingshot). It just had to be a dogwood. I made bows our of hickory saplings which I shaved with an old Barlow knife and cured behind Mama's cook stove.

It's interesting that I remember so much about spring and the long lazy days of summer, and I don't remember as much about winter and coats and boggins. I remember every detail of snow sledding and those days. Using socks for gloves and coming in soaked and froze and steam rising off the pants ad socks and shirts when Mom hung them near the stove. As soon as they were anywhere near dry and I was warm, back out we would go. I loved Mama's snow cream. I don't think I've ever even come close to having any as good as hers. May be just cause I knew she loved me just like I was.

Live was so simple and easy to me then, and I'm sure it was to you. Having crushes on girls who didn't even know it, I remember walking by a group of girls more than once and they would giggle. I'd turn red and keep her moving boys. I never did figure out what the giggles was about. The Lord knows I slicked my hair down and tried to look cool. I couldn't figure them out then and I ain't much better off now...

Now a lot of you know how much fun it was in the '50's...Man we had the Yankees, Mantle, Maris, Yogi, Martin, Kubek, Ford, and Hank and Moose and Gil—what a team—We had a black and white TV with a test screen and sign off at 11pm but on some Saturdays. We had Elvis, Johnny, Jerry Lee, Drifters, Platters, Brenda Lee, Supremes, and so many more great singers and songs—like shimmy shimmy co co pop, or yakety yak. How about Last Date or one of my favorites, A Summer Place? I remember me and Eddie standing behind Mary Ruth and Martha and they played Last Date on the piano. I thought Ed was in love then, and maybe he was. Us boys was all scared of pretty girls. We kicked the ground and turned red often.

Don't get me wrong, I love springtime and the new-ness of life; but I really love the mountains and the joy they have brought into my life. From camping to sang hunting to squirrel and rabbit hunting as a boy, From fishing in the creek to running through the woods, Mama's cook stove and funny books, burying my high school sweetheart and 3 children and ma and pa and cousins and grandpa and grandma and two brothers and favorite uncles and aunts has taken a toll on this old man. So I hope I don't bore you with my canoe rides. It's where I go and it helps me to love and be loved if that makes any sense. Well, I'm through—I loves the mountains, I shorely does—and all you mountain folk too. You are unique and blessed. From an old song—wake me up early, be good to my dog, and teach my children to play......

Lids and Screws and Music

Everything seems to be getting more difficult. Like getting out of my truck after driving for a ways. Or climbing a ladder. Or taking a screw out of something. Or keeping up with where things are. Seems I spend half my time hunting stuff. Taking a lid off a pickle jar requires Herculean strength seems like. What's up with all this junk going on anyway? I used to 'jump up there' and 'jump down there', Now I have to 'climb up and climb down'.

My mind seems to be pretty good its just my body has gotten lazy or something. Wonder if a facelift would help? I guess I'm slowly dying cause I have to use deodorant and 'Old Spice' to keep from stinking. Oh well. Least I wont have to put up with this stuff in Heaven. But my mind is okay I think. Some says it is and some say I'm crazy. One thing I have no trouble doing is riding the rivers of my memories in my old canoe; Surely you have a memory lane you can travel for a little rest from the journey, or a dream that you still hold on to.

Well yesterday I musta rode and paddled a thousand miles. And some of you all were with me on the river. We went up to Wytheville Va. to the Waufenhaus dinner theatre. You are served a wonderful dinner which begins 2 hours prior to showtime. In the theatre. And the performers are the servers etc. Then you are treated to an excellent show of some kind. Yesterday and the month of April has been 'Back to the Fifties They did 71 songs. Of course not every verse but some part of 71 total songs. It was a fantastic trip down memory lane. Wake up little Susie.

I could see the drive in there on the left before you get to the old Enka plant site. I could see me in a white t shirt and a rolled up in the sleeve a pack of Luckies telling her Dad with a shotgun that we 'fell asleep and our goose is cooked', and him believing it--like he wasn't a teenager at once was on Blueberry Hill and I was the Leader of the Pack doing the twist with Peggy Sue. At the prom all dressed up trying to dance with 3 left feet and a red face. Seeing all you all, all cleaned up looking gorgeous and handsome, ready to graduate and conquer the world. You girls with your low cut gowns and heels on and us boys talking about '57 Chevy's and stealing peeks at them bare shoulders and legs. And dreaming.

They woke me up with Chain Gang and Jailhouse Rock and Elvis. Orbison showed up and The Everly brothers... Corina and Will You still Love me Tomorrow, Who put the rah in rah ma rah ma ding dong, or something like that. I never could keep up with that song. When A Man Loves a Woman, and Do you Wanna Dance seems to always bring good feeling with them. And on and on for a couple hours.

Taken to so many old scenes and places in my mind...To South Hominy and Pisgah and on to Enka High and on to the prom at Erwin. And singing Elvis in Medford's old pulpwood truck with Steve and Larry and Asheville's former sheriff Bobby all crowded in that rickety old dodge truck.

Music and Song. Boy what would we have without a song? A song to make us cry, a song to make us laugh, a song to take us back someplace warm and friendly, 'Our song' Where you 'Lay your head on My Shoulder', and the two of you take on the world. And its because of 'Just a Dream. Just a Dream'. Boy, I couldn't make it without a song. My truck or car gets serenaded to every time I get in them. Especially in the morning. Just like a daily devotion, a song gets the day started off right... Gaither's 'He Touched Me' is one favorite Gospel and of course Elvis's Gospel. You all do realize old time southern Gospel is fading away. Seems only us old folk keep it going.

Now that's sad, but yesterday was no different than that. Saw one couple in their 20's. Everybody else had gray or colored hair-my wife said as long as they made color I wouldn't see no gray in hers- But our old time rock and roll is rocking on out--so put on a CD or find an oldies station and take a trip down memory lane it will do you really good. The theatre is doing Beach Music next month—I'll shag some at least I call it that.

An Axe and a Longrifle

I said many times that our people came across these hills from every conceivable walk of life. They had a dream: find a spot of good land and build a home, be a free man, to be fiercely independent. They had the rifle in one hand and the ax in the other and a Book under their arm. They would find a holler that had water and a place to raise a garden and wood for building and heating. They would claim it. The more affluent ones had mules, horses or oxen. The first unwritten 'rule' of mountain folk was you helped your neighbor; so if one of my folk had a mule, you had access to the mule. They took those axes ad a strong back and cut trees and hewed logs and built a shelter; first for them, then for their animals and chickens. They would help each other from daylight till dark every day except Sunday.

After the cabins and barns were built, they always built a place to worship. This cabin served as a schoolhouse as well. Cause one thing was for sure, there was going to be lots of children. One thing they needed hands to help farm and work and log. The womenfolk needed girls to help with the gardens and milking and washing and canning and sewing. So much work to do, all day, every day, except Sunday; which brings me to my thoughts for today: Worship.

Lots of communities did not have a preacher, and when one wasn't around they read scripture and sang shape note music. Now there were circuit-riding preachers who would travel from church to church and preach. He might get there at daylight so the 'church bell' would be rung and folk would come hear the preacher. Then he would go on down the road, usually on horseback, to another community; and as long as his voice held out, he would repeat this process all day. He was not limited to only Sunday's. Whenever he came the bell would be rung and the folk would gather. These men would be paid rarely in cash money. I've often wondered how they carried eggs and butter and food, because one thing was sure, the people appreciated the parson and they took care of him.

I remember 50 years ago going to a little church on Laurel and hearing shape note style music. The preacher got up, a tall lanky mountaineer, and opened the Book. I sat there in awe. Whenever he finished reading scripture he commenced preaching. He never stopped for half an hour, and he was a 'hacker'. The only breath he took was between sentences. He was loud and I did not understand very many words he said. No notes, just preached. I didn't know what he said, but afterward the people hugged him and thanked him and said, "great sermon". He was soaked. That impressed me.

The Presbyterians build churches and hospitals around and were a major influence in Shelton Laurel. The folk there had more access to education and the communities were so much better off because of the help the Presbyterians brought to the table. My mom got me to go to the 8th grade even though she did not get to stay with her brothers and sisters and her dad. On the other side of the county my dad only got to go to the 3rd grade partly because of less opportunity and also the need for hands to work the hardscrabble farm he grew up on.

One circuit rider preacher came across the mountain every week to Shelton Laurel and one week he was late. Story goes, they asked him what happened and he said his horse got sick. Well you're riding him, so what did you do? He said I laid hands on him and prayed for him. One fellow said you mean you prayed for your horse? The old preacher said, "Son, I wouldn't serve a God who couldn't heal a horse." And that was why they did what they did. For little or no reward. They still worked and farmed just like everyone else, but there was a fire n their bones and they had to go tell the old old story of how a Savior came from Glory.

Some of the churches/schoolhouses had fireplaces in them, and some in later years had a wood stove in the middle of the room. You might as well hug a firebug up by his legs for all the good it did. So it was very common for folk to either leave a quilt there or bring quilts with them to every service in wintertime. Look at those homemade benches in the picture and you can see why no one went to sleep. Course the preacher woke the dead preaching Hell hot, and Heaven sweet. They usually baptized in the summer time unless someone was on their deathbed then there was an urgency to get er done...I suspect that frigid mountain water had something to do with sprinkling as opposed to immersion. There were tremendous revivals where whole communities were revived and the lost were saved and folk would be plowing and God would hit them and they would fall on their knees and get saved. Same thing happened all over the world, in England, and the great Wales revival. God Himself was in these mountains and He was ever present because he was exalted and honored by the God fearing men and women who lived here.

Our religious heritage is one reason mountain folk are the salt of this old world, which has turned away from God. It is another heritage that is fading into the fogs of time. In just a few years the worship and fear of love of God has slowly faded into the background. A lot of our old time churches are social gatherings now.

They came across these hills from everywhere. Scott-Irish, German, and European and all parts in between. They saw these beautiful mountains and valleys and sank deep roots into the soil. They worked from light to dark, grubbing, chopping, sawing and building. They came across the hills with a broadaxe, a horse or mule, a few tools, and a deep need for freedom. They mostly all had an old KJV Bible in these. They used it for worship, for their guide to life.

They first helped each other build a cabin for shelter and a shed for livestock. They had to get a crop in the ground for wintertime. They had to make corn crops, and hay. They used every part of their corn: the ears for food...Hominy, corn-meal, mush, and to kick-start their work animals. My grandfather would plow the hillsides so steep if you had a tractor you couldn't use it, and the old mule Fred and him would stop at dinner and he would give Fred an ear of corn-for reloading he said. It was enough that the old mule would work day to dark. Sweat, stink, and fart...

Ginseng and Cash Money

The smell of sweat and leather is unforgettable...Those old barns smelled like work. They used the cornstalks for feed and the shucks sometimes were dipped a bit n coal oil and used for light—we get the phrase 'light a shuck', going home in the dark or to the barn or outhouse maybe—Anyway, after the cabins were built, next came the school-churchhouses. Though our ancestors had little or any education, they still realized the importance and most wanted it for their children. Most had large families for lack of birth control but also for help on the farms. Everyone worked...Large families meant more preparation for winter, more food to can and store in the root cellars. Our ancestors were independently fierce and proud people. They would probably disown our great country if they were aware of the mess we are in now.

There was very little cash money. Did you know that one source of cash money was wild American ginseng? I've heard that Daniel Boone had Indians digging for him. I don't know about that but I do know that history teaches that it was valued hundreds of years ago, and it is still here. Poachers and fools have practically eliminated it in lots of places but it's still here. I can see my grandfather with a little sack made out of a feed sack tied to his waist with a biscuit or some such in it for food. He had a sang stick 6 ft long probably and he kept it sharpened for balance as well as for digging. Heading off up a holler for higher ground and "cash money".

Can you imagine, you've just had a brutal summer making sure you had firewood for cooking and for heat for winter; you've canned and stored food for winter as well as food everyday. The hogs are getting fat, fences are repaired, harnesses are repaired and oiled, roofs constantly fixed, hay has been cut and stumps are burning on that new ground. You get to go to the woods and hunt for the most beautiful plant in all the world. I think it would be like a vacation, better than a vacation. I suspect lots of old timers put some things off just to get in the woods. I would have…

Think of that great heritage we come from boys and girls. Next time you look across a holler and there on the other side a long way off you catch a flash of red, and you feel that surge of 'joy', 'excitement'—think about your ancestors feelings those many years ago…They almost had to find that gold. I live on sweet memories a lot at my age, and my hope is you make yourself some memories worth keeping this season….. Leave some in the ground—they did…you be blessed, you hear?? As David says—grow, grow, grow.

Brown Paper Pokes

One thing of importance to me even after 60 plus years, was the brown paper pokes that we kids (and grownups) got at Christmas at the Open Bible Church on Davis Creek in Hominy Valley; an orange, an apple, some hard candy, and usually nuts (English walnuts usually). Now this was a treat sometimes almost duplicated in the socks hung up on the mantle at home... and these treats along with a little something on Christmas morning was Christmas for us kids...But you know what, we were so full of anticipation and the spirit of the Season that I was never disappointed. I loved hunting a tree and putting popcorn strands and angel hair on the tree. I do not recall being overly religious at the time although I know we were very aware of the Reason for Christmas. I wish we could have Christmases like those again—this commercial stuff is way off base—give me a paper poke again——

Now, it's 2015 and the memories of Hominy Valley and Christmas are fresh anew this morning. I woke up remembering the brown paper poke full of goodies many times and usually there wasn't much left. But the sock was usually loaded with the same stuff; and a present of some sort, but the joy of the season is still fresh. The beautiful music, The Babe in the manger, (there's a new kid in town), The dawn of Grace, A life of Faith, new beginnings and hope for all people. To the lowly shepherds first, then to me. I must confess that for a period of my life, I wasn't very nice. I came out of the air force with a drinking problem.

Any of you who had those problems yourself or in your family know about the mental abuse to those who love you —and those you love; but one thing that kept me 'together' was home. The Homeplace. For me one was the rented house of Hollis Robertson's on South Hominy, and the house on Curtis Creek. My grandfather's place in Madison County. Finally, the home dad bought in Woodfin. All homeplaces of my heart. I think that is one reason they all mean so much to me—the memories of a wonderful time to grow up. Those things and a family ho loved me helped me to get up one morning with a pint of liquor beside the bed in a 3 room apartment and say to my soul—there is more to life than this—I walked to the sink in the bathroom and poured it down the drain.

I was 28 years old and now during this wonderful Christmas season I am a blessed 72, and I have never tasted another drop of alcohol. Don't misunderstand, it wasn't me with the strength altogether—The Baby n the manger was the real strength for me; and I didn't even realize that for a spell. Listen children, leave the porch light on, light the tree in the yard—that prodigal may be coming today—and he may want to use your sink—I love you all for your blessed friendship— be blessed, you hear me? God spared me this year when death was 92 percent certain-what do they know-He is Christmas— love each other this year like you may not be here next year— and be blessed...

This Old House

Where was you raised? I mean what kind of house do you remember first? What age can you recall? 5 years old? 4? I don't remember 4, but I do remember 5; and I remember some specific things. I remember this dog I am holding very well, but not the cat. I remember when the dog died-Dad suspected poison- and I remember Laura, my sister, crying but not Leta, my other sister. Oh well, she might not have cared. I remember cutting the tip of her forefinger off with the lawnmower. An old push-mower that she wanted to push I guess, and I said no. She put her finger down on the mower, and I pushed the mower. Blood and screams for a spell. I do not remember getting my innocent little butt whipped either. I was five. I remember throwing a hammer up in an apple tree (horse apples) and looking up and the hammer hitting me in the top of the head. Blood was everywhere. I do not remember what happened next. I remember running through the cemetery at White Rock Church because I was afraid of black racers that would grab their tail and chase you rolling like a tire. I do not remember who fed me that whopper either. But I never walked through that old cemetery either.

Oh my, don't you recall the houses? I do not remember how many rooms or even where the outhouse was at the Warren House above White Rock Church; but I do remember sleeping in the "hall" on a rollaway bed. One time I had the whooping cough and Aunt Dewey came to stay with me cause Mama had an operation. She made me cornbread and told me to chew each bite 60 times. I think she told me that to keep me shut up for a spell; and oh boy, I remember Violet, the 11 or 12-year old who "made" me play house with her. First time I fell in love. I was in Glady School in the first grade. A one-room schoolhouse, now a church.

Oh yeah, we drew water up from the spring on a pulley. You let the bucket down and it dipped in the spring and you wound it back up the hill. I think about a half a bucket. Mama was out at the outbuilding getting some canning jars when she tilted a box on the top shelf over a copperhead fell, jumped out, and just missed her face. She screamed. And I heard a 12-gauge go off sometime. I'm not sure when, but Dad killed the copperhead. I do not remember being poor. I was never hungry. I had clothes. I had shoes for church in the summer and shoes for winter. We had little and did not have a car then. And then we had to move.

A White house with a basement with a dirt floor. The front porch was high and there was a set of steps up to it. I spent many an hour reading funny books on that porch, that a girl across the way let me borrow. I loved this place—a mountain came down to the back of it and there was a creek just down the hill. What more could a little boy possibly want? Well, maybe for Violet to have come with us. But I soon fell in love with Patsy, Byrdene, Christine, Barbara and Laura Sue— maybe all at once. At this house, I was in the second grade the first year. I went to Stony Fork School. Where recesses are embedded in my mind. Marbles, Cowboys and Indians, dodgeball and baseball and teasing all the girls I was in love with.

At this house my everyday job was firewood and kindling. Keep the boxes filled before I could go to the creek or to the woods. I didn't mind the chores cause today I love working and I think it started in the woodpile at this house. What I would give if the walls of these houses could talk. Laughter and sobs and singing and quarrels and romance would prevail. Some things probably wouldn't want to hear. I loved and still love the farmhouse that my Uncle Bud and Aunt Mary owned in East Tenn. An upstairs loft to sleep in where my cousin Jerry would tell stories and cause me to pull the cover up over my head at times. To me it was more than an old farmhouse...It was a warm, open, family home...

We moved to Curtis Creek just down the road maybe for the 7th and 8th grade and I walked home from school most days. I loved this place too, and I made friends at all of them. Walker Hinson, a farmer, took a liking to me and took me with him cutting and bailing hay..He was good to me...The house had indoor water, the first one, but still an outhouse down the hill a piece. I was in the 9th grade before we had a place with water and an indoor toilet. I love the outhouses and the Sears catalogue. I was halfway through the 9th grade at Enka and one day Dad said we are moving to Woodfin. Leave all these gorgeous girls and baseball behind??? Dad and Mom finally bought a home and now I am glad they did. I don't mind telling you but this teenager cried when we drove away from Hominy Valley.

I miss each of these old houses still. I jump into the old reddish canoe that leaks a bit now and paddle down the rivers of my memories and almost every time on or all of these houses comes to mind. I went back to the Davis Creek house owned by Hollis Robertson a few years ago and it was empty. I looked through the windows and a bathroom and water was added on, otherwise it looked much the same. I went into the woods where the hog lot was and the outhouse and then I climbed the steps up to the front porch. I slid down against the wall and closed my eyes. I could "hear" the house. Emotions rolled in and tears rolled down, and then laughter and memories and tears came and went. I was there over an hour and I remember finally standing up and laughing out loud and yelling "Thank You Lord" as loud as I could. You say, "Jack, You're crazy,"...I say yes, but don't disturb me, I enjoy it. There is laughter in the walls, even where you live now...but if you be real quiet I'm sure you can hear the old houses you grew up in and around, perhaps your grandparents houses/cabins, calling you to come visit and sit a spell...up against the wall with your eyes closed.

Just Raise the Sails

I have traveled life's road on a whim and a prayer at times. I have gone 'against the grain' out of stubbornness before. I have done lots of things the hard way. I can visualize a white and black dog (good and bad) fighting inside of my soul for control of me. Whichever one I fed the most won. You know what I mean don't you?? The two commandments —Love God and your Neighbor—feed the white dog. Doing things my way fed Blackie...Oh we have been friends. I know the enemy; I've done enough business with him.

Another way I try to keep in check is checking out the waves. I think my life has been a boat ride. You all know what a boat is, don't you? Well, I have paddled against the wind so much and labored fruitlessly till I was wore out and sunburned...contrary to the wind. Now as I've gotten older I have learned a couple things that will help us; riding along on the rivers of life, we can use the contrary winds and get through them without so much labor and suffering. I raise the sails and let Him take me home.

Are you like me—rowing with all your strength and going nowhere, or are you sailing along eating fried chicken and tater salad?? I thought yesterday I was called to preach— I woke up not wanting to go to work and craving chicken— but Bojangles fixed all that. I am so thankful that He teaches us thorough preaching and His Word...how to raise the sails, sit back, and enjoy life.

The old black dog? I keep him on a chain. Sometimes he

gets loose and I whine, I gossip, or I complain some, and I find myself rowing again—so what to do—chain him up, use the sails, and this—if my people will humble themselves, pray and seek my face, I will hear from Heaven and heal their land…this is where our once great country is—lets raise our sails—.

Content or Satisfied?

Contentment is not satisfaction. There is a real difference. Contentment is sorta being grateful, and perhaps using what we have to help ourselves and others—whether it's little or much. Maybe to have the most and best in life, by making the most and best of what we have. And that, my friends, is what mountain folk are all about—or used to be and some still are. You simply make do with what you have. If you enjoy what you have to the upmost, you will be content. Satisfied? I know and have known lots of folk who had little in material things but are the most contented people in the world. I have some friends who lack for nothing and some are not happy. Somehow there is a fear of losing wealth and a desire to have more. I've never experienced those emotions—I started out with nothing and still have most of it. I've promised God if I win the lottery, I'll give Him half, and spread the wealth. So far he doesn't seem to believe me.

I and a lot of you have suffered many tragedies and setbacks, yet we move on and have that peace that don't make any sense. Why? It all started when most of us were took to church 9 moths before we were born. We memorized scripture and we sang songs and we played in the Christmas Play's and we heard that loud preacher, especially when he talked about hell and demons. But, somewhere along the line, that seed was planted, and it was watered and the High Sheriff warmed our hearts and we said 'yes, Lord.' We can be content based on that decision many moons ago. I'm not satisfied. I want more. I want to be better, I want to do better, I want to be a better role model for whoever is looking; but I am content. I have lots of regrets and fears (not death, death has no hold on me), dreams that haven't come true, trips I haven't made, a Yankee uniform I didn't get to wear, children and loved ones gone on—but I am content. I told my multi-millionaire friend that I beat at golf (really content here), Frankie, that though his bank account, and houses and all that was so much bigger than mine, that Our graves would be the same size…What do we have in common you ask?? We both know where the good stuff comes from…

The Biker and The Parkway

I quit worrying about things a long time ago. I love people—I really love characters—Like that biker I told you about on the parkway—rough looking and I spoke to him... and he opened up. He had terminal cancer and was making a circle around the US and back to Maine to his wife—if he made it. We talked for awhile and I was blessed. He was content... when we parted, I said 'you be careful and watch for them bad drivers'. He wheeled around and pinned me with his eyes, and said " I ain't worried about that, when the Lord is ready for me, He will come get me." And he paused and swallowed hard and looked away for a moment, then turned back and said 'I hope He don't need me till I get back to my wife, I need to kiss her one more time.' He touched his forehead like in a salute and we watched him go down the mountain road out of sight. I was content in that moment, but I wasn't satisfied. So I bowed my head and literally begged God to let him get home to his woman. I don't know if he got home, but I am content with that and I am also satisfied with that—You see, I did the very best thing I could do for him, so I'm satisfied. Hay, I bet there are folk you know that you should, need to, will say a prayer of contentment for...you will sleep better, I guarantee it...You be blessed this day and always—you hear me?

The Listening Post

Some days I feel like I can do a little marathon. Other days, I can lean on my listening post for hours. You don't know what a listening post is? Well, it is a round wooden post with a flat top around chest high that is placed in a strategic place so you can observe all your surroundings. Who knows when hostile Indians or Bears and such may be lurking around? So you be diligent and fold your arms on top of the post and watch.

Another form of listening posts is called a rocking chair or a recliner; but everyone needs some form of a listening post. Sometimes I can get out of the car and walk normal and upright, other times I would never be the first in the swimming hole. You would think I was getting old if you didn't know me. I think at times me and Auther are getting too familiar with each other; but I have determined that the only thing golden about the golden years is your pee.

To me the golden years were the years of yesterday, particularly the fabulous 50's and 60's. What with the Yankees and Dodgers and Elvis and Jerry Lee and Johnny and the Drifters singing to us sinners, it was exciting. Bobby sox and crew cuts. Winks and the first McDonald's on tunnel road. Waking up seeing Pisgah shrouded in fog and the patter of soft rain on the tin roof. Going to the outhouse with your dog and cat trailing along, and the wet grass on your bare feet—You knew the creek would get up a bit and the rock dam you made yesterday would be gone with the wind. O well, plenty of time to dam it up again, and again.

As I stand here leaning on this well-worn post, I realize I am running out of time at a high rate of speed. One day, I won't give a hoot if the grass is well manicured and my truck is washed—uh-oh—I don't much care now—Gosh I've got to get off this post, the creeks running and I must go make me a swimming hole—see you soon if I can find my reading glasses —.

Barabas and The Pardon

There were 3 in the dark, wet rock room. They were huddled together by choice and by chains fastened to the floor. They listened with increasing terror as boots thudded on the rock hallway, and each trembled with fear—Is he coming for me? He opens the door and unlocks the thief's chains and takes him down the hall and out the door. In a few moments the screams began as the 9-tailed whip tore out chunks of flesh...40 times, and 40 agonizing cries of pain.

The sounds ceased and the boots came again. The remaining thieves trembled with fear for they had been found guilty also, and sentenced to scourging and the most cruel death of all—crucifixion—The boots came and took another one and the screams were repeated. The sounds stopped once again-and the boots came own the rock hallway.

In the dark wet rock room, Barrabas trembled with fear. My turn-I bet he wished for death at this point. The guard unlocks the chains and Barrabas stood on watery knees and wet himself from terror. The guard says 'you are being set free.' He didn't hear him for the fear was all consuming—the guard twisted his head around and up and said

Look at me, someone has taken your place, we are setting you free.' He sank to his knees and said, 'what? Why? And finally, who?' The guard said, I don't know why, but I heard it was someone named Jesus. The thief on one side said, save yourself the mockery, the thief on the other side said, this man has done nothing.

Now I don't know which way Barrabas went-which

thief he followed—but one thing I do know—When He came to me, and took my place I am so thankful that by His Grace and nothing more, and nothing less, He set me free. This is mostly my theology and don't go looking for untruths—leave the passion in the Book-It bleeds from Genesis to Revelation— He has taken, or will take your place also—Make Him Lord in your life today.

I Love Porches and Green Beans

The porch was wide with white columns and a plain tongue and grooved floor. The house was a blue house painted white!!! There was a one car shed out back behind the wood shed, where I spent many an hour splitting kindling and stove wood for the cook stove and the heater. The car shed held dad's '50 Chevy, which he was proud of; but not so proud that he wouldn't use a piece of tape on it most anywhere he thought he needed it. Down the hill behind the house was the outhouse. I was a frequent visitor except when Mom wasn't looking. Down below that was the hog-pen with a nice duroc in it being fattened up for winter. There was a creek just down the hill called Curtis Creek. I had torn up one muskrat's leg trying to trap them and I gave that money making venture up out of sadness seeing his leg.

Sometimes my sweet mom could light up a Christmas tree with just a look. I was easing my Schwinn bike that dad had sacrificed to buy me for this past Christmas, out from inside the woodshed. She just looked at me through the kitchen window and I had enough sense to put it back. And man, it was a Schwinn; Chrome fenders and a light and horn on the side and whitewall tires. I had added little squares of pasteboard attached with clothespins to the braces on the fender, and it sounded like a Harley. I was wired to go! But you know what my sweet dad had done this gorgeous Saturday morning? There was four, that is 4, FOUR, bushels of half runners sitting out on the front porch; and on Saturday morning. There was the swimming hole where we gathered and prayed some girls would show up and go skinny-dipping with us. There was baseball in the cow pasture or down at the field at Pisgah Elementary just a couple miles below the house. There was fishing and running in the woods, and tagging after Walker Hinson and his hay baler. And there was that sang path I was keeping an eye on, and three big 4 prongs that needed looking at, Lordy, Didn't dad know better??? But beans?? What an insult to my imagination. And no doubt Roger would ride by on his JC Higgins from Sears and toot his sorry little horn. He knowed not to laugh cause I had a good arm and could flat hum a rock, or a baseball. Until I threw it away pitching for the Junior Deputy's. They didn't know little fellas need to warm up and shouldn't try throwing curve balls. Ruined my dreams of playing for the Yankees. But we sure had a lot of fun hitting rocks with backer sticks and playing baseball in the pasture.

Well, nothing to do but swallow my pride and swell up and get on the porch. I had me two pots and some Grits papers and I usually sat with my back against the wall and drug over a bushel of them sorry beans. It usually took me an hour or so to unswell and join in the talk that always went on…My sister Laura had already moved to Georgia and for the life of me I can't remember my other sister Leta on the porch. One thing I am sure of, if she wasn't there I gave Ma an earful of 'why ain't she out here'… Now with halfrunners you string them with the grain, and then break them in short snaps. All evidence of strings had to disappear or Mama fussed. I remember her making me fill the woodbox over full. She always had an apron on and she sat in an old straight-backed chair and broke beans at about the speed of light. When she had enough for a run, she went in and put them on and when they had cooked enough she packed them in jars and put the lids on. Then between times she was back on the porch. Dad had no right thumb but that did not slow hi down either. But mostly I remember the silence. Just the sounds of beans breaking and being thrown into the pots and pans. Somehow or other doing those kind of things together gave you a sense of pride and accomplishment. I always had to get more wood and carry the strings and such down to the hog pen. Stack up the baskets and put them in the shed in the dry. And I remember sweeping the porch off. I suspect Leta was busy with Mom. But somehow it taught me to finish what I start, to clean up my mess. And there was even satisfaction hearing those jars pop and seal.

Four bushel that day—four of us. On a porch in the mountains. Ma and Pa and Leta and Me. I forgot about the bike and swimming and even baseball for a while. I was looking for the bottom of those bushel baskets. Keep in mind sometimes I would be the only one out there—Dad usually lifted the cookers and chunked up the wood and Leta washed jars ahead and helped Ma some. And dad could take his time when he chose to. You know what? This is one of my favorite times right here. IT wasn't many years till I was a freshman ad we moved to Woodfin. And I guess it may seem funny to some that when I go back up there and the house is still there with the wide front porch, that I stop across the road and I can still see us laughing and talking and pouting and breaking them stupid beans on Saturday....

When the time came and Mom had some stewed Potatoes and some of her delicious slaw and an onion with cornbread and she broke the seal on those half runners with a chunk of fatback, I was so 'proud' that I had had a part fixing them...Especially when I took a bite. I guess for all of us, when things happen we don't like or even in really hard times three are lessons to be learned. I want my half runners broke short and with no strings. But if you bring four bushel here on Saturday or any other day I will personally send you up to Hickory to my sister Leta and Vernon house. I still don't think she did anything........

Open Bible Church

Some of us have went to church our whole lives, haven't we? We memorized and learned verses. We have been blasted with "Hell is waiting on you to mess up boy" to sow a seed and get wealthy and your miracle is just a dollar away....I have concluded that none are completely correct.

Death, sickness, sorrow and heartache, along with joy, happiness, peace, and love are all part of this life. Along with age and wear and tear and breakdowns. God Himself decreed life to be 'what it is'. The very best Hope we have is to go peacefully, suddenly, and to work it out when that last check we write bounces...But when we were born, death was not far away, and when it comes our friends and family will say we are dead. But we who know Him will not be dead; We will have have passed from the temporal to the eternal. What a quick trip it seems to be now that I'm old...But I am determined that until the trumpet sounds I will try to say or do something to help others. My prayer is "Lord just give me the opportunity to help someone". I was dead over 20 minutes and I never felt any heat or did not see any golden gates, so I guess that is a sign to me to help others.

The days of our lives on this wonderful place created by our Master, has increased over the years...From 3 score and 10 to 4 score and 10. Greedy doctors keep us alive when we should be let alone. The generations crowd each other now and the sand is oozing out of the hourglass faster and faster. So some beautiful daybreak with the red and pink and gray hues brilliantly displayed on the horizon, the real wonders of the world will fail to do their job. The doors of our lives will finally close and the window blinds will be drawn. We won't SEE the sunrise, we won't HEAR the song of the mockingbird, we won't FEEL the warm touch of a friend or lover, we won't SMELL the sweet smell of the Carolina Jasmine, or honeysuckle, we won't TASTE that first cup of good coffee. And that special surge of emotion when we love with abandon will not be felt. Oh My, God's unseen hand has written on the wall already, and I reckon it is good we cannot see the writing...If we are right about the hereafter we have nothing to fear.

I would like to go back to South Hominy and Open Bible Church and hear the leather lunged, white mouthed hell fire and brimstone preaching of Berry Watts again. I never really listened, I was thinking about fishing, and slingshots, and sang and marbles. I'd really like to go to homecoming there again. I doubt the dater salit and nanner pudding will be as good as then, but I'd just like to seem them tables full again.

As an afterthought—what if we were wrong? There is no Heaven or Hell? We have followed the precepts and guidelines of the Book for nothing. We could have robbed, killed and stayed drunk with no moral consequences. Come on, you and I know better. It's a better life even if there was no promise of Heaven. What's wrong with posting the 10 Commandments all over everywhere? Don't kill, Don't lie, Don't cheat are pretty good standards. But I am like Paul, I didn't get knocked to the ground physically like Him, but I hit the dirt anyway; and I am certain that in whom I have believed will take me home. This little tirade is somewhat a downer but every once in a while I remind myself that "In my hand no price I bring, Simply to the cross I cling? I can face anything, I hope you can cause we may have to before the sand runs out...Be blessed, and be ready.

Cicadas and Lightning Bugs

Well I been taking another ride in my old wore out reddish canoe that has sprung a couple leaks, down the never-ending rivers of my memory. "I hold them to my chest and find them ever gentle, ever sweet on my mind." I couldn't stop if I wanted to. I am saddened for folk who had bad experiences as children. Some don't or can't go back. I was out in the yard with a 5-year old and he found a cicadi-locust, 17-year locust, lying in the grass. With a little help he finally picked it up and has carried it around for a while. I didn't tell him it was dying, but I explained it needed to be put back I the grass and let go. Which he did.

It was so refreshing to see the awe and excitement in his face over this locust. And of course I went back to Hominy Valley when I sat down on the porch. I was probably 7 years old when the 17-year cycle happened there. It was a tremendous 'song' ringing through the trees. I got me a quart jar and collected the shed shells that were stuck all over the place. I had them things everywhere. And I remember the live ones lying around here and there, unable to fly and dying. I took the shells down to the old oak bridge and I would float them down the creek pretending they were cowboys sneaking up on the Indians. It's amazing how we entertained ourselves for hours and hours, never having to say, "I'm bored."

There were a lot of these cicadas that season and they gradually disappeared. By the way, they come out of the ground and shed their 17-year-old suit and climb, fly up into a tree and on a slim branch lay their eggs under the bark. The twig dies and falls to the ground and the eggs hatch and the larva go into the ground for 17 years; and the mature one dies. What an unusual act of nature! 17 years of dirt and finally see the Carolina blue sky, and drop dead. Kinda like some folk who finally retire with plans made and have major health problems. That's why we need to live now...

Hugh Watts used to come and play with me and Connie. He was bigger and always got to ride the white horse and when he shot us we had to hit the ground. We always missed him when we shot him. Now when he didn't come I was the older one and I rode roughshod over Connie. One day I was the Lone Ranger and my dog Butch was Silver, his horse. Other days I was the Cisco Kid and I would let Connie be Pancho, my sidekick. Hopalong Cassidy and Lash Larue was heroes too. And by the way we didn't grow up shooting folk just cause we had cap pistols. Connie had cap pistols; I usually made mine out of wood. I've also told you many times that I was an expert switch cutter, and even tough we literally lived in the woods, I had to go father and father to find suitable material that suited Mom. I also devised a system of making a small cut about a foot and a half up the switch so that after a few licks it would break. Oh I was slick I thought. Them good old red marks on my butt and legs never caused me to need counseling or take out warrants on my folks for cruelty. They did cause me to think about what was going to happen if I went on with my present course of action. Sometimes I thought the risk was worth the switching. Now, girls wouldn't consider that. Usually one punishment was all that it took to get a point across; but us boys didn't think that way. I figured a switching didn't last long and I could whimper and act like it was killing me and get a new clean page to start over.

As I got older, I realized that is exactly what Christ did for me…The page was black and wrote all over and there was a book of it, but one day I opened to a new chapter and the pages was blank. So since that time as I have 'matured' as much as a nostalgic, canoe riding, romantic, dreamer can, I have been very careful what I write on the pages of my life. Not out of fear of a switching, but because of a desire to please and point to Him. Though, I do 'fear' the consequence of bad choices. I have no clue why I got off of bugs to this, but it just seemed to fit. Perhaps seeing this wonderful little 5-year old boy squatted down thrilled about a bug made me think about what is really important.

Catching those fireflies, and tying strings on june bug legs and hunting wasp nests for fishing was a wonderful part of another time. Insignificant and of no consequence to anyone but those of us who did those things. I'm going to make sure we go out firefly hunting just to see how much fun he will have. He has a tablet and is in kindergarten and we played a game on his tablet and he beat me 18 to 6. I will bet good money that I can catch more fireflies than the can though——

Jimmy Skunk or Reddy Fox

Shirley asked me when I started reading. As soon as I could put words together. When I came to words I didn't know I broke them down. I mispronounced a lot of words; like Yos-sa-mite- not yo-sim-a-tee. Pen-a-lope not pe-nel-a-pee. I called a lady at church by that first rendition and she bowed up and said, "My name is Pe-nel-a-pee." The ladies at church still laugh at me about that.

My dad read the Bible and the paper. He only got to go to the 3rd grade. He went to work on the hardscrabble farm I reckon. He interpreted the Bible just as he read it. Anything that was fun was wrong. I am not downing him or judging him, he lived what he believed to be true. Mom, raised in another part of the county got to go to the 8th grade. Thanks to the Presbyterians who came into Shelton Laurel and built churches and schools. I heard a lot of emphasis was on teaching the young girls. Mom liked to read everything including those lady books and romance magazines. Dad disapproved, so she read them and hid them.

I started reading Thorton W. Burgess books early on. Old Mother West Winds Children, Reddy the Fox, Peter Rabbit, Jimmy the Skunk, etc. They were wonderful reads for a little boy and I read them over and over. The Black Stallion Series, Walter Farley was favorites; But Jim Kjeelgaards dog stories were my favorites. Big Red and Outlaw Red and Haunt Fox etc. I read funny books over and over. The Lone Ranger was a favorite. Archie and Veronica and Hopalong Cassidy. I read the advertisements and the grits papers. I would crawl in behind Mom's cook stove in the winter and read. I was taken to other places and I pretended it was about us in the stories ad I was the White Knight and the hero. Lad, a Dog is still a favorite. I have some of these books that I have found here and there. When I want to know why Jimmy the Skunk has a white streak down his back, I go to the garage and my bookshelf and get Old Mother Wests winds book down and re read it.

I love reading a book that stays on my mind for a while. I don't know if our younger generations will read actual books with dog-eared pages or not. I have Kindle, but I like to hold my Bible or a book in my hands. I'm old fashioned in more ways than one. I also like to say Grace and eat at the table or bar together. Sometimes it happens.

Man I wish I could crawl in behind Mom's cook stove and read about Silver, The Lone Ranger's Horse. I hope he gets away from that mountain lion. One of the highlights of being a boy who read a lot was meeting the bookmobile once a month at Clay London's Store on Saturday. After a while they knew me, and what I was looking for. I can still smell that old yellow box van. Coulda been every 2 or 3 weeks—I can't remember everything…..But I remember the joy of reading—real good.

Cut the Stupid Cable

Sometimes I wonder if I even got the ability to think or if I just give up and give in to stuff that really makes no sense. I am thinking seriously about cutting the cable cord. You know, that cord that sucks dollars out of your meager bank account every month; and mysteriously every other month goes to a higher rate with no reasonable reason. The owner's dog had to have a hysterectomy, or their refrigerator tore up, or someone ran over their mailbox, or Johnny needs a new winter coat. So the bill from these lifeblood suckers goes up. And I keep paying for the dog. I shake my head and clench my fist and try to represent my Christian Faith but I doubt I could get into the 11th chapter of Hebrews. Listen, I have over 170 channels of cable that I wouldn't watch if they sent me a check every month. Storage Wars and how to manage your money and the daily stocks report are useless to me.

I don't have no stock except three Holstein steers and I should have Time Warner so our cat Theo could get this aids thing treated. Why am I paying for stuff I will never stop the remote at? The only good thing for men is once we get settled in our easy chair with our beloved remote we cruise channels for a long time then we throw a mild tizzy about there is nothing fit to see, but then we go back through the channels like we think something has changed. It never does. But some wives will pay for cable just so their man is occupied for a while. And the tizzies don't really bother them that much. We get red faced and settle on treehouses for a few minutes till we get dizzy then go over and laugh at Hillary's new book until nausea sets in.

No wonder cable is driving some men to drink. Recliner sales are way down and will probably get worse unless things improve with the remotes. They have designed the remotes to resemble racecars and guns and even beer bottles but it hasn't helped yet. I think it is time to cut the cord. Get a smart antenna and the local news and forget about Pawn Stars and Poker. Besides that my fixed income is getting fluid and slip sliding away. I have hated to admit this cause I know all my friends on here are not as dumb as me. Probably no one else pays for 200 useless channels but me. I could put that extra money into a book on how to please your wife when you don't have a remote.

Well it's a good day to have a confession, I feel better about myself already. Oh Lordy there they go again, they just asked me if Melanie had on high heels or sneakers. And I don't know—I was searching for Foghorn Leghorn or Wiley E. Coyote to no avail...Shucks, I'm getting the scissors. Be alert for shouting and dancing not associated with the church. Free, Free at last......you be blessed this day and everyday and lay the remote down and remember how blessed we really are.

A Caneback Chair and A Porch

Well, I been on the porch again today. I was paint-ing in our nursery after cleaning off a bank and mowing it and getting too hot, and my little mind drifted down the river in my ole canoe again. Chauncy Fender from over on Laurel had a farm and a neat white house with a nice front porch. Chauncy also had a mule because a tractor was basically worthless on those hillsides that those folk farmed on....He always wore overalls and he had a wry sense of humor native to mountain folk. He would stop at 12 each day and come in for dinner. After-ward he went out on the porch and leaned back in an old cane back chair and rested, dozed, sharpened his case for about an hour. He said he could rest on a porch. There was a tall steep mountain in front of him; there is a branch funning at the foot of the yard. Not much else to see, but it was so peaceful just sitting there. Most wouldn't see but a mountain, a small field, a yard, a branch...I say what else do you need to see?

I loved listening to Chauncy when you could get him to talk. It was a good porch....Sometimes you just sit on a porch not looking for anything or even noticing what's going on around you. For me a porch has been a place of resting, medi-tating, reading, doing nothing, looking for nothing, expecting nothing. I do not think I've ever sit on a porch and not enjoyed it. Shatley Springs restaurant is always crowded because it is family style, served at your table. By that I mean bowls of food just like in the country when you were growing up are served. And you never run out. They have a huge front porch with rocking chairs. The last time I was there I thought, boy this is the way to wait for a table. There is also a railing to put your feet on.

Whenever I go out in the evening especially, I notice folk on their porches. There is not as many as used to be for sure, but there are some and it is about all I can do not to stop and talk. Porch folk are worth talking to. And you know what? I can't imagine if He has mansions, that they will have huge porches with rocking chairs. It's so peaceful sitting on the porch with someone you like or love and never having to say a word....

The last porch I want to mention is on Oklahoma Road in East Tennessee. It isn't a real big porch. And it don't get used much. But it is a good place for me. I have always been drawn out to the porch when I go to visit my kinfolk. It overlooks the dairy that he used to run and just past it is a hillside and a grove of trees on the left. Usually corn or soybeans in the bottom. Nothing spectacular for sure....except to me. I loved sitting out there with my cousin friend Boyd Chandley and just talking, about this or that. It was an easy time, a special time that I can't really explain easily; Just a porch with feeling. It will be difficult to go sit out there by myself but I got a feeling the porch will make it an easy time. I miss my friend. I am thankful that he was home. I am thankful that he did not suffer much. I'm grateful that he has his family all around him And I'm really grateful that he was a Christian. I am also grateful that when he built his home, he built a front porch—or me....and didn't know it.

Moms Thumb Cleaner

I tell you what, a brillo pad didn't hold a candle to Mama's thumb when it came to cleaning up the corners of my mouth or dirt on my cheek. She would lick that thing, and being allergic to water, I would shudder, for I knew what was coming. Seeing this post today with the tubs of water and the kids taking a bath brought back a multitude of images and memories of like situations. I found out pretty quick that if there was more than one to take a bath, you needed to be first. But I was the only boy with two dratted sister pets and of course they ganged up and said I was the dirtiest, therefore, I got the tub last.

I was around 7 on Davis's creek in South Hominy. We lived in Hollis Robertson's rental house right at the base of a wonderful mountain and just up the hill from a wonderful creek that always needed damming up or to be fished in. It was a constant battle which one to do first. And of course Connie Gene and I played a great deal of cowboys and Indians on the side. He was younger than me so he was usually the bad guy and I was the hero. Man I'd like to saddle up and meet him down at the creek, and we could go running thru the woods, beating our sides and yelling and having great fun. With one eye on Con's big whiteface bull—which didn't like me much anyway......

Back to the story, it's so easy for me to go off on them side rabbit trails because they were special times that I store like gold nuggets in my mind and when I recall them and reminisce about those simpler times—I am blessed. All the tragedy and sorrow and grief have to go...And that's how I deal with sorrow. Anyway, we had an outdoor well with a hand pump. So on Saturday evening it was bath time. So I helped pump the water and we carried it into the house on the wood cook stove and got it hot. We even had to do that in the heat of summer, which I told mama it was too hot. She never did listen to me much. Anyway, you fill the tub up about halfway. It was in the kitchen. And the first lucky one would get in and sit down. If I tried to sit down in a tub now, it would have to be a dump truck for me to get back up. When they got thru washing usually some more water was added to heat it back up and Leta was usully next. When she got thru it was baby boy Jack's turn. Mama made sure the water was really hot and much to my dismay made sure I got in. And she always inspected to see if my 'rusty' feet was clean. When you went barefooted all summer they were considered 'rusty'...

Anyway, part of the water was used three times. And especially after I used it, it was dingy for sure. Seem like I remember a 'skim' like on top of the water. Well I ask you, when you stood up some of that stuff stood up with you...No amount of complaining about dirty water or wanting to take a mountain bath (a dab here and a dab there) had any effect. Then the tub had to be emptied a pail at a time and threw out in the yard. Then the tub had to be cleaned and rinsed and hung up on the back of the house. Spilled water wiped up off the floor. It was an ordeal I'll tell you. I hated baths but I feared Mama's thumb worse. You see you couldn't waste water. The wells were not deep and water was a blessing even if you had to "run and get it."

I remember washing every night with a dishpan and soap and a rag—but Saturday was bath day. It's funny you know, I know neither my dad or mom could get in a tub, and I don't recall them ever washing. I mean, I know they washed every day, I just don't remember that part. Shoot I wouldn't mind a tub bath now just for old times sake. You talk about 'sight'—see a bunch of us old people have a tub party and have prizes for who could actually sit down and prizes for who could get back up.....what you all think??? You be blessed now, you hear me??

Just Mama

I remember her standing over the old white wood stove with the water warmer and the bisquit warmers. I remember her wiping her forehead with the apron. Mountain kitchens get hot in the summer, and when there are up to three meals cooked each day, they are usually warm. I remember crawling in behind the stove in cold weather; sometimes reading funny books, or books from the library. Knowing that Mama's baby boy Jack was going to get something good off of that old stove.

She was the best cook in the world, I thought. I know now she had to get tired of it, but I never heard her complain about it. My job was kindling and stove wood in the wood box. Mama could hear me breathe. I would try to sneak a wooden kitchen match out of the matchbox holder on the wall and she could hear the rattle a quarter mile away. I would roll me a rabbit backer cigarette or corn silk and she could smell it a half-mile away.

She could wash me better with her thumb than I could with a washrag. She insisted my hair be combed and my clothes ironed and neat and that I stayed clean. Even though we walked to church sometimes and there were a million rocks to throw. If I misbehaved in church (every service) she would get that little hangy down part under my arm above my elbow between her thumb and forefinger and twist it. Some thought I was getting 'in the spirit'...I musta cut a thousand switches for mom. She never got tired of switching me either.

She ironed my blue jeans, bed sheets and all that. I got sick of being so clean. If I heard her say this once, "wash them rusty feet before you get in that clean bed," I heard it all summer.

She loved water and soap and I only loved the creek water minus the soap...I remember how she looked at me with softness in her eyes. And sometimes she looked at me like that right after she wore me out with a switch...She could tell when I was up to something before I even knew it, yet she told folks I was her baby boy, while she was cleaning the sides of my mouth with her thumb, or digging in my ears 'places I missed'.

I was Mama's baby boy and I didn't really realize it until many years later...and I loved every minute of it. She was a mountain woman with a remarkable story of survival and really educating herself through books...She loved me, I was her baby, she was my mama, and I miss her...

I Miss My Mama

My mother Ella Pauline Chandley Burris…and my aunt Zoe Chandley Henslay. Zoe was quilting into her '90's. Someone had made her a small frame out of PVC that she could do small sections at a time on her lap. Both of these remarkable women sewed the tightest little stitches and made some beautiful quilts. Zoe sold hers for as much as 200 plus and minus but she liked me and gave me a beautiful one, which I see about everyday.

They are the daughters of Lonnie Henry Chandley and Hannah Shelton of Shelton Laurel. When their Mom died they were put out to live with whoever would take them. Mom was around 8 she told me. Zoe married Coleman Hensley and Mom married Charles M Burris from Bull Run, near Marshall. Zoe raised 11 children…Her husband Coleman killed a man who 'picked and ridiculed' him often—I guess he couldn't take anymore….He served less than 7 years and Zoe every 2 weeks for all that time went from E. Tenn., where her son Milton had moved her, to Brevard NC to see him. Some say he worked 'just enough' and ginseng hunted and made some mountain koolaide. I don't know for sure.

There were 7 in the family and they were scattered all around the community; the epitome of mountain spirit and integrity, honest and trustworthy to a fault. Times were tough then and Lonnie had remarried Daisy Franklin and evidently there wasn't room for all those kids, and some say they moved off and just left them here and there. I suspect the latter.

Later on all made peace with Lonnie and his 'new woman' Mary. My mom made real pace when she was 90, but that's another story—I took her to the graveyard on that day... All of them are gone now and us cousins are swindling down. One is under Hospice care now and I love him like a brother...I love in Statesville, NC, and He lives in Telford, TN.

Time gets away and I wish we had all asked more questions...Maybe most of us who love looking back and digging up the past wish we had been there.....I don't know about you all but I loved growing up in the '50's...to me that was the golden years in America. A time and memories fast disappearing...Sad.

Her mother Hannah died at 32 years old. She had 8 children, one child died. Her father after a spell, decided to remarry. They were from Shelton Laurel, NC. Mountain folk, farmers, moonshine, tobacco, ginseng, and anything else that helped support the families. Upshot of it was after Lonnie remarried there wasn't enough room for all those children and hers too. So my Mom's dad said you have to go somewhere else to live, you and your brother.

Some say mom was 8, and someone else said she was 10. She told me she was around 8. She went to her aunt Delph's for a spell, and wound up with her grandmother. That family had 10 in it. This is a shortened version of this but Mom was upset at her dad to say the least. As a little boy we went to visit and I never knew the story till much later. Mom would give my dad 'fits' sometimes and I often wondered why. He was a good father and provider and gentle. I think, looking back that she never completely trusted men, even her husband and lover and father of all of us.

This was a way of life in the early 1900's. You did what was best for the family, or what you thought was the best. I've often thought though that those boys could have kept the family together. My mom never saw one of her sisters again. She said I think I passed Gladys on a bridge one time, but we didn't speak. Gladys passed away at a young age and she was gone.

I was going to share this story along about Saturday but when I got to thinking maybe someone needs a lesson in forgiveness.....When my Mom was ninety, she said I want to go to the cemetery Saturday. I said fine, I'll come up ad we will go. I presumed she wanted to go to Marshall to Dad's and my brother's grave. She had went to Rose's and gotten flowers and such...So Saturday morning My wife, sister Laura, Mom and I loaded up my van, and mom had a folding chair she wanted to take also. I said I don't know if we can get up to the graveyard at Longbranch. She said I want to go to Shelton Laurel.

Well, we got to the cemetery, which they are always on a hill, usually hard to get to, and that was because any decent piece of ground was tilled, or pasture. Mom said, get my chair and flowers and put them over by Lonnie's grave. She said, You can't stay here. There was a huge elm tree on up the hill and I pulled the van up there and we got out in the cool shade and not a word was said. I knew I was seeing something on this warm summer day that was a life lesson. I looked down the hill and this old gray-headed mountain Mom was sitting in that chair and leaned over a bit and she was talking. I could not make out the words (I have wished so many times I knew what was 'exchanged' that day.) It felt like something broke and started running inside me, and I began to weep, just like right now......

After a bit she motioned us to come down and she got on her knees and fixed his grave and put flowers on it.....90 years old before she forgave and buried the hatchet...And she said, I'm ready to go now. and she was—for she died not long after. And the thought came to me, Mom you shoulda done this 50 years ago....If anyone is bitter at your Mom or family, think about getting it settled before Sunday. You can be like my mom—ready to go....

I never knew about this. Mom was too busy protecting me, changing my diapers, kissing my boo-boos and making them all better. She thought castor oil would cure anything. She could hear a whimper through 3 walls and be there instantly. She had x-ray vision—"what you doing in there" and she already knew. She had eyes in the back of her head—she saw everything I did in church and she never looked around...I still wonder how she did that...

She was a time keeper—get gone or you'll miss the bus —She was the referee between me and my sisters—she believed in the laying on of hands at an early age. She was overworked and underpaid. But she never complained. She cooked, cleaned and took care of us relentlessly. She washed clothes outside by the well, kept fires going, and she was the best cook in the world. She didn't have time to harbor those resentful feelings. But she did. She was my Mama. And I love her for her toughness. And I love her for the softness I her eyes that said I love you and I'll take care of you. And how many times did I hear her say things like, "you fall off that old bridge and break a leg, don't come running to me." But Mom, where else could I go??? I miss my Mom——

I miss my Mom

Moms Agape Love

In 1998 I got up off of a mat I had on the floor I the den and went into the kitchen and made a pot of performance enhancing drugs. Cream and splenda to calm it down and I went out to the screened in porch that looked down through the woods toward the creek. My mountain place in Statesville. I had walked past a hospital bed with my first wife, who was in an end of life coma. My insides were jittery as the coffee I had. A heart transplant had given us 10 good months, and she caught a bacteria that got into her bloodstream and killed her....

Going down I-77 to get her, I pulled off the road crying I challenged God in a non-Christian way. I said, "God, what in the hell are you doing to us?? You give us a heart, then 10 months later you take her away...I don't understand, she was devoted to You." Why? Why? Why you do this???? And in His way and not audible either, He spoke to me in my confused spirit and said simply; you had 10 more good months didn't you??? And that was it.... It was what it was, and I accepted it there beside I-77.

In the bedroom behind me is my Mom. She is old, she is tired without dad, and she is ready to go home. But she is my mom. She came to stay with me these couple weeks and to say good-bye to her daughter in law—whom she loved dearly. The comfort she bought to me is indescribable. She didn't feel well, yet she acted like she was fine. There was sadness in her eyes and a stoop in her walk. I know what she sacrificed to help me. She was simply my mom. She had been there from the get go, and she wasn't going to drop me now.

She tickled me when we would be in the dining room or on the porch, she would say, "I'm going upstairs now and rest a while." The house was one level, and I think by the time she walked past the hospital bed and down the hall it seemed like a hard hill to climb to her. She held on to me the morning death came and she sobbed way down inside herself and I really realized how much she loved us both. She was Mom. And I leaned on that old gray-haired mountain woman those two weeks and she stood up under the load....Thank you Mom for loving us...

I took Mom this doll for a surprise, just to cheer her up a bit, and she loved her. She sat the doll on her dresser and it stayed there until Laura gave it back to me. She said Mom wanted me to take her and give her to someone else if I wanted to. After Mom went on, I brought the doll home and put it up on a shelf in the closet. About a year went past and one day we were cleaning some and I got it down and opened the box. What I found in the box put me on m knees, weeping. It was a long time before I got past the first line of the note she left me. Here is the note—her handwriting was shaky and she didn't even feel like it but she wrote it for me—Thank you Mom—

My Darling Son

> I'm so sick I shouldn't be trying to write you. I want you to take the doll back. I've loved it, so gad you gave it to me for a little while. So you can keep it or give it to someone else. I know you will never forget me, so don't grieve over me. I've already suffered too much. Your Mom, Love you.

How could I possibly forget someone who loved me when I was the prodigal son? I wasn't always the darling son except to her. She kept the porch light on. For me. I can't hardly get all the way a hold of that sometimes...So I try to honor her in my small way—No Mom, I will never forget you, and I'll read this note from time to time and I will cry all over again....Not because of grief, but because I'm so thankful that you was My Darling Mother.

Sunday is Mom's day—Do something good for her and yourself—Nobody outside of Heaven ever cared for you like your Mom.

Mama and Quilts

Under the watchful eye of Pisgah, my Momma used to make quilts out of flower sacks and old shirts and anything else that was good material. I remember the quilting frame hung from the ceiling at Hollis Robertson's rental house where we lived. They would let the quilt down and I remember four ladies around that quilt sewing and talking. I cannot remember who any of them were except Mama; but in that time everyone helped each other. If you needed a shed or a barn or company, and folk knew it, they would show up. Just like at some deaths. Folk would sit up 'with the dead' for ever how long it took. You just helped each other. We don't do that much anymore. Everyone is too busy I guess. I remember getting down under those quilting frames and playing.

One day I got sent home from school with the pink eyes, and when I got there mom wasn't home. I think they were quilting somewhere pretty close. Well I had seen Hollis setting tobacco and I figured he couldn't do it without me... So I went over there and dropped tobacco plant into the setter, and carried water for it. You all remember those don't you? You drop a plant down the chute, stick it in the ground and squeeze the handle. It set the plant and watered it. Course the ground had to be loose and ready, which is another couple days of hard work.

Anyway, I got lost in tobacco setting, and Hollis said here comes your mom. I could tell by the walk she was not happy with her baby boy. She smiled at Hollis and pinned me with those eyes that were so loving at times. Not this time children. I had to cut a really nice switch for a little adjustment that she made in my thinking. Later on after awhile I would cut a little place about halfway up the switch and it would break usually after about 2 or 3 licks. I thought I was smart, but I'm pretty sure she knew all my little tricks. Like she could hear me sneaking a match out of the matchbox on the wall by the cook stove from incredible distances. She could smell rabbit tobacco or cornsilk or tobacco from a quarter mile I think. It was hard for me to sin, but I worked at it.

I'm sure my sister Laura learned quilting working with mom. She is a master quilter. I'm talking about little stitches and not the perverbial sewing machines. There is something magic to me just crawling into bed under this quilt mom made for me. I cannot tell you how much it means to me and just the comfort of it. In the note she left me in the doll box, she said you won't forget me will you? If for no other reason, the quilt makes sure of that. I made a full size quilt in about 1993. I sewed birds on every square. It wasn't very good but what thoughts and emotions went into that—I tell you this, I admire quilters. Hand sewn quilts. Back then you piled them on your bed until you couldn't hardly turn over. The bedroom was never heated so you got into this cocoon and when you breathed you could certainly see your breath, and ice on the inside of the window. Them covers made the difference.

I would read until I couldn't see. Dad said lights out. And after several dozen acts of disobedience, I cut the light out when I got into bed... Remember the string run from the light to the bedpost? Best piece of string I ever saw. I could hear dad or mom coming and cut the light. But you know in them old houses the light shined under the door anyway. I got tired of switchings before they got tired of doing the switching. But you know what? They loved me. They never stopped loving me, even when I wasn't much good to 'man or beast'.

The porch light stayed on.

They have been in a better place for a while now. But one thing for sure, I miss them whenever I get in my old canoe on the rivers of my memories. It pleases me when they get in and take a ride with me. I can see Mom's thimble and the needle sticking in the quilt where she stopped to fix supper. Man I hope its taters and beans and cornbread and onions and creasy greens——

Master Cook

Life's evening sun is sinking low

A few more days and I must go

To meet the deed that I have done

Where there will be no setting sun

    I watched my Mama cook so many times. I never learned anything, but I always knew something good was about to happen. Mountain folk know how to cook taters in so many ways that you don't even realize that you ate them for two weeks straight. I've seen her take a bowl and put flour in it and I think some Crisco and milk and knead it up and pat out bisquits. She always took a finger and depressed the center a little bit. Now what else she used I don't know. But it hurts me to say that those frozen 'grands' are really good bisquits too. I was behind the cook stove if it was winter and usually reading whatever I could find. I loved getting back there. Of course it was my job to keep the wood box filled, and I did.

    Mama's gone on home now and I can't remember when I ate her last bisquit. Her and dad had bacon, an egg, jelly and butter and black coffee saucered every morning along with canned bisquits in their later years. You know you and I don't ever think about losing loved ones when we are young and know everything. One day I awoke and it hit me that if we live long enough we get old. Now getting old is better than the alternative for sure; at least most times. Part of aging is burying loved ones. Not only do we lose those we love, we lose a way of life—we lose history...We seldom realize that they had dreams and wishes that they didn't achieve either.

I didn't think of mom and dad courting, falling in love, their first kiss, the hard work and sacrifice of dreams to raise us; Now, here I am, the old man. Ma and Pa and brothers and so many already gone, why in the world didn't I ask more questions? Anyway those homemade bisquits were the perfect place for a slice of termater and mayo; or honey and butter. If I knew where a wood-burning cook stove was, I would go crawl in behind it. And I would smell those bisquits.

One Room Schools

I am reminded today of another time, a simpler time when kindness, caring, and helping our fellow man was much more evident than it is today. During times of sickness and death neighbors came with food, support, and lending a hand to the chores. Fresh baked bread and home cooked food filled the tables; Fresh butter and buttermilk, made in an old fashioned churn, and cooled in the cold waters of a nearby spring. Old times used to say, 'give me a tater salit and a nanner pudding and we can have a wedding or a funeral'.

There was one roomed schools, a rare automobile, pulpwood trucks held together with baling wire, There was always churches; Lots of times with a wood heater in the middle of the room. Every woman probably had a quilt to stay warm, cause you might as well have hung a lightning bug up by his legs for all the good the stove done. There was quilting bees, barn-raisings, homecomings and music. Shapenote hymns in church and bluegrass everywhere. These folk worked so hard for so long that the music was an outlet—a getaway, a time of rest. So many great songs, ballads and gospel music came out of the hills.

An outhouse? Not a rarity in the mountains. I was in the 9th grade before we had an indoor bathroom. This outhouse is near a cemetery in Shelton Laurel. There is a small family cemetery there. Some of the graves have a rock with no name on them. There is a shelter there and I suspect it's used at Decoration Day and perhaps other times each year. Most of those old time mountain folk were loved and respected. They preached their own funerals with their hard work, giving ways, and honesty. And the folk just do not forget, year after year after year—graves are cleaned and flowers put out.

Nowadays we can't wait to get the ashes and dump them somewhere and get on with living. And I do think funerals are way out of need—expense wise and rules. If I could get one wish 'I would be rolled up in Mamas quilt that I use and dropped into a pine box and dirt shoveled in. Flowers before I die: I have made this request but she acts like she can't hear me. These canoe rides down the rivers of my memory are not always 'pleasant'....but I am 'old'. And I wish sometimes I knew what and when is going to happen—and it don't really matter...But something is coming and what happens is predicated on a encounter with Him one Easter Sunday Morning...

I died once for 18 to 20 minutes and my wife and friend saved my life—next time no one may not be around—so if one of you would, come over here to Statesville and steal me and build me a pine box, roll me in mama's quilt and sing 'Go rest High on the Mountain" I'll write you a check—you hear me?

Mamas Hands

I've tried to put down 5 tributes to my Mom this week. I think my idea was to honor Mom's memory and to somehow help maybe some other 'younger folk' realize how important it is to 'love' on your own Mother and Father while you can. One day will be the last day. And Hindsight, Or "I wish I had visited more" or like me "I wish I had asked more questions about their life growing up", all these regrets will be too late. Being mad at family and holding grudges only causes you to lose...And being sorry as an after thought isn't worth a hill of beans—

I remember her hands today. Sewing tight little stitches in gorgeous feed sack and cloth scraps quilts for her family. I remember her hands after washing clothes outside in an old wringer washing machine with two rinse tubs. She or I or my sisters ran the clothes through the wringer twice, her hands would be red. Funny but I remember her plucking a chicken for Sunday dinner. She would have feathers stuck to her hands. I remember her at the kitchen woodstove, cooking, strong hands with a dishrag to lift and move pots and pans. I remember her with a hoe chopping weeds and hoeing beans and corn and tomatoes for her family...And with an apron on, full of half runners and the precise way of breaking beans the same length, "so they were pretty in the jars". But mostly I remember her hands when she was combing my hair, or holding my hand or caressing my cheek. The softness of her eyes was relayed through her hands, and I knew she loved me.

Then I remember that anger and disappointment was also relayed through those hands. The thumb that when licked would become a brillo pad. The soft hands would become hard and strong around a switch, which she used with bad intentions...Or she could simply reach and get me by the arm and I knew what was coming. But you know what– whether soft as a babies touch or hard like flint, I still knew she loved me. And both the loving touch and the discipline equals "I love you but you will not misbehave". I think the old paths of discipline worked then, why not now....Mom had it right..

On November the 10th, 2000, I woke up in Statesville and had the incredible urge to go to Asheville to see Mom. I told my wife I had to go. When I got there I went into the bedroom and Mom was so weak and sick. We talked just a bit and I sat down in a chair and just looked at her for a spell. Those strong loving hands were now weak and she was picking at her cover and I knew I was losing her. And I also knew she wanted to go 'Home'. I think she had wanted to go mostly ever since dad had died. She was not a complainer, and I had bought her an oversized blue tee shirt that said on the front, I don't do mornings. She wore it often and she looked the part, and that memory gives me reason to laugh every once in a while. I stood up and got her right hand and caressed it and my sister Laura came up to the other side and took her hand, and My Mom took her last breath there. And I cried.

It wasn't entirely grief but maybe in part relief for her. I knew she suffered and I couldn't stand that. So I had told her awhile back to not worry about us, we were fine. Everything was in order. I knew she was at peace especially after making amends with her dad awhile back...Rest Mom, you deserve it I am overwhelmed at times how Our Lord takes care of us. He gave us Moms to show us an example of His love toward us. Her love wasn't based on whether I was good or bad, just like His. Someone said if we went to heaven on unconditional love, then our dogs would go and we would stay out....I don't think that applies to Moms. Prodigal or saint, the porch light was on. He woke me that Friday, a cold November morning, so I could be with her and say good-bye...

I love you Mom and I miss you. Tomorrow is Sunday. Honor your Mom–either in memory or in deed. If there are family issues get over them at least for a day. I know there are "bad Moms". If you know someone who needs a word of en-couragment, call them, take them to lunch—be a "Mom"...No one ever cared for you like your Mom. Happy Mothers Day.

Mount Pisgah and the Creek

I've been loved. I know love. I love 'love'. Sweet love, intimate love, agape love, puppy love. I've experienced it all. And at various times I have abused love from those who loved me. Memory wise that hurts way on down deep; but one thing I have learned is no one loves you on this side of Heaven like your mother. Here I am 4 years old, restrained, protected, and "clean" and loved by my mom, Ella Pauline Chandley Burris. Now you know it ain't normal for a 4 year olds hair to be that combed in place, and a white shirt? That my friends…took doing for sure. After all I had a cat named Boots, and Laura's dog, named Tippy to run with…

We moved to Davis Creek in South Hominy shortly after this photo. It was a most wonderful place to live. There was a creek, outhouse in the woods, hog pen and smoke house and a chicken house and a huge garden. An outside well with a hand pump just off the back porch, it was Heaven for a little boy, especially with Pisgah looming overhead. The woods that surrounded the house was full of prime switches which mom was fond of. It was okay for me to carry a barlowe knife with the handles gone to cut the switches with, but it wasn't okay to rock my sisters, or fight with Connie Gene Davis, or to 'sass' mom. Go cut me a switch was heard often seems like. I finally devised me a trick and I would cut me a little place about halfway up the switch, and after two or three licks the switch would break. I thought I was so slick but in hindsight I think she knew all my tricks and may have even gotten a laugh out of them...Disgusting....

I came home with the pink eyes and mom had gone to town on the bus to pay bills or such and I threw a book on the chair and I had seen Hollis setting out tobacco plants across the way and I figured he needed help so off I go. I saw mom afar off and she wasn't coming to hug me and put a ring on my finger and shoes on my feet either. She was so nice to Hollis but when she cut them eyes at me they had fire in them...I never went off again without she knew where I was heading.

She cried when I graduated from Erwin High. She cried when I got on the Greyhound going to the Air Force the next day. She cried sometimes when she asked me to come see them and I didn't go. She cried inside when I was drinking and losing my way. I don't think she realized how ashamed I was of myself and I hated her to see me like I was. She went to work cleaning in a motel and saved her money and made her life better and she never drove a car. Then one frosty morning I came to myself and I said, just like the prodigal that I was —I will go home.

I was married with 3 children but the porch light at Mom's was still on. God not only changed my life that morning but He put a deep desire to be the son and Baby Boy that my mom knew I was all the time... My mom.... That old gray-haired tough sweet woman loved me when I was unlovable....And when I came to myself and began to "try to repay and make amends"; she never one time mentioned the past. One thing that even now makes me tear up is the softness that was in her eyes when we went 'home' and the words she always asked after the hugs was "do you want something to eat???" No Mama, I'm just glad to be home. I miss you all the time....

Micheal and the Treed Cat

One of the highlights of my life happened in the 90's. The 90's were very good years and they were heart breakers. Literally. There was tons of laughter and joy, and there was barrels of tears, especially in the later 90's. I lost three that I loved, deeply.

My 3rd son Micheal had diabetes from the time he was 7. He took shots every day of his life after that. He was very smart and school bored him. In the 11th grade he went to Mitchell and zapped his GED and said that's it...Well he also went through a rebellious spell when he did what he pleased and he had a doll baby hanging on his arm. So you can imagine being a teenager and "in love'. It wasn't easy always eating right when all your friends were partying. Anyway the diabetes affected his eyes and eventually he lost his sight. Well during this period he met Debbie at church and they were introduced and 2 hours later they stopped talking for a short spell. It was a spell on him. They got married and I gained two step-grandchildren. Vince and Sarah Benton are a bright spot in my life. They both are super smart and handsome and beautiful to a fault. We had great joy having them around and going camping and church and horses and all that. Vince went into the Air Force and after several years decided to go on to college. Sarah is in New Jersey (Egypt) working and raising her son Michael. I love them both.

Anyway, Micheal planted a garden and tied up his green

beans by feel and I would see him on his knees working the ground and I almost always cried. No body much knew it but I went off in the woods and cried many times. Anyway one day I was standing in the road and looking up in a maple tree at their cat way up there, and here comes Micheal with his staff feeling his way up the road. I said where you bound, sonny? He said is that my cat I hear? Yep, it's up the tree with no visible means of transportation. He said hold my staff. And feeling around he went up the tree. He got on up there and got to the cat and picked it up and put the cat on his shoulder and started back down, by feel. I'm standing there with my mouth open and crying again. I am a big baby. You cry, I'll cry. Well about two thirds of the way down his foot slipped and the cat of course sunk them claws into his shoulder, holding on. Well he reached up with his hand a picked up his cat and said which side has the fewest limbs? I said over this way. He said see you later tree-climber, and tossed the cat out and away from the tree. The cat was unhurt of course and took off home. Micheal came on down and got his staff and took off home.

I stood there a long, long time with thoughts bouncing around in my head.... His sight didn't get him down, so why was I doing all the crying??? Anyway that is who he was. They were in Chicago for Christmas with Debbie's family and he had spent the afternoon passing out food at a shelter, bread I think. They went home and he took a shot and checked his sugar and went to bed. I was lying in bed at 6 AM studying my SS lesson when the phone rang. Sarah screamed at me we think Micheals' dead!!! And someone either took the phone or told her to hang it up, cause there I sat with a dead phone. My wife said what was that. And I repeated what was said, and she said maybe just low sugar. Well I had no phone number and it was a bitterly long 30 minutes or more before I got a call that Micheal was dead. I had him brought to Statesville and there was a huge snowstorm from there to here. The Lord helped Debbie drive through all that and come across the mountain with no trouble. A miracle I think. He was a good son, fiercely independent, (don't know where he got that) and a serious Christian. The highlight he left for me was the grandkids. So even with sugar so bad the Lord honored his service and love by giving him a family, and that helped us to bury him.

Then after that I lost my high school lover to a bacteria in her blood stream after a 9-month very successful heart transplant. She set the bar for how to be a lady and have love and compassion for others. She loved me for some reason. I hated to see that casket go down into that vault and the dirt flying in. The flowers were many and beautiful, but they portrayed death to my eyes. My Mama cried. I have a card my Mama sent Peggy. It says, thank you for loving my son and for being my friend. I cried again. Then next came Mom. I got up that morning and had that feeling. Go to Asheville. So I told Gerri I had to go and I went. I held her hand and she took her last breath. She was tired and she was sick and she missed Dad. She wanted to go on for a while. I miss my Mama and I miss Micheal, and I miss Peggy.

Oh don't go there, I am happy now and The Lord has blessed me with a wonderful woman who has helped me with honey for the journey. There was things that happened during the heart transplant that could have only been divine in nature—Let me share one—A girl came to the hospital waiting room hunting the heart recipient. Now they are not supposed to do that, but the head nurse liked me and told me about her. I had met her in the hall and felt something in my soul by the way she looked. Anyway I went down to the cafeteria and she was there. I introduced myself and she said it was her brother in law. Here's what floored me and I cried again. His name was Micheal and he was 28 years old, same as my Micheal. Coincidence??? I don't think so.

We had church there in the cafeteria... She gave me an angel on a chain that I pick up and just stare at every once in a while. Another small 'thing', I took her back to the hospital on the same day we had went the year before—August 1st, I brought her home the 13th of August-13 days—she died 13 days later—on my birthday. Only two things here but there were several more and maybe sometime I will tell all of them...I don't see Vince much but Sarah comes down a couple times a year, she is still a Carolina girl....

Down this old river of memories on this day in my old wore out reddish leaking canoe has been a mixed journey—I have enjoyed the trip even though I cried some more. My feelings are not hid in the closet, it is what it is—like suppertime in the mountains—two choices—take it or leave it.... I love you and hope you see Him through your troubles and heartaches. He is the Man of Sorrows.

Mountain Folk

I wanna tell this separate from my trip to Haney cemetery today. I went by the store and was going to stop but had an 'urge' to go on down the creek for a ways and I stopped and piddled around for a while. I don't think this old man I was destined to meet was there yet, so I had that 'urge to go on by...I wasn't exactly sure where the turnoff up the hill was and last time I was there you had to take a fence down to get to the cemetery. So I went back up the road and stopped at the store and there was this older fellow on the porch and I said do you know where the Haney cemetery is? He said why sure I do. He said it ain't been too long ago, you could ask a question around here, and no one would answer you. I said I know all about you cantankerous old mountain folk.

He liked that and said who you got in the graveyard son? I said grandparents and kin. What is the names? I said Lonnie Chandley was my grandfather. He said oh I remember Lonnie, I was just a young fella but I recall him. He said I run a store just down the road for 45 years. I said is the store still standing? He said shucks son, I live in it. He said I had a time with insurance cause I got two kitchens and two bathrooms, they thought I was renting out half of it. He chuckled about that.

I love these old time mountain folk. They will size you

up, listen to what you say for a spell and make a decision if they like you or if they are through talking. He musta liked me. I think he said he was 86 or 87. He said that there lady in the store has got that roll bologna (baloni) and its is really good in a sandwich. So I got her to fix me a quarter inch slice with mayo lettuce, and mater...not even fried. It was outstanding. Well I truly believe the Lord sends these folk my way. I love them. I said well I'm going on up the road and just past that paved road at the first house on the left there is a trail, road, and path up to the cemetery. It coulda been mountain style directions—wal, son go a few mile and where the big sycamore got lightning struck be on the lookout for that white rock in old man Shelton's pasture, next to the barn that burned up, you will see that old shed just turn left, Heck son, you can't miss it. They got a fence around the cemetery cause folk are dying to get in, ha ha. No it wasn't like that, he gave me precise directions.

But when I got ready to go he said wait a minute, you can follow me up there, I was going that way anyway. I said you don't have to go out of your way. He said I ain't. I'm going up to see my girlfriend. And I thought, my, my that's alright right there. Now listen this 'old' man had a new looking Ford escape SUV. I had to hustle to stay up with him. He pulled over at the road and rolled his window down and said I'm hanging around the store about every day some, so stop again and you have a good time with your folk. Bye Now. I watched him out of sight.

I said thank you Lord. And we did have a good time together. When I came back down the road I stopped at the store and got me a half pound of boloni, quarter inch thick. I'll try it fried with good thoughts of my time on Shelton Laurel where my mama walked and skipped about and worked and courted my dad from Marshall. I stopped where White Rock School was and sat for a while and I could envision a little girl walking there to school. It was all good for me today....

Baccer, Mountain Gold

See The pile of sticks on the ground, Some of you will know without me telling you what these are. They are an integral, necessary part of our mountain heritage. Or let me rephrase that—they used to be a part of our past. I was living on Curtis Creek and Walker Hinson took a liking to me. Walker had cows and a whiteface bull that I rode on the back of a few times. His back seemed to be 2 ax handles wide...He also had a whiteface bull that was a show bull of sorts that I led down to the creek for water on occasion. Now I was 10 or so and that bull was big and red and white—and a little scary... But now I know that Walker knew that and used that, those bulls to 'educate' me...

Walker also grew tobacco like most everyone who had a bit of land. Some folk didn't want to raise it so they would lease it out for a percentage of the profits; probably the best way. That way you didn't have to build a bed and gas it and cover it with canvas and grow your plants. Then the ground was made ready and when the time was right the plants were set one at a time. Most times with a setter that you dropped one plant in at a time and the setter had a water reservoir and you jammed it into the ground and pulled the 'trigger' handle and the plant dropped in with a dose of water. You held the handle open and lifted the setter and the dirt settled back in around the plant. A strong arm and back and grip were needed for this. But man it was cash money down the road.

Back then you hoed the plants and kept the weeds out and cultivated them when they were small. Of course then down the road there was tobacco worms to kill and then the suckers grew out and were 'suckered', cut off and then the baccer was topped. Black, sticky hands that was difficult to get clean. Not too many folk I knowed enjoyed topping and suckering. Then of course the tobacco was cut and a tobacco stick was stuck down in the ground, (you didn't have to put them deep in the ground cause the stalks stabilized them. You put 4 to 6, depending on the size, to a stick by putting a 'spud' on top of the stick and driving the spud through the stalk and sliding the backer down the stalk.

Then after a day or two the tobacco was hauled to the barn on a sled usually and boys and men would get up on the tier poles and hang the tobacco in the barn to cure. Then when the time was right it was taken down and handed into hands by grade and tied and stacked on a basket—ready for the warehouse on River Road where the buyers bought it. Quite a process and a lot of work—but rewarding most times—and relief when the auctioneer said 'sold'...This huge pile of tobacco sticks in this field on Shelton Laurel have their own story to tell. I did not see one single field of tobacco. In fact I didn't see much of any kind of farm goods except hay...

I used tobacco sticks for something much more important. I don't have a clue how many I broke, carried home or lost. I hit rocks with them. I would stand beside the road and hit rocks. Rock after rock after rock. I would pretend I was a pitcher like Whitey Ford, tossing them up in the air, and I would pretend I was a hitter like Mickey Mantle. I wasn't the only boy around who liked to play major league baseball with a tobacco stick and a road full of gravel. You know Walker never did say a word about his sticks.

When I passed this pile of sticks I had to turn around and go back. I sat there for a while thinking about the stories they could tell. One thought I had was how many are there? This is way more than a seven tenths of an acre allotment. And I though why are they stacked out here in the weather? They'll rot for sure. Then the sad, to me, thought was, what difference does it make, no one needs them anymore. Now because I write about another time in our youth doesn't mean I am advocating using tobacco. I know the dangers. But it was a real vital part of our heritage... I figure, looking at this pile of sticks, I figure I can stand in the edge of the road for at least 20 years and still have sticks left.

Oh well, Mantle and Ford are long gone and I reckon my rock hitting days are too. I'de probably strike out anyway. How'de you like to hang all them sticks in a barn boys?? Some of those old barns up and down the creek groan and creak in their memories of simpler times, their tiers were hanging full of golden leaves...No more—won't happen again—no one makes sticks anymore-and what there is, is stacked up beside the creek, rotting...Lordy You be blessed in your memories, you hear me??? Now of course some of you know that these tobacco sticks will hold up tomato plants too. They are made alike. I prefer to think of them as backer sticks for my own memories and good pleasure.

Kerosene and Salt Pork

I remember the 8th grade this morning. We thought we were something. Graduating. Going to high school. We had arrived. It was mysterious. Exciting. We were grown up. Ha.

Same excitement graduating the 12th grade. How naïve we were.

Dad was in his '40's and I thought they were so old. And I was smarter, I thought. Amazing what I learned after that age when I knew everything. I remember sitting against the radiator at Pisgah that last day and looking at the gorgeous girls all dressed up and excited. I also remember a bit of sadness too.

This morning I feel a bit of sadness too. Our joys and hopes and dreams way back then was in a period of time unlike any before or since. Nobody that didn't experience it can't "feel" like we do. For instance I told Dr. Bradford last Sunday in church that Elvis was dead and I didn't feel good.

He looked puzzled and said, "What's Elvis got to do with it?" I shook my head and said, "Forget it Doc, you're too young." This old canoe is floating on the high waters of my memories this morning.... I love all of you who were there, and it's good to see you today...Be blessed.

A Boy and A 12 Gauge

The rain let up just before dawn and a foggy mist hung over the hickory and oak saplings and thru the woods all around the old, faded logging road I was walking on. It was so beautiful and kind of eerie and mysterious too. A few song-birds were telling the age-old story of God's great creation.

I was 12 years old and I had my dad's 12-gauge shotgun and two shells. I was once again after a ruffed grouse that had been 'beating' for a couple weeks. The grouse gets up on a log and beats his chest with his wings. It is absolutely incredible how far away you can hear them; and I eased along when he was beating and stopped when he did. I did not get that one that morning, but I got something much more valuable.

The sun coming up over the mountaintop and peeping through the trees amidst the fog was simply wonderful. And I am so thankful. As I walk back down that old logging road in my mind, I am reminded that the beauty of nature is a gift from God, and ours to preserve for our children and our children's children. My eyes are often closed when I am riding in the old canoe on the rivers of my memory, but I can still see that fog creeping down like a sleeping cat, and settling on the shoulders of a young boy, in a most beautiful place, and I am blessed.

The Quail and the Coonhound

Do you remember the musty smell of tobacco in the barn? What about the silent fellowship of grading and tying the tobacco? No words were needed. Do you still have friends you can sit with or ride around with and never have to say a word, like the family and friends working tobacco? Do you remember the slick, worn counter and floors at that little country store? How about the smells that assailed you when you opened the door? The smell of candy, apples, bananas, cloth, leather, salt pork, kerosene and others? How about the soft, soothing patter of rain on a tin roof in the old barn where we played in the hay? Or how about the endless chore of trying to dam up the creek?

It is so funny how much these old memories mean to me, now that I am old and well past the age when I knew everything. The mournful cry of the dove, or the cry of the redtail as he heads toward Hickory—shucks, he's already there. The whistle of the Bobwhite —almost gone—or the coonhound or beagles hot after something... My, my, I love to ride in the old canoe on the rivers of my memories, and hear and smell this poetry. Poetry you say? It doesn't rhyme, but it can still make you smile—or maybe cry, or maybe just close your eyes

Jack Burris

and take a little ride down your river of memories.

The Pulpwooders

I knew they were coming. Walker Hinson told me they were coming. I viewed this information with mixed feelings. I squirrel hunted in those woods and loved it. At the same time I knew a bulldozer was going to make a road and I was interested in seeing one in action. Walker told me not to get in the way and to be careful and try not to be aggravating. Well the day came and the bulldozer came and it looked huge. He began cutting a road up to the woods, and then he went around and up. Needless to say when that thing cut off and he left, ole Jack was up on it pretending to move some dirt. You say, who was coming? Well the dratted ole pulp-wooders. They were going to rape the mountain of the oaks and hickories and pines. It didn't really bother me then cause I wanted to jump in with both feet. It was worth laying out of school for. But fortunately school was out...

Anyway in a day or two here comes this old dodge truck, it sounded like one of them wringer washing machines. Wham-a wham-a-swish-wham-a. The thing was missing a front fender and there was a 5-gallon dope can for the passenger seat. And it leaned sideways. Them old pulpwood trucks were held together with baling wire, hood be wired down, muffler, if there was one, would be wired up. I was grown before I knew that they actually made new pulpwood trucks. All of them leaned over to the inside of the road. And you always knew one was coming up the road. Anyway I do not remember the three men's names who cut the wood. They had one of them huge McCulloch chain saws and one did the felling and cutting up with it. One trimmed the limbs, and one drug them to the 'yard'.

The yard was a large place, cleared off so the truck could turn around and the wood was all brought there for loading. Wasn't long till I was helping trim limbs and petting the poor ole workhorse. The men took a liking to me and usually shared food with me. Oh, I was in high cotton! Wasn't long till I knew everything about logging and told everybody that I did too. Now listen the owner, boss was a big ole fellow with a sailor's mouth. I heard words I did not know existed. He would look at me and wink sometimes for some reason. I think he knew he was shocking me. After all I had been saved a lot of times, and I never heard such talk from my dad or kin. I really liked him and the other two. He rolled Prince Albert cigarettes with one hand, and he would put it in the corner o' his mouth through the entire process of smoking it, It's funny sometimes how you remember things of little consequence.

When it rained sometimes they would drag the truck to the yard and drag it back out with the dozer. I was getting educated. They talked some about their lady friends. One thing one said has always been around, He said his woman was hotter than a sitting hen in a tow sack. I didn't know exactly what all that meant, but I had a pretty good idea. I do have a point to make, but my ride in the old canoe has stirred up some things I had misplaced somewhere in the corridors of my little mind...

Well the boss lived at Candler and he had a tobacco allotment. So one day he asked me if I wanted to go home with him and help hoe his tobacco. I remember saying I would ask Mom. He said no, I'll stop and ask her. He did and she let me go. I was in high cotton bud. You just didn't get to go all that many places in the early 50's. Well we got down to his house and it was near dinnertime, and I remember going out on the back porch and washing up in a wash-pan with a towel hanging on a nail. There was also a bucket of water with a dipper in it. We took our shoes off and went into this clean, and neat house somewhere in Candler. Two of the cutest little girls ran to him and he dropped down on his knees and hugged and talked to them. Somehow this big old rough man in overalls, who smelled like oil and wood and sweat, who could wilt a tree with his choice of words, Sitting here in the floor hugging his two girls did not fit my picture of him or his home.

Anyway his pretty wife, with her apron and a smile for me came and kissed him. You would have thought I was a special guest. She treated me so good I was kicking the floor and turning red. And the two little girls crowded around and asked me 6 zillion questions. What really floored me and my Hellfire and Brimstone teachings was what happened when we sat down, as a family to eat. In the early 50's he said hold hands and lets say Grace. And honey child, he said a powerful Grace... know cause I was looking at him as wide eyed as a calf with a new gate. I thought in my mind, he has repented and got religion.

It was the nicest dinner and I can see the girls and him and her in my mind today. We sat on the porch with them dratted girls hanging on me, so I was glad when he said lets go to the patch. I recall distinctly going down the rows hoeing that green gold. Seems there was several of us and a lot of laughter and chatter. He had emphasized being very careful and not cutting any plants down. Well you know me I clipped one off but he wasn't looking so I straightened it up and moved on. I have often wondered if he knew I cut it cause by the next morning it would be wilted.... I learned a great lesson up on that hill.

The next day or two when the loggers came back, I was anxious to see the boss and how he acted. Well, the truck got stuck and he peeled the paint off the fender with his professional conniption. Borders on a tizzy. I never did ask Dad or tell anyone about the "two sides" I had seen. But I sure thought about him a lot. I finally figured that he loved his family and that he knew the importance of prayer, so maybe someday he would quit such doings.

I've never forgotten him or the wink when he started a fire with his mouth and he would be watching......I've used some of those words before, but it has been a very long time. By-Grannies suits my style. By the way, when you was young did you ever see a new pulpwood truck??

Be blessed this day and every day...wake me up early, be good to the dog, take children to church, and don't let the loggers come......

Papas Only Icee

Well another Father's day has come and gone. For some it was a wonderful time, with hallmark cards, hugs, and love in abundance. My son Greg, who the Lord blessed 4 years ago so wonderfully, with a Kidney and pancreas transplant, gave me a card with 5 dollars in it. He said you and Gerri go get some ice cream. He couldn't have done any better. How many of you remember making home made ice cream? Turning the crank until it got too hard and dads finishing the job. How sweet that ice cream was. I know one thing; it would 'freeze' your head.

Reminds me of a trip we took to Douglas Ga. to see my sister Laura and her family. We stopped at a 7-11 and dad got an ICEE. He drank it like a coke I guess, because he laid down across the front seat of our '53 Buick, holding his head and moaning. I never knew him to drink another or even taste one. Those old White Mountain freezers would do the job and still do. I have one I bought about 30 years ago. I enjoy making it for memories sake, and the kids, and me.

I really envy some fathers I've known. John Matthews comes to mind. They tried so hard to have children and after some disappointments wound up with 5....4 gorgeous girls and an outstanding son. He is a real dad. Of course I know many more who are great fathers. I guess I've not been a very good father. I started out wrong and that early influence on young boys is so important. Dad set such an important example for me too. He was simply put, always there....But there is no thing any of us can do about things past, so while I wish I could do some things different; I am realistic, and know that is not possible.

But I tell you something children, when you bury three children and a wife it takes a special touch of Grace to move on. And He has given that Grace in abundance. So I say to all you dads; You are special and blessed. Don't work all the time, take some time to see the flowers and to smell the sweetness of life....Like the soft patter of rain on the window, your presence brings calmness and warmth when its needed. Remember to hang your work on the tree limb outside your front door, and pick it back up when you leave. And for goodness sake take off them muddy shoes—you don't need to take bad stuff into your house. Just inside my front door is the safest, warmest place I know of. I look forward to coming home, and my attitude at home is one reason why it is a 'good' place. I've been a better grandfather, than a father. I've learned so much from my mistakes that I can't wait to see what I learn every day.

Well it's been around 100 degrees for the past 3 weeks. I think my last large concrete job is about to be finished. We have poured 622 yards in 5 mini storage buildings and the parking lot the last 3 weeks. It's Saturday and I'm home and it's raining because I did a rain dance. I wish I had the energy to get the ice cream maker down, but I ain't. I bought some half runners and some peaches. The beans and taters are done and she made me a peach cobbler. I had squash and cukes and onions and taters and maters from my neglected hot garden. I don't know how it grew, what with no rain and the heat. You can bet your bottom dollar I say Grace... Well again I do enjoy these little forays down the rivers of my memory, in my old canoe...You take care and be blessed this day, you hear me?? And don't fret a lot about the stupidity of the so-called Supreme Court. Just pray for us all...

Pisgah Mountain and Barefooted

Standing here high up on Pisgah, standing all alone,

I can't help but reflect and wonder, where the years of my life have gone.

Hominy Valley, I can see down below,

Reminds me of another time when summers were so slow.

I'm always in awe at what I can see,

Even when my eyes are shut, still seeing through the trees.

Stand here on our mountain, where the red tails have flown,

Wondering where the years of my life have gone. JB

  I got in my old canoe today and took a cold ride down the rivers of my memory. Some old friends showed up and things got warmer. Sometimes I am amazed at the difference in folk. Some could care less about the past and old friends. I can't really put into words what those long lazy wonderful, barefoot days of summer meant to me. Oh not when I was young so much...Got to busy with work and children and debts to reflect much.

  Boy its all piled back on in the last few years. What would some of you do if you could go back for a few hours and play some of those old time games. Jacks, Hop-Scotch, Cowboys and Indians, Marbles, Baseball, Hide and Seek, Tag and I got lucky a few times and played Spin the Bottle. And what about that first kiss? First date–and Last date. Break-ups and make-ups. I think I started some arguments just to make up. And how did we go camping with so little? And it was wonderful. We took kids to Davidson River every chance we got. And every single one of them have said it was the best of times.

I took the preachers grandson one time and he ran through a briar-patch somewhere on a bike and got scratched all over. Then he wrecked his bike on the asphalt and tore up his nose and the side of his face. When I took him home the preacher said he looked like he had been to "h—" and back. I was shocked. But you know what, the boy said he loved it and couldn't wait to go back...You cannot go wrong spending time with kids. When my lady had her heart transplant we had planned to take the kids camping–and she didn't feel well and insisted I go on and do it. I took 7 young folks to Davidson River. I took these kids ginseng hunting. I think they loved that as much as anything we did.

My Granddaughter is 29 now and said the other day "we need to go ginseng hunting again". My grandson is 25 and in college at Western Carolina and every so often he asks me when are we going to the woods and find some sang. I had a van, a pop-up and a tent. They had a blast and I did too for a couple days. At 3 AM Dean came and beat on the van and said Peggy is having seizures, you got to get home. You know I woke those kids and said we got to go. I never heard one word. In minutes we were out of there. That has always blessed me so much for some reason.

That was the last time I got to take all of them. It was 1998. They have been riding with me today. I made three of them a scrapbook for Christmas. I put some photos of sang in the book. They loved the book and they cried some and that caused me to cry too. I don't think anything would of meant more to them. I want them to know and remember those long lazy days of summer when they get old and smile and maybe even cry a bit at times. I love it when folk show up to ride in my old canoe. Its old and the paint is faded and it takes on a bit of water, but most everyone still wants to go for a ride...And for that?? I am so blessed...

Fathers Day Thoughts

Father's Day. A day of old spice. A day of hugs and Hallmark cards.

It seems strange at times that my father is not at home in Asheville; because he was always there, especially when I needed him. But he is buried under an oak tree in Marshall, NC.

Like a warm fireplace in an old farmhouse, or a cool drink of water from a spring; he was a source of comfort. He always seemed to be going to work or coming home. I would go to the road and wait for the Enka Plant work bus to drop him off. I remember being barefooted and trying to step in his tracks and walk like him. He was my father. My first bike, baseball glove, Mickey Mantle Louisville slugger baseball bat, my first girlfriend, and football—they all had one thing in common— dad was there.

Life went pretty smooth. The bills got paid; we had a house and food and decent clothes, and a whole lot of love. So for me growing up was what God intended it to be. There was laughter and there was woodshed discipline that had a tendency to produce tears. Like most families, we are short of pictures of dad because he was usually behind the camera. Dad read the paper and bible almost every day. He broke up fights between me and my two sisters, he joked and told stories and just did what a father is supposed to do—just be there. He taught me how to shave and how to pray. He taught me to work and to be on time.

Oh he didn't sit down and go over it step by step, he did it all by example. He was a father. All you dads need to know that somebody is watching you and walking along behind trying to follow your tracks.

I remember dad once in awhile. When I smell old spice aftershave I remember him. And sometimes a funny story or joke will make me chuckle and think about how dad would like that one. Dad never did tell me his life story, or tell me about love and marriage or how to be a man. He just showed me. And for that I am grateful; Like a warm fireplace on a cold, cold day, or a cold drink of Mama's sweet tea—some things give comfort in any season of life.

The winds of age took their toll on Papa; his flame flickered and died leaving only memories. So like today, occasionally I get into the canoe and float down the rivers of my memory, and once in awhile Papa rides with me. And I am blessed. I hope all you fathers had a great time with family and friends...Be blessed in Christ today.

Outhouses and Sears Catalogues

I'm in my old worn out canoe that leaks a bit this morning, floating down the rivers of my memories. Dang, I didn't expect this ride. It's taking me to some of the old outhouses I have visited. If I'da knowed this I would have used some of dad's Old Spice or Vitalis. Sometimes the smell is peculiar in these things. My first stop was at my grandfather's in Marshall. His was down the hill from the house and a kinda rickety looking outhouse, but it had one of my main attractions. There was a Sears-Roebuck catalogue on the wooden shelf and inside that huge book was semi-soft paper that was suitable somewhat to use for cleaning purposes. But over about halfway was the toys; beautiful red tricycles and wagons and guns and trucks and such. I would endure smell, flies, mosquitoes for long spells and drool over them toys.

My next stop is the outhouse in South Hominy. It was out in the woods, a fair distance from the house. I had no problem going there in the daytime, but I never did make it all the way at nighttime. It was scary out in them woods. I got more switchings from running out in the night barefooted and running back in with dirty feet and piling back up in the bed. Not for not making it all the way, but for messing up a perfectly clean bed. Mama had a thing about cleanliness and I attracted dirt...

I built two outhouses over in the woods where I used to live. I dug holes and they were usable, fully functional, and complete with Sears-Roebuck replicas. Built in wasper nests and some black widows. Now really how many folk do you know that ever got bit by a spider sitting in a relaxed position?? Yesterday the pool was full of kids and I saw boys and girls run over behind he bushes. Now that's natural, right there. And they don't even care that here is an outhouse in the house. My bride spent 15000 dollars on one bathroom. I'm afraid to use it. I tried to build a good one here but she wont let me. That bathroom is gorgeous, tile and cabinets and super soft paper—I'm afraid of it. Shoot for 15000 I could of built 10000 real bathrooms.

I am now floating in East Tennessee. One of my all time favorite people is my Uncle, Bud Chandley. He had on top of the hill above his house, an outhouse. I do not know for sure where he got it, because I don't remember it being here in my youth. Anyway we went up there just to visit and pretend we had to go. We like the old paths. Now what has floored me about this one is, it is a three seater. And it has vent pipes out the roof. And I ask you, who in the world is going to go into an occupied outhouse and pull their pants down or skirt up and sit down beside somebody else???? The holes are so close together you would probably touch. And what if you had gas?? Or the catalogue was empty? Or maybe extra offensive odor??? Who would do such a thing??? Why build a three seater?? Or a two seater??? Now I know girls don't have any problem sharing a bed to sleep. But boys??? Never. I take 20 men to play golf at Myrtle Beach and separate beds are the only option. The bed could be 40 feet wide and two men ain't gonna share it. And if they did try it and just almost touched, one would go sleep in his car. An outhouse??? Never.

Looks to me like a wanna be carpenter got carried away. Maybe advertise Bed and Breakfast with a Three Seater with built in Vents. No extra charge. As you can see by the pics Bud and I took turns just getting our picture made. And the vents, like the odor is going to run right out the vents and be pleasant and smell like Old Spice and Vitalis. Oh and by the way, if three of you were in there what would you talk about between grunts and moans? "Billy's doing good in, ugh, school." Or "Excuse me, we had corn for supper last, ohhh, last night." Or simply " pass me the catalogue, I wanna see, oops, that latest tricycle."

Well I gotta get out of this old canoe, It's getting deep in here. You all be good and where two or more are gathered together, somebody will probably stink things up...You all be blessed this day and every day, you hear me? And don't be so serious, lighten up, you know its the truth...Unusual ride today, hee hee.

Milton Price, A Mentor and Friend

Well when we moved to Woodfin and left South Hominy it was devastating at first for me. I was in the ninth grade and knew no one. But Eddie Bartlett lived next door and he quickly became a friend. My dad had some block to lay in our basement and through church he found someone to lay them. His name was Milton Price. He belonged to Lessie, and one son named Ted. Somehow or other Ted and I met and became friends. We had some terrific ballgames in the pasture across from his house. A lot of the fellows came and played ball with us, so I got to know a few more.... But Milton sorta took a liking to me and became someone that I admired and looked up to. He took both Ted and I to work in his concrete company. He taught us how to form and pour and finish concrete. Ted was more meticulous than me, and a better finisher though he was younger...But man it was fun going on those jobsites and producing something that you could be proud of—And I loved it. The first job Milton left me and Ted to finish was just above their house and we musta troweled that thing 10 times, and it was slick as glass.

Ted and I both loved music and we lifted some weights and we boxed some and had some fun growing up. Well, I went off to the service and when I came back I worked at Enka for about a year and hated it...So I looked Milton up and went back to work with him. I was drinking too much and he didn't like that. Ted had gotten married and built him a house and I was envious. But man, could we pour and finish some concrete. Well anyway we eventually parted ways; and at some point Ted went to work for the railroad, and retired there. He was smarter than me. I finally got settled down and tried contracting around Asheville and about starved. But after an Easter Sunday morning meeting, I really settled down...especially when the Lord said 'son there's a better way'.

So I moved to Statesville and worked for the flour mill for a while and started pouring concrete on the side —I hauled forms out the window of a 70 Plymouth fury. Then I started contracting and have been at it every since until this heart failure mess...Racing was really getting going here and I poured concrete for about all the NASCAR drivers including Dale Sr., Buddy Baker, Wallace, and on and on—but one individual that really helped me through the years was Butch Stevens...probably one of the smartest men in auto racing, I worked for him off and on for 30 years He called me 'no crack Jack'...

I have loved this trade and have taught it to several others who are contracting themselves. But it all boils down to Milton Price—He helped me along and showed me things I never realized until I was older. Milton's been gone awhile but I still think about him now and then, and I smile. And Ted? He's around Asheville and he finally got on Facebook and that has brought a lot of memories back. Hay, Ted, lets call Eddie and Gene and Jeff and the Chandler boy and George and the Medford's and some of the others and lets go crawl through the barbed wire fence and play a little tackle...What you think??? I loved your mom, Lessie, and I loved your dad— We had a good run for awhile—you be blessed, you hear me???

Hog Killing Time

This chill in the air takes me back to another time this morning. Especially after traveling through the Smokies yesterday. The early morning fog rising off the creek and seeing folk with jackets on said winters coming. I can hear my dad say to me along about 6 pm, 'Jack go slop the hogs.' We had two on one particular winter morning. When we first got them they were so cute and I used to get over in the pen and play with them. But the bigger they got the less I did that, because I was told they would bite you and wouldn't let go. Kinda like the tale that a 'mud puppy, alias water dog wouldn't let go till it thundered. I'de see one of them in the creek and dodge it for sure.

Anyway, when pop said go slop the hogs, it meant picking up the bucket that had left overs, and what ever else had gotten accumulated for them to eat that day. And most folk poured warm dish water in the bucket. Sound good? The hogs loved the stuff. It was a real chore to lug that bucket across the yard and through the woods to the hog pen. They would be squealing and hungry. Sometimes I cut and pulled weeds and grass for them. And of course dad bought feed and corn for them.

It led to one thing; Bacon, ham, tenderloin, lard, livermush and such. On a cold frosty morning we would build a fire under a barrel and fill the barrel with water. We had running water. It ran after you pumped it up and into a bucket. Many trips later the barrel would be filled about 3/4 of the way up.

Dad made a tri-pod with a chain hoist in the middle to lift the hogs. We borrowed a horse, I think from Con Davis, to drag the hog to the barrel. First, of course dad would take a 22 and shoot the first one between the eyes.

I remember watching that process and getting a little sick at my stomach. We dragged the hog to the fire and hoisted him up with a chain horse and dipped him into the barrel! We usually had to turn him and dip them twice. Then you scrapped the hair off. Smelly and hard work for a little boy. Then the process of raising the hog up off the ground and washing him off and then butchering it. You always took a piece of tenderloin to mom and usually the feet to cook for dinner. Despite the process that was the best dinner you ever ate. Hot bisquits and fresh tenderloin.

Well we and everyone else had a smoke house so the meat was taken into the smokehouse and put on tables. Dad would salt and salt the meat down for curing purposes, and then it was ready to hang up in burlap sacks (the feed came in them). Later in the winter dad would take a knife and go out and cut off whatever he wanted to eat. Lane Watts helped us two times I know for sure and of course you either helped them or shared the meat.

You may wonder why I choose to think about this bloody process. Well for one it was a way of surviving winters from the beginning of time. No gardens until way up towards summer so you had to can and can stuff, and the root cellars best be stuffed with potatoes, apples, sweet potatoes etc. Mom and Dad would process all of the hog. Everything.

We were blessed in that dad had a job at the Enka Plant so we had cash money. Lots of folk struggled through the winters. So it was a mountain way of life. I wouldn't take anything for those memories of family time, for feeding the hogs, the labor of helping contribute to the family. No wonder Dad always said grace at the table. You were thankful. We throw away more than we eat these days... I don't want to go kill no hog this morning, but when there is a chill and the first heavy frost hits the ground, I think about it.

I can see Dad, in his 40's, (I thought he was old then), Black hair combed back with his sleeves rolled up, with a knife in his bloody hands laughing at something Lane said. Now Chats worth something to me I wouldn't mind a tenderloin bisquit this morning, one without steroids and antibiotics, one from a 'slop' bucket and feed from the grist mill. You think that was an easy chore? You try dragging a bucket across your yard and up a little hill and through the woods to a couple of squealing hogs It might just make you glad when you see your dad get the 22 out. Wish I could ask dad what the joke was that Lane told that this morning—I shoulda listened and asked more question back in that other time, for sure....

A Prince Albert Can and Worms

It's later than you think. Everything is farther away now, and there's a hill to climb now. I've quit running stairs and am taking the elevator. Steps are steeper than they used to be. Have you noticed the smaller print they use in the newspaper now? Nobody can read them anymore without glasses. No sense asking anyone to read aloud. Everyone talks in such a low voice I can hardly hear them.

People are changing, people look so much younger. On the other hand, people my age look much older than I. I ran into an old classmate the other day and she had aged so much she didn't remember me. I got to thinking about the poor girl this morning while combing my hair. I glanced in the mirror at my reflection, and confound it, they don't make mirrors like they used to either.

I was around 8 years old and I remember going out to the chicken house with a Prince Albert can and digging red worms. Sometimes I dug up a wriggler- which was not good bait. The intense joy and anticipation of going fishing is a feeling I miss these days. I have a bass boat and I bass fish some but I really like to catch crappie. They are delicious fresh, and rolled, and fried ....I like to go when I can at certain times of the year more than others. Crappie lay their eggs in the spring and also move back into the shallows in the fall. I love to see those ultra light bobbers go under—either with jigs or minnows. It's fun. But I've lost something along the way somehow. The joy and excitement have abated. I find myself talking to myself with words like this—now watch your step, old man its wet and you might slip; or don't go jumping down out of the truck anymore; make sure the life jacket is out and put it on.

Somehow this careful stuff is depressing. I want to jump up there and I want to run over there and so what if I fall in; but that old enemy of mine—time—has taken a toll. These knees won't climb a ladder like they used to and the ankles hurt a bit when I jump down; and this old metal shoulder ain't what it used to be. My heart is strong, and my will is good, and I am strong and my mind works well at times—It's just this old body—It feels like a '50 Ford and not a 2014 Cadillac....I don't do well on low octane, though gas is no problem. And sometimes after a trip, and sometimes after a short ride I kinda have to roll out and get my bearings and legs headed in the right direction....

But you know; this is the emotion known to man. Late mortgage payments, car wont run, child is sick, parents need us, letters from school, doctors with bad news, doctors with good news, funerals and vacations mark our calendars permanently. Tragedies and Victories write their messages on our hearts and they are part of the reasons we cry at weddings and laugh at some things that aren't even very funny. I am glad to be here, and gray and tired at times. I don't intentionally try to be depressing but this is life isn't it?? The autumn years when we can say I'm sorry or I love you and really mean it—because most of us don't put on anymore—what's the use?

But I want to experience that wonderful anticipation and excitement like I did way back yonder. Bill West was coming and we were going to Enka Lake, brim fishing. I went around the house and smokehouse and outhouse and chicken house and found a couple wasp nests and knocked them down without getting stung—I want to run like that again—here he comes and really he is in love or something like that with Laura, my sister. And I probably begged and groveled to get him to take me, but he did. We sneaked out on the pier and caught brim and crappie until we got run off...Then we went to the other end and fished from the bank; seems like hours. Now that my friend, was worth the excitement. I wish I could hear that old '46 Ford coming again—shoot, I can—just closed my eyes and listened...

Like I said I am grateful to be here-I don't deserve the Grace that has been shown to me. Just to work and paint some and listen to good music and see my kin folk and see a baby's little foot and dream about the hills, and have love in my life, and the truck still runs today and to still pour a little concrete and to catch a crappie should be enough for me, shouldn't it? It's not. It's not enough. It all is wonderful, but it ain't near enough. This right here is.

I reckon I'll just trust him to get me there—after all, He got me here, beat up and scarred by my side tracks, but He, not the babe in the manger, but the Lord who walked out of that tomb, took care of me. You be blessed this day—you hear? And take a child fishing so you can at least see that joy and antici-pation that has faded in some of us—Take them to Church first, then take them fishing——

The Bookmobil at Londons Store

I wrote this before heart bypass, but most of it really hits the nail on the head—I thought my heart was strong— then I was probably 2 minutes away from staying dead—no warning or chance to hug somebody or tell Gerri I love her —I don't think I'll pour any more concrete, I think I'm going fishing or to play golf...and I know I'm going to be more thankful....you be blessed and hug someone this day.

Did anyone besides me read Burgesses Books on Old Mother West Wind- and Jimmy the Skunk, and Reddy the Fox and all those wonderful stones he wrote??? What about Jim Kjelgaards Big Red, Outlaw Red, Haunt Fox and so many more?? Lad- a dog? I think I read all they ever published many times along with Jack London —

The book mobile came to London's store on Saturday— I do not remember if it was every Saturday or not-but I would walk, bike, crawl or run to get there-Do you believe I can still catch that smell once in a while and it will remind me of that old yellow van type truck—they got to know what I liked and would try to have something for me-If they didn't I read some stuff over and over and tried all kinds—

Man I wouldn't take anything for those books-Did I mention Walter Farley and the Black Stallion?? A whole series of those...I have ridden the Black Stallion many times—I cannot remember who lived in the brown house beside Hollis Robinson, bur we traded comic books-she always had new ones and I mostly just took hers back but she never let on or seemed disappointed-I devoured those comics-I read every word on every page-advertisements and all-remember selling grits??? I couldn't give them away-Thank God for writer and books and good words—we will talk about music later—there has to be a book and a song-

Country Stores and Porches

If I look closely down the road a bit I can see a man and a boy on the porch of the old country store having a RC cola and a Moon Pie–Me, sitting on the edge of the porch Walker Hinson took a liking to me and I went with him to cut, rake and bale hay. We would always stop at the store for an RC cola and a Moon Pie–I see my stubble and gravel toughened bare feet dangling from the porch– I mostly chased rabbits and carried tools for Walker when the bright red New Holland baler acted up.

That old country stores front porch was and is a place of great enjoyment. Walker was good people and I will always be grateful that he helped a little boy along the way—a little honey for the journey—I rode the back of his huge whiteface bull and fed his calves and led his show bull to water in the evening.... I took this hill for granted then, but I soon realized how blessed I was to have Mt. Pisgah always in the background —What a wonderful place, this valley in the magnificent Smokies.... I've been blessed man; I wish I was barefooted with a RC and a Moon Pie.

The RC and Moon Pie Store. Walker Hinson was so good to me. He took a liking to a little boy, and he didn't have too....

The Creek

While sitting here in Novia Scotia, Canada, looking out over His magnificent creation, the old canoe came floating down the rivers of my memory and of course I took a ride —my thoughts turned to Davis Creek that I waded in, spent hours damming up, fished for hog suckers and hornyheads in, skipped rocks on and sometimes just laid on the bridge and looked down into the clear cold water and dreamed-and dreamed-and dreamed—This ocean and beautiful scenery there?? Doesn't hold a candle to that creek and what pleasure it gave a little boy such a long time ago.---Lordy me

Don't Smoke

This here hernia business is taking its toll on old Jack. I'm so sore I can't even think above a whisper.... He said I may get home tomorrow or Sunday...I walked to and fro like an old man in the hall...Slow and easy.... I think this hospital stuff has gotten out of hand the last two years...I never thought I'd say that I can't wait to get 73.... Go from never been sick to 3 surgeries is outta hand, I'd say.. I'm afraid to cough...Oh well, don't get me wrong, I'm still blessed way over and above all that I can ask or think.... So I guess I better quit whining and man up...But if Mom was just here for a few minutes she could kiss it and make it all better...My sweet lady is so good to me... I am so thankful for the doctors and nurses, and I make double sure that they know that......

I've had 6 hospice patients over the last 5 years...all had lung cancer....only one had never smoked....my very first one was a multi millionaire and scared of dying... me and the chaplain tried to help him find peace.... all the money and prestige he would have given up gladly for peace with God—we can have both you know—the redtail hawk that died hung up in my fence brought back this sad reminder—some struggle for success and get hung up on that and never make peace with the Giver of peace—and die like the hawk—struggling—

The other five patients? Some had quit smoking for awhile ...two had struggled with it up till sickness came—but all were at ease and at peace with Him...It's the first one that I can't get off mind at times...I'm convinced death bed repentance is possible— but I am equally convinced that it is very rare—make peace now friends—and for family sake quit smoking and dipping....lung and mouth cancer is terrible

Teasing The Bull

Decisions! Decisions! My bare feet hit the wood floor and I have major decisions to make. I won't wear shoes again but to church and such till school starts back, in August. It's summer time; around 1951, 52, 53. What to do first?? Maybe I'll go pin hook fishing from the old oak bridge, or maybe I'll go get Connie Gene and play Cowboys and Indians, or I could run through the woods riding saplings down and having great fun, or probably the creek needs damming up first, or I could go out and lay down in the tall hay field and look at the Carolina blue sky and dream of playing for the Yankees, or maybe go over to the Shooks house and trade for her funny books (I hardly ever had any new ones but she always did and never mentioned it was mostly a one way deal), then I could sit on the high front porch and read every page including the ads over and over, The Lone Ranger, Silver , his horse stories, Lash Larue, Jughead, Archie and Veronica, Superman, able to leap over tall buildings in a single bound—and Hopalong, Roy, Cisco and Pancho and on and on...

Which will I do first? Maybe go tease Con's bull again till I get scared. Uh oh, gotta do chores first. Cut some kindling out of the chestnut we got off the mountain behind the house, split some stove wood and fill the wood box. Feed the chickens and get any eggs, and at times do damage to the occasional black snake in the hen house; carry slop to the hog or hogs—now that was a chore, the hog pen was in the woods and to get the slop bucket there was work...I would get me a stick and scratch their backs and I believe they loved me–they would grunt and squeal, and I guess that was why It was sad when the 22 went off at hog killing time–but those tenderloins and bisquits for dinner soon erased my anxiety.

Oh, Lordy, it's washday. Gotta pump the tubs and washer full. I'd pump with both hands and it was a chore...Then wash the clothesline-twice-not washing it one time got me a switching for the ages, so now I had to wash it twice. Crime does not pay–Then help carry and hang out and take in. Lordy I can hear the creek gurgling my name. I guarantee you it was a prettier sound than a phone or tablet or some game starting up...

Finally, we finish up or so I thought. Now got to go in the garden and pull weeds and be so careful not to step on anything... I can't remember my two sisters ever doing anything...but I know they swept, and cleaned and helped with the washing. They learned to sew and to cook. My Lordy they washed their hair and combed and brushed all the time...And they were always looking in the minors... Enough to make a little boy sick. And they even kept their shoes polished and shined up, and white socks rolled down-disgusting stuff, all that primping...Finally I'm flying down the hill to the creek and let the adventure begin. I've decided to shoot water snakes laying on those limbs with my bean shooter–I can't ever remember killing any but I knocked--scared a lot off those limbs....

I figure I'll stay down here as long as possible, I heard mom say to leave the tub on the porch. That meant her baby boy Jack was gonna have to wash his "rusty feet" sometime in the late evening. Mom would come to the back porch and yell 'Its supper time' or time to come in'...We would sit at the old wooden table and perhaps dad would talk about him and

George Suttles getting behind an AC unit at the Enka plant and eating lunch; and having a prayer meeting right there. Mom might mention quilting with some neighbor ladies, and commenting the beans were almost ready to pick. Or she might need some more mason jars this year...my sisters might talk about boys and school. They said they couldn't wait for school to start back–how disgusting is that?–Especially at the dinner table–Then I might tell dad about the crayfish I caught or the hogsucker, or about the snake in the hen house.

It was family time–no phones, tablets, I-pads or TV.... We had each other and didn't realize how important that was. I rode around some last Saturday and began to notice and look for kids outside playing. You know how many I saw? One little girl on a bicycle. No baseball or basketball, no horseshoes, no tag, or hide and seek, no hopscotch–nothing. Technology has come a long way and we have seen tremendous things since the 40's. I'm just not sure its all that great for families....

Oh well, I can still dream. Think I'll stay in my old canoe on the rivers of my memories and go out on the porch and dream once more of throwing a 100 MPH fastball and playing for the Yankees with Mantle, Ford, Martin and the rest.... You be blessed this day and every day, you hear me?????

The Lone Ranger and His Horse Dog

This is my dog (silver) Butch. The cat was Boots. The chickens were eventually Sunday dinner; and I got something besides the back when that dratted 'ole preacher didn't come for Sunday dinner. I never did like him. This was at Hollis Robertson's rental house across the creek at the foot of the mountain, just across the ridge from Con Davis's. I was Jack (alias: The Lone Ranger, or Lash Larue, or Johnny Mack Brown, or the Cisco Kid, Hopalong Cassidy maybe—but never Roy Rogers or Gene Autry—they sang to much for me. Old Butch would play those games until I wore him out, then he would crawl under the smokehouse and pretend he didn't know me. He was my pal. He followed me to the road one morning to catch the school bus and tragedy struck a little boys heart.

Laura knows what happened from her river of memories; but seems like I tried to carry him home, and there was blood and dirt all over. He was too big. I couldn't get him home. I have this memory of mom showing up (could of been Laura) and hugging me and I was bawling. You all know what bawling is; don't you? It's when your insides are shaking and you can't get a hold of it. Then the snubbing begins. You do know about snubbing don't you? Anyway dad buried my friend, and the playtimes were difficult for a spell. He's still around--In fact he just took a ride in my old canoe on the rivers of my good memories.

Some say if you have one good dog and one good friend you are and have been truly blessed. I've been blessed for sure. Con Davis's had a son named Connie Gene. He was one year younger than me, so I bossed him around. We played together a lot. He had two cocker spaniels that I despised, so I aggravated them. And the red one bit me. But honey child I carried two bean shooters most days and I was deadly with them things. I shot more rocks at them dogs but they still chased me. I think looking back that they enjoyed the game; same with his whiteface bull. The fence ran right beside the road and I would take a red rag and run up and down the fence yelling in my cowboy outfit and homemade wooden pistol-See it in the photo. That bull would paw the ground and come to the fence and walk up and down the fence--usually by that point I was moving on sonny.

I don't think I was 'mean' through and through, just a little mean streak. It was a quarter mile to the road and a few times I come across there at dusk—and walking beside that fence made the hair stand up on my neck, especially when the old bull was close and I could hear him paw the ground. 100-yard dash?? I set many records. I went back there awhile back and laid down in the hay field and looked up at the wide blue sky and wished the old bull or Butch was still around. The old wooden bridge made out of oak logs was where I spent many, many days with a pin hook and sapling and string and a can of worms in a prince albert can, was gone.

Replaced with a concrete bridge. I couldn't hardly look at that cold thing and I've been in the concrete business 50 years, seems like. The outhouse was almost gone and the smokehouse where we cured the hog or hogs, was gone and the well not used. But the house looked about the same outside and memories flooded in and I just sat down in the woods there and laughed and cried some. Connie Gene got a toy rifle that puffed smoke when you shot it, so I took it away from him. I laughed at that memory because I had to make 3 trips to the woods before I came back with a switch worthy enough for the crime.

I guess I cried because I miss those long hazy days of summer, a good dog, a good friend to play with and fight with, sisters to aggravate and I guess just family, when things seemed simple and folk were kind. Life is fast isn't it? And we have accumulated all this stuff to take care of and its gotten even faster. Yes sir, winter is on the way in more ways than one. But, I reckon, I'll keep riding my old canoe on the rivers of my memories, until it freezes over. After all, I'm still dreaming —hope you are too-now you be blessed this day you hear me?

The Dirt Roads Are Paved

Beside a singing mountain stream near Pisgah somewhere, I've knelt down and drank the clear, cold water so many times. And many times I would turn over a rock or two the see the black lizard (salamanders) scoot off. I would catch the slick little jokers sometimes for the fun of it, just because they were hard to hold on too. Sometimes I would just lie back in the leaves and listen to the gurgle of the water and look up through the leaves at the beautiful Carolina (Duke) blue sky. I don't know of many places more relaxing and pleasant than that was, and is. Maybe a redtail hawk would be soaring overhead or a blue jay telling on me. Of course a lot of those times were squirrel hunting days, but mostly I was ginseng hunting. Sometimes I just wanted to climb a mountain.

You know those times that we enjoyed so much, help us to 'relax' and take those pleasant journeys down memory lane. Nothing like just closing your eyes and hearing the laughter and shouts at Pisgah Elementary on the playground, Or walking down the halls at Erwin and Enka High and wanting to impress the girls and be macho with a pimple on your nose. Or sitting in class looking out the window thinking about playing for the Yankees or making a million and leaving your mark on the world.

Well some things change don't they—the dirt roads are mostly paved, the tractor has replaced the mules and horses, Ipods have replaced the 45's. But one thing hasn't changed. I can go to Pisgah today and climb up the slopes and lay down by a singing mountain stream and look up through the leaves at the blue sky and catch me a spring lizard—Think I will take off now—you be blessed—you hear me???

Lige's Store

Lige Pressley's store on South Hominy was a typical country store. I was just a little fellow but I remember the worn slick wooden counter and floors. Of course the stores had distinct smells. Always the smell of candy or at least I thought I could smell candy from afar. Country ham and wood smoke and kerosene and salt pork all blended into a familiar smell. I don't remember Lige like I do Clay London. I remember buying groceries at London's store. Everything from flowered feed sacks to ammunition. 20 dollars was a good weeks worth of groceries. Brown paper pokes full of food and such. Barefoot boys and girls looking sideways at the candy and bubblegum on display...

I could chew that bubblegum forever. Put it on the bedpost and get it again the next morning. It would turn white looking and tough as whitleather. Nothing has been good enough to do that since. Remember the light string that ran from the light to your iron bedpost? It was convenient for jumping in bed then cutting the light off. Particularly when you warmed your butt and ran to the cold bedroom and jumped in before you got too cold.

I used to read all the time and I know some of you have read in bed under the covers with a flashlight. You didn't burn the overhead light for that; and dad or mom see it on. Money was tight and light bills were kept to a minimum. Dad would beat on the wall when there was no school and I would have to get up and get the fire going in the living room. And lots of time in the kitchen stove too. Cold? I would put kindling first and when we had that little can of kerosene handy, honey child I would pour it on and light that stove up...Then you would turn your butt to it and then your front and run back to bed as fast as you could. To this day my most dreaded sound is someone pounding on the wall at 5 am on a cold winter day. Insulation? Ha. Quilts.

Kinda like that stove in the middle of the church when everyone had quilts and such trying to stay warm. If you was 3 or 4 pews away you might as well hang a firebug (lightning bug) up by its legs for all the good the stove did. But it was a great time in rural America. I look for old stores and old barns and old churches. If the walls could talk, what stories we could hear. One memory I've repeated often was at Lige's store. There was an older fellow who sat out front and inside by the stove sometimes and he had a genuine Case, yellow handled pocket knife; something to drool over for a little boy. I bought me one later on in life but it didn't have the magic then like it had at the store. This old fellow would say, "I got a case boys, and he would smile and say, 'Just in case'". And wink at me.

Even then in overalls and barefooted I knew what he implied and what he did not say. Them old time mountain folk were and are simply the best people ever. And I am grateful for that time of growing up under the shadow of Pisgah....You be blessed you hear me???...

Frost and Squirrel Hunting

I woke up this morning and the frost is on the ground. It always brings back a flood of memories. And always some I had sorta forgotten. Squirrel season opened way back in the 50s on October 15th. Rabbit season usually on Nov 1st. When I was 9 or so poppa let me take his 12-gauge hunting. I still have the gun, and usually shoot it at New Years, though it seems to kick harder now than when I was a boy.

When I first got to go hunting he would give me one shell. No. 5 shot, 12-gauge. So you can bet I didn't shoot until I was pretty sure of hitting something. I used to take an old broom over in the woods and sweep me out a trail up the ridge. Then I could go creeping along thinking I was as quiet as and Indian. You could hear Mr. Squirrel cutting a hickory nut a long way off. When he was eating I was sneaking. If they saw you they would get on the backside of the tree. So I learned somewhere than you could throw a stick on the other side and they would run around to your side. Kaboom. Squirrel and gravy. Not for me but dad liked it. After awhile of responsibility with one shell, got two, then three etc. I became more selective too.

I hated to kill one as soon as I got in the woods, when I only had one shell. You see, it wasn't just the hunt and the kill; it was being in the woods. The leaves turning and crackling under your feet gave Mr. Squirrel a pretty good chance. Though with a 12-gauge, not much of one. I finally got me a 22 Remington bolt-action single shot. This may be some kind of record, because one season I got 82 Squirrels. Now you do that with a 22 and you can say you are a woodsman and a hunter. I thought I was equivalent to Daniel Boone. I think it was in my 'blood'.

I haven't been hunting in 45 years or so. But these first frosts bring a smile to my face and I think on it. Back then I contributed to the family. We didn't waste anything.

Dreams About Baseball

Well I took a ride in the old canoe again and floated down the rivers of my memories-and as usual I smiled some and was saddened some--The junior deputies came to Pisgah School and started a club--Man, real sheriffs with guns, and blackjacks and stories, and cars with long antennas and sirens. Of course I joined up. They tried to teach us that crime doesn't pay.

Well, I took that in somewhat but I was really interested in playing baseball on the team they started. One of my favorite dreams was to play centerfield for the Yankees. Mickey Mantle and the Yankees were my dream outlet. I would imagine showing up at Yankee stadium from out of nowhere and becoming the greatest Yankee ever. That's one reason I loved the movie 'The Natural' with Robert Redford.

We would go to the Asheville tourist's games, Larry Medford, Bobby Medford (sheriff until) and me with his uncle in the back of a pickup truck. We would get behind home plate and down the left field line and fight the black boys for foul balls. We had 13 one time. Now that was a big deal to us then. Funny, I don't know what happened to those balls. Any way we played ball down below the school and other teams would come and it was marvelous.

I distinctly remember when my baseball dreams got busted. I was playing center field, Robert Hinson was in left and I think his brother Larry was pitching. Anyway we got behind and the sheriff-coach called me to come pitch...no warm up and you can guess the result--I threw my 'arm out' I had to hold it up it throbbed so bad--I could never throw hard again without pain...oh I knew in my heart I wasn't a Mickey or a Whitey Ford anyway, but I had a dream.

Anyway I played all summer with a sore arm...should I have quit dreaming?? Lord no. We need to dream and have wants and goals. I still have dreams-- "I've dreamed many a dream that never came true, but enough of my dreams have come true to make me keep dreaming on—I'm 70 now and I wouldn't trade those times of dreaming as a barefoot tousled headed little boy for nothing. Zig Zigler said If you help enough people achieve their dreams, then your own dreams will come true' So find out what your kids and grandkids are dreaming about---who knows, you just might help some of them come true.

Things Change

Well while I was up on the parkway this past week, I took several pictures of family and the mountains. Its almost like you can't take enough. I know some of those pictures were of scenes I have taken many times; but they sorta take my breath, especially when the fog is rolling from a thunder-boomer along the valleys. Then I dropped off down the mountain through Glady Fork and left up Davis Creek. I've been in a quandary ever since. I was going to show my grandchildren where I had so much fun growing up (if I ever have)...

But when I looked over to the Robertson house, things were so different. Organic gardening I guess had created little plots all over the place and the house looked different. I couldn't hardly look...I figure it oughta stay the same at least till I die for goodness sake. I did ride down to the bridge (A stupid concrete bridge now) and show them the creek. The banks were even growed up and that got me too. And of course Con's old whiteface bull I used to tease in the early 50s was not there —O well....

But what really got me was on up the road where we used to walk to church and where there were lots of rocks to throw and pretty pastures and some apple trees was all growed up and some deserted buildings and old trailers. And on top of that Chester's is just a shadow of what it once was.... And Open Bible Church is brick for goodness sake.... I am so sad...It made me realize 65 years have really passed in a hurry-...Things never stay the same.

I go to Belk's and happen to glance in the mirrors (they oughta take them down) and think "my heavens Jack you're an old man, you ain't as tall as you was, your britches sag, your hair, what there is of it is white, you can't hear as good, and you had heart, and hernia surgery all this year...What's next old man???

Then I go to God's Country, South Hominy, and things all of a sudden sadden me...And time goes on—seems faster and faster.... Don't get me wrong I'm still going to go out in my old wore out canoe that leaks a bit and travel the rivers of my memory and remember how it used to be...And I will smile, especially when I think about a good coon dog on the trail, or those brown paper pokes we got at Christmas, or homecoming and tater salit and nanner pudding, and marble shooting, and falling in love at least once a week, and that first kiss, and the senior prom and all of those wonderful faces of folk I went to school with...

Wonder if they are all as old as me...Sometimes I think maybe its better just to remember how it used to be than try to go back...But I won't I'll head back that way again and remember the good times...After all, those times are what made me who I am...How in the world do you forget those things and people who gave you so many good reasons to remember them???? I reckon I'm stuck in 3rd gear.... Maybe I need to move off South Hominy and tell the rest of the story.... you be blessed this day and every day, you hear me???

Running Barefoot

Well I betcha spring is on the way. In fact I would guarantee it. But you know what—? These springs are coming way to often and at an alarming rate of speed. But there is something about spring. The time of renewal and new beginnings. The caterpillar will once again build a cocoon on a branch, and in time a gorgeous butterfly will emerge...And the fragile butterflies will beautify our flowers and yards, free of charge. The robins will appear maybe before the last snowfall and remind us that its time to think about a garden.

When I was a little fella a long time ago (doesn't seem so long sometimes) spring meant getting out of them dratted ole shoes and running barefoot at a high rate of speed. Lots of girls went barefooted too; so don't act like you never did. Kids today wouldn't think about that—they are more into Air Jordans and 'looking good'. I go outside every once in awhile barefooted and grimace when I step on a rock or something. The sounds of our feathered friends whistling, chirping, and singing just for us is enough to make spring special. Spring means buds burst open and yellow bells and green leafs appear and a song is in the air.

In my other life on South Hominy, spring meant cleaning. Quilts and blankets washed and put away. And sometimes just hung over the clothesline and beat. Mom would wash windows and leave them open and the smell of spring in the fresh air was the best deodorant in the entire world. The wood box would be moved out of the living room for the summer... Thank God for that; but the supply of wood for the cook stove was a never-ending chore. I wish I could carry in some wood for my mom one more time. If you listen close to the echoes in the wind you can hear the ring of axes and the adze as new barns and log homes and sheds were built. Springtime: new beginnings...

Listen close and hear the sound of the scythe as the first cut of hay was gathered and haystacks appeared. Our people with weariness from constant 'battle' with winter and being 'shut in' laughed and 'got in the spirit' when the sun began to warm their homes and souls. Listen close and you can hear singing and preaching about Heaven and Hell ringing through-out the hills. Look close and you can see the moms, exhausted from cooking and putting up with the old man in the house for the months of winter, and sewing and repairing clothes and quilts, and being the doctor and nurse—look close and see the smile as she sits in the sun and sees her man plowing and getting ready for another winter. It was a hard life, but it was home, and spring with the violets and trillium blooming made the spirit rise.

No better folk than mountain folk who were born with nothing and kept most of it throughout life. But they had love, and faith, and loyalty. They believed in each other and helped each other. Listen close and you can hear the banjo, fiddle and guitar and harmonica in the warm spring evenings when supper was over and the firebugs were lighting up the yard. The music and song echoed into a time long gone. Listen and hear the sounds of the kids as they play hide and seek in the night. Look at the lightning bugs in the Mason jar. Listen and hear the sweet sounds of Grandma as she sweeps off the porch with a birch broom—she's singing into the wind and the sweet sounds come to me in my old wore out faded red canoe as I float these rivers of my memories....

I once was lost, but now I'm found, was blind but now

I see. No sweeter sound. I see my grandma, little wisp of a woman, a midwife a long time for extra cash money—I smell the snuff and see a brown stain on the corner of her mouth— but what I really see is the light in her eyes when she sees me and she hugs me like I'm the only little boy in the world...my face buried into her shoulder.... Spring—makes us alive as a young mule on a frosty morning. So be on the lookout for yellow bells and buttercups, and listen close, you will prob- ably hear my old canoe sliding off into the river, and I'll prob- ably be smiling....

Is It The Last Time

When I was at Niagara falls and out on the 'mist' (boat) when it was sleeting and the wind was blowing, I knew I was seeing it my last time. When I sold my house 3 years ago that I had built except for the electrical-and I almost did that but I didn't know all the codes on the electrical box. I went down to the creek and the cabin I had built down there and sat in the rocker and figured it would be the last time. I looked at the initials I had carved on the beech trees years before and some kind of moisture rolled down my cheeks. I ran my hand over them and knew it could well be the last time. I went into my outdoor toilet and got the sears catalogue out of the plastic (for squirrels) and flipped to the tricycles and went back to another time, for the last time in that one.

Out west I stood on the hill at Custer's last stand and could hear the war cries from a people we robbed and slaughtered. A proud fierce people who won that battle but it was the end for them—I knew it was my last time there. I marveled at Mt. Rushmore and thought how in the world do you figure out how to do that and make it work so excellent—It was my last time there. When in 1983 I walked out on the grass and set down by the flagpole in Okinawa and pondered the fact I was going home the next day, I had moisture in my eyes again —it was my last day and last time there. I held our little girl named Lisa Suzanne in my arms for the first time —and the last time...two weeks before due date —the cord—

In 1967, I took 300 dollars from a boy and he took my maroon '57 dievy-2 door-out the drive and I saw it for the last time—It was such a blessing to hold Mama's hand when God came for her-the last time...Those hands had made me take baths, cooked and sewed for me, felt my head for a temperature, made me take castor oil for all that ever ailed me, and those hands that wore switch after switch out on my sore behind. Those hands that would pinch that little hangy down part under you arm above your elbow when I 'cut up' in church... Some thought I was in the spirit.... Hands that quilted tight little stitches, ironed my blue jeans and kept a cotton picking comb somewhere and was always parting my hair and wetting that thumb and wiping spots wherever I had need...brillo pad thumb—

I can't remember the last time—I wish I could recall the last time—They come and go unnoticed don't they?? A friend or family dies suddenly and we try to recall, the last time...I bet we would approach a lot of things differently if we knew when those last times were.... I surely wish I could have a few more last times just one more time...October the 30th 1998. Our anniversary and she was in Carolinas Medical Center on 'life support' for her heart. The nurses decorated the room and they got extra pillows and they worked out the meds and they made a cake and we had a party. Then they closed the door and I got into the hospital bed and spent the night with her. The last anniversary. 38 years— It just happened to work out the right way, that last time. And for that I am thankful...really thankful.... I mean really, really thankful....

Well I expect I could go on for a spell but another day I will do this again. I hope it has encouraged us to hug a bit tighter, get out the good dishes for all who come, love a little stronger, be more forgiving—it may be the last time—and like only Dolly could say it: most of all I wish you love—be blessed and be a blessing....

The Chimes Of Time

For a lot of us old folk, and especially those who have lost loved ones, the loneliest times are between dark and bedtime; and those times during the night when sleep eludes you, and memories come flooding in. Seems like we are in a relay race of sorts doesn't it? For a period of time (if all goes well) we have our Moms and Dads, and then one day they are gone, or we move out and the plate gets broken, and we realize they have passed the baton to us. And for a time we are alone making plans and strategy for the coming years.

Then children come along in the next relay and we become engrossed in giving them 'better than we had'. And we run that relay and all of a sudden we don't know what happened to our 30s and 40s and even 50s. And we enter another relay of life--the children are grown and move out (and sometimes or a lot of the times come back and bring someone with them) but we have passed the baton to them because we are tired and want to rest from the race of life some—

Then if we are really blessed another relay begins--grandchildren–Oh what a joy--Not burdened with all the side events and trauma-- my neighbor is 70 and is raising her 4 year old grandson–her race is a hard row to hoe sonny–and its happening with much frequency, more and more grandparents are raising kids when they aren't able and shouldn't have too. I say Keep them, spoil them and send them home and plop down in the recliner pooped-raced out!

And then the final relay comes quickly along--autumn has come; the chill of winter is coming--we ache, we can't do what we could do last year. Then the cold hand of death takes one of us--and the race is suddenly almost unbearable. No loneliness is like the loneliness of grief. And those times of a night when silence sets in no matter if the TV and stereo and telephone are all going at once--the silence of loneliness cannot be drowned out....

Two things help——time and Faith. But I have a suggestion for you, why not leave memories for your family–or just write for yourself. Your grandchildren and on down the line would love such heirlooms. It doesn't matter where you start--but if you are in that relay stage it might be the best and sweetest thing you could do for your family–Listen I hear winter coming, and I think it's coming at a high rate of speed---I have started a memory book--and I laugh some and I cry some–And I have been remarried for 14 years now but how or why would you forget people who gave you so many wonderful reasons to remember them—

So start--Get a really thick good quality memory book or journal, black ink pen, and if you need to go on line for suggestions, do it or get a grandchild to do it, they can do anything, even getting the flashing light off of the VCR.... Hope He really takes a liking to you and yours----Trust me it would be a treasure--

Not Raising Hogs

You know what, I've been spending more than I'm getting...So through the fog that I seem to look through, a wonderful thought came to me. Seems everyone else gets everything they want but our brain dead congressmen are afraid to do or say anything... So I have come up with a plan that will surely increase my income substantially. I heard about this years ago and it just popped up, so now must be the best time to get started....

The government has a program that helps keep products from not having enough, to not having too much.... On a level keel so prices won't fluctuate so much. Well one program is that they will pay farmers not to raise beef cattle. So that is the business I am getting into. I may expand into other fields if this works out. I am trying to find out what kind of beef, whether Whiteface, Angus, Holstein, etc, not to raise. And I also need to know how many not to raise. There are lots of questions...How much hay do I need not to harvest and will I be paid for that? And another thing, how big a farm do I need not to raise these beef on. I figure I will start out not raising 200. Just to get a feel for the labor cost and return on my investment.

Also, will it make any difference if I don't raise calves and just don't raise grown cows? These grown cows that I don't raise will weigh more and should bring more money, for not raising them. And will I need to not drill wells for water? And I should get compensated for not drilling wells...This farming is hard work and mentally challenging. I mean there is tractors not to buy and corn not to plant, But I really hope this works out. If all goes well I hope to expand the operation to include not raising hogs. I've always been partial to not raising hogs. I think duroc is a good breed not to raise. And again, not building pens and not raising feed should be included in the compensation.

I have heard about not raising soybeans and corn and I am excited about that too... I just need to know how big a farm I need to not raise the beef and hogs and corn and soybeans on. I'm so excited I think I will go down to the bank and see about an advance to start not raising beef. Don't you love this government? And also it would be a real blessing to have this farm that I don't raise beef and hogs and corn and soybeans on, in South Hominy, just at the foot of Pisgah.... Maybe I can work in some time to go and not dig ginseng. Should be some really good money in that. You all be blessed, you hear me?? And laugh once in awhile, God shorley knows there is enough to cry about.

Pisgah View Ranch

I went to Pisgah View Ranch around 20 or so years ago and rented a cabin for a couple days. The place was wonderful. There were guests from every-where. Some of them came every year and had made it a longtime family vacation. Of course the country kitchen made a big impact on guests. Served family style and bountiful, you just didn't want to miss the mealtimes. But I travel back there occasionally in my wore out canoe on the rivers of my memories, and have always found it to be peaceful and the memories bring a smile to my face.

There was music on Saturday night, usually good blue-grass with a mix of southern gospel throwed in. The judge, tall and distinguished, was always busy talking to guests and tell-ing stories and such. The founder, Chester Cogburn had passed away and the 'judge' ran the place. But there was something about the place that had a calming peaceful effect on you. Sitting down by the lake in the early morning or at sunset, and looking up at Pisgah was absolutely wonderful. And I had lived near there for about 15 years before we moved to the Woodfin-Newbridge area. But the time I spent there was still as fresh and new as if I had never been there....

In the very early morning just before sunrise would find me walking up the logging roads on the mountain behind Chester's. And of course sang was on my mind. I dug a lot of ginseng there and over on the slopes of Pisgah. I always re-planted the seeds and hoped it grew back. Perhaps some little boy would come along who knew the history of the place and would discover the magic of just being in the woods of Pisgah. I cherish the memories of the small branches that had the beginnings way up on the mountain. Drinking that ice cold water and just laying back resting and looking up through the leaves at the caroling blue skies and hearing the birds singing to me and the shrill call of the redtail high overhead, was some of the things that made that time so special...

I cant climb some of those really steep places anymore without knees and ankles acting stupid, so I avoid those places where the ginseng hides and gets big and is so gorgeous, but I can see it when I close my eyes. I'm going up there in a couple days and check out Pisgah View and I'm thinking about renting a cabin for a couple days when the sang berries turn red as blood-and that means you could find me, before daylight, heading up stream ever looking for my favorite plant and for that 'spot' to eat a can of viennas and drink from that fountain of youth that will be still gurgling and talking to my senses nearby... and I will miss that country dinner that is so good for that time which is far, far better for the body and especially the soul ......

I've been pouring concrete the last couple months like I was young and could. It has been so hot, so I have had concrete on the job by around 6, so as to get poured out and finished before the afternoon came around. I usually had a couple changes of clothes because I would be soaking wet with sweat in no time at all. If this makes any sense it felt good to work and things go well. So I am so thankful for decent health and a strong back (some would say a weak mind)—I don't know how I would do to get up with nothing to do. You can only play so much golf and to hot to fish in the middle of the day...

When the sweat was rolling and the shade called to me and there was no time to stop and lollygag around, sometimes my mind would go back to the mountains, and that cool cove with the branch running full of cold, cold water, and I would think, 'Are you out of your mind?? What are you doing out here in this heat at your age??? Get in your truck and go to the mountains and quit this foolishness. - Too late, old man, you got to finish what you shouldn't have started to begin with. But then we finished the 5 mini-storage buildings and the parking lot with 750 yards of concrete and the contractor and owners were 'tickled to death' with the time spent and the quality of the work. So all is well I reckon.

So in the next month or two look for a grinning, gray headed old man with a sharpened stick somewhere on the slopes above Chester's, or you might find me sitting in front of the lake looking at Pisgah. Or I may be down at Pisgah Elementary thinking about old times and friends—or over at Erwin walking down the halls listening to the laughter and talk and lockers slamming and reliving that last day of high school. Thinking about dreams that never came true, and old friends that never call, and Ma and Pa and a wife and youngans who have gone on—But some dreams have come true, and some friends do call, and the ones who don't call are still my friends, and I'm pretty sure where the loved ones are who have crossed over Jordan. So for this day-It is well with my Soul—you be blessed this day and everyday-you hear me? —Shirley it is so good to 'hear your voice' again. Love you in Christ, my friend

Mamie

You can be in a beautiful place and have ugly problems. The man at the gate called 'Beautiful' in the Bible. He had an ugly problem; He was crippled—at least until the Lord looked at him. I was in Novia Scotia, a beautiful place, and I was thinking that this can't hold a candle to the Blue Ridges and the Smokies...But at least for short times we can put our ugly problems on the back burner and rest some.... Except today, answers are soon coming about tests and biopsies, and I want to hear and I don't want to hear—

When folk you love and admire are in rough waters, everybody is in a ugly place...And you and I could well be the next one needing prayer and encouragement.... I've been there, I know the comfort friends and family bring.... please, when you have your devotions say a prayer for my friend and family over in East Tenn..... Ugly problems can be fixed... If we talk to the "Fixer", we have pretty well done all we can thanks...

Well I rode over of East Tenn. yesterday and visited a couple cousins. My Aunt Mary's sister was over there. Her name is Mamie. Mamie is 92 years old and her niece and my first cousin Lois was with her. Lois is 86. Mamie has a large Toyota SUV. She is the driver. She parked that thing behind my SUV on a steep hill and got out, (it is not easy just opening the door on a hill) and come on up and into the house. She said I don't wear contacts or glasses and I go to the y 3 times a week. Swimming is part of it. She said (just don't hear very well. Her face is smooth and she has no weight problem.

I watched from the porch as she and Lois walked back down the hill and opened those doors and buckled up and took off. Not at 15 mph either. I thought, man here I am at 73, wondering about 74 and she is having a ball--at 92. I say, hats off to you Mamie and I surely hope I get to come to your 100th birthday. You can come and pick me up—I'll ride with you. Shucks maybe even 110.... Wouldn't surprise me. And was nice to see Lois also—She and I and Junior played golf 20 or so years ago and she mentioned that I loved Aunt Mary, she's gone on now, and her family.

One of the sisters and there was a few of them, would mention getting together and next thing you knowed there would be tater salt and nanner pudding everywhere.... lots of love and laughter I miss that. And those that are left still get together as often as they can—I hope the youngans carry on that family tradition. One of my favorite people is my cousin Jerry. He had 5 bypasses this past week; He is home and getting well, thanks to Carol. The first day or so he cautioned her to be careful going out the back door and not slip. She assured him after 10,000 times she knew how to go out the door without slipping. He "said" I was more worried about me. If you fall and get hurt who will take "pet" care of me???? That's my boy...

Then I followed Mamie up to Rena's and visited a short spell with her. My friend and cousin Boyd passed away awhile back and He and Rena were my Tenn. family when I went over. Always said my bedroom was just like I left it. They were best friends. They worked side-by-side making a successful go of dairy farming. Long hours and hard work. We have teased Rena about waiting on him hand and foot. But the truth is if he hadn't treated her the way a man is supposed to treat a lady, I doubt his ear of corn would have got buttered. I felt the loneliness and sadness there.

But I also saw him and his 'touch' on the home.... So there is no way to forget someone you loved with everything you have. Why would you want to? They give us to many good reasons to remember them. Grief and sadness work themselves out...And I suspect a garden will get planted and she will be canning and cooking and time will ease some loneliness. Thank the Lord for a good strong family, especially their two, Karen and Richard, and their special grand daughter and grandsons. And we are thankful that her surgery went well and we believe all will be ok. I love all you Tennessians....

The Nolichucky

Some things just take your joy and hide it from you, don't they? Bad news travels like wildfire, and good stuff travels slow seems like. I can't even watch the news anymore. Everything is bad; terrorists, police killed, murders, rapes and suicides and dope dominates the news. I can't pinpoint just when America that I knew as a young man began to go to pot. I don't really know what happened, but I suspect the government had a lot to do with what has happened to us. So now we sit and watch and are amazed at the violence and anger that is taking hold. Best keep your guns looks like. But I don't want to discuss these things because I have read the last page.

You and I know that we are getting on up in years and one day the roll will be called. But knowing its coming doesn't make it any easier to swallow. When our family and friends come to that place a part of us shrinks up and sorrow and sadness permeate our thoughts. We don't want to lose nobody. And we are smart enough to know that tomorrow could be our day. So we take one day at a time if we got any sense. I have a friend who said he would make it to 95 because his folks genes are strong and they made it to their 90s. I hope he does, but ole Jack ain't gonna make such a foolish statement.

I tell you what I learned this month... If you feel the need to make a phone call or to go visit someone, you best be saddling up your pony, cause it might be the last time. About three weeks ago I got this incredible urge to go see my cousin. Gerri couldn't go so I went to stay a couple days. We had the best visit; we talked, laughed and shot some bull and ate oh so good, and even went over on the mountain and found some ginseng.... He was planting a huge truck patch and already had a mile of sweet corn in the ground...I've been going over there for 60 years—and staying with him for the last 40 I guess.

I love East Tenn. and the mountain range and the Nolichucky River and the beautiful rolling hills and dairy farms.... Good people You know I have never heard my cousin say one 'bad word'-not even close...But I did hear tell he gave a Yankee a green persimmon once, and there was a few choice words said about that...Good people, them cousins—and my joy is hid from me today.... He is fighting for his life and the prognosis is not what we want to hear...And I can't do a thing...

Life is wonderful and oh so cruel sometimes. And we are never ready to give up good people. They make us better. He has done that for me-I'm a better man for knowing him—I hope someone can say that about me...I just ain't ever going to be ready to give him up...l can't for the life of me, imagine East Tenn. without him...But at least I pretty well know where he is heading, so there is some comfort in that... good folk don't need to suffer, but I reckon that's life too.... thanks for listening to a sad ole man this July...

The Skunk

I was somewhere in between 6 and 8 years old. One of the highlights during that age was piling up in dad's '35 ford and riding down to Marshall and out to Bull Run...Between Marshall and the grist mill at Petersburg. My grandfather and grandmother lived on a hardscrabble farm (I've always liked that word, along with gumption and fixing as a verb and a few more good ones). He had a horse named Fred and a mule that I can't remember his name. I loved the smell of the barn. Leather harness soaked over and over with sweat, tobacco always smelled musty, Hay and yes horses and their smells. Using his outdoor toilet and the sears roebuck catalogue was always in the plan cause I don't remember the catalogue at home. And the red tricycles and guns was so good...

The other attraction was my Uncle Bill who liked me and once in a while rolled me a Prince Albert cigarette...And another attraction was my cousins lived on the farm. Danny was 2 years older than me and knowed everything. Well on this particular trip he (and I) sneaked out the single shot 22 rifle and planned a night hunt for coon or anything else that we would literally stumble upon.... So we played all day in the creek and barn and chased the older girls around. There was a rock chimney that we could climb up into the attic; which had a cot and other stuff in the room. It was great fun climbing the chimney and thinking we were getting by with something....

So it finally got night time and the adventure began We sneaked down from Danny's room and out the back door and was careful not to slam the screen door—which had a couple wads of cotton out of pill bottles in the screen door to plug up holes in the screen...I'm sure some of you remember that when you take the cotton out of your medicine.... Mountain folk had and have a use for everything...Well we took off and climbed the hill above the house up to the top. There was some moonlight so we could see a little bit. We didn't have a dog but we did have a flashlight, which we didn't use except for when we shot at a lion or tiger or possum or sound...

Well we come upon a skunk in the middle of the path and Danny said lets shoot it. Well he was the leader so on went the flashlight and he aimed and shot the skunk. And we thought he killed it. So we laughed and so on and did what stupid kids do...You would of thought it was a grizzly. Unnecessary murder was what it was; but the night was far from over. Well, we eased up to the skunk and my stupid leader poked the skunk with the 22-barrel. He sprayed us both. It was like a fog and you couldn't breathe.

We ran backwards screaming I guess and rubbing our eyes and face...Danny said lets go to the spring and wash this off. We left the 22 and flew down the hill to the spring and proceeded to wallow around in the water. Well we got most of it off or we thought we did and my leader said we can't go into the house, we still smell and it will go away by morning. So my leader suggested we sleep in his dad's car. Now Uncle Dan was a salesman—he wore white shirts and neckties. I don't believe to this day I have ever seen anyone get whipped any harder or longer than Danny did that next day...

It scared me to death and he told me to get gone and

never come back. I wouldn't even look at my Uncle Dan for a long time.... We had gotten used to the smell I reckon. They made me strip and wash and they washed my clothes and we went back to South Hominy earlier than usual. I was thinking in church this morning—we got used to that skunk smell sorta like we get used to sin in our lives—and we think it wont hurt nothing—And then God puts us back on course—sometimes gently and sometimes not so easily...either way it leaves a bad 'odor'.

Later on when I got the nerve to go see Danny he said he went and got the rifle and the skunk was gone He said the rifle stunk awful...Shoot, I slept pretty good in the car and really loved sneaking out of the house and carrying a gun around and shooting at real 'game'? Exciting to a little boy.... But you know what, seems like something is always stinking up a good time...you be blessed this day, you hear me?

Genuine 16 Ouncer

I went up to South Hominy Friday. And everywhere I looked, sweet memories flooded the river of my mind. From Glady and the 1st grade in the one room schoolhouse to Stony Fork and the very first picture show. I think it was wild horse mesa, or something like that. At recess everyone wanted to be the hero, but the biggest and baddest boy usually got to play the good guy. I always played the good guy in my mind anyway. We would slap our sides and gallop all over the field for days. Then it was back to marbles and such, and getting grass stains on britches and wearing out the toes of my shoes, and cutting switches for mom.

The little store at the entrance of Davis Creek had two 16-ounce drinks in the freezer of the little fridge- or maybe just one; I'm not real sure. 8 cents. I rarely had all of it but we would pool and run and kick and scream to get there first. He enjoyed having that drink for us and watching us go after it. Many times we couldn't get it for lack of funds; but it was fun. I found a whole dollar bill one day and I knew mom would make me take it back to school, so after me and Leta and Laura got off the bus I ran ahead and pretended I found it in the road. Aw, bubble gum fit for a king and a whole 16-ounce drink with ice in it—Lord knows that was heaven to me.

I have tried and tried to see that name on that drink

bottle but it is a blur. The thrill and wonder of boyhood in the mountains to me is like a cold drink on a hot day–refreshing– Gosh I wish I could jump off of that old school bus and run into that old store bounding and jerk that freezer door open and find that treasure!!! Lordy, I just did—in the old canoe in the river of my memories just floating along–thanks for riding with me today. I hope He takes a liking to you and all yours this day.

Boyd Chandley

Well I went to Tenn. today to see my cousin (brother) who is sick. It was a mixed, emotionally draining visit. I am thankful that I got to see him when he knew it was me and Gerri. He was at that place where your body begins to shut down. Volunteering for Hospice, I have seen this situation a few times. It was heart wrenching today. Cancer is no ones friend. It hides until damage is done then rears its ugly head. 2 to 4 weeks without treatment-4 to 6 weeks with chemo and all that worthless junk. He said no.

So he is going home with Hospice help. I hope I am wrong but I think their time frame is wrong. Small cell cancer has spread everywhere except the brain. Even into the bones. It started in the lungs and he has never smoked or chewed. A dairy farmer, expert at lots of trades, superb fisherman and outdoorsman, expert rifle shot, outstanding integrity, Husband of 63 years, father and grandfather—friend to many— Just an outstanding American who believed in work and fairness for all. Excellent dairy farmer, opinionated to a fault, and would tell you what he thought, a church man.

I am selfish today. I don't want to lose him yet-80 doesn't seem all that old anymore. Course time rolls on like a freight train out of control... It wasn't so long age when my Uncle Bud was the patriarch of the family...Has it been

20 years? Or more? Time is no friend of ours. Each day kills another dream I won't accomplish.... A month ago He was in the garden, preparing for another winter.... But here comes ole time. It is ironic how you can have heart trouble and manage that oh so carefully—then cancer comes along. The old reaper, called the providence of life, he shows up...It happens to good people and bad people. I am so thankful even with cancer all over, seems like, that there is relatively no pain. My prayer today is that pain is not an issue until God sends for him....

I count it the greatest honor to be his friend. I miss him already, and I know that he probably will not know me even if I go back this week. But I will know him. I won't forget our fishing trips to Canada and Alabama. I won't forget about my "bedroom" in his house. I won't forget the laughter and the talks about our families.... I won't forget going shrimping in Fla. at night and talking and laughing under the moonlight...Those things mean a lot to me—How could I forget someone who has given me so many great reasons to remember them????? I love you Boyd and I'll see you down the road...Could be the Lord likes to fish—Anyway that's how I see it...

East Tennesee

I remember a time in my younger days that had a tremendous impact on my life. My Uncle Bud and Aunt Mary Chandley lived in East Tenn., near Telford... I used to go stay with them some in the summer. I remember riding a Greyhound over there from Asheville when I was 12. Aunt Mary had several sisters and if anyone just mentioned food they had a get together. I mean a real, old-fashioned, southern, eating meeting-some of the best cooks in the world... Just the epitome of what families are all about. They loved much, and often.

Their son Boyd was in the army and I didn't get to know him very well until many years later. Two other sons, Jerry and Johnny, were at home and their daughter Jean. Jerry soon became my hero-he was older than me (not much older but when you are young a year or two is a big difference). Besides I think I've passed him now. He was the best storyteller I ever heard. When he talked about fishing or hunting I felt like I was there-we slept upstairs in the old farmhouse with the huge kitchen and he would tell stuff-and sometimes I wanted to close the window when he talked about wildcats and such...

Jean was older too, and she was a long legged dark haired gorgeous girl who seemed so mysterious-she had a boy-friend (Jack). I think that I could not figure out what she saw in him-he wasn't good enough for her-Anyway, Randall came along and stole her heart and he is almost a Chandley. Certainly a really good man. Jerry and I would go frog gigging and

Johnny wanted to go so bad and we would tease him and we called him froggy-Aunt Mary didn't like us teasing her baby boy, but it was fun, One time Mary's sister had a party and we went for food cards and ice cream. I fell in love briefly with a red headed beauty named Joan. I remember we kissed under the tree at Martha's and Joan had a fever blister-romantic memories huh?

Anyway they came to Bud's and I hit the back field and Joan came back there and found me-and as we passed the kitchen window holding hands, I glanced over and Aunt Mary was pointing and laughing and talking-about us I guess-I was beet red for sure--Jerry got in his share of comments about my courtship too—I wouldn't take anything for those memories or the freezer pies Mary fixed for me...I loved this family and their way of life. Their love for each other, their respect for each other (they could each have different opinions, and usually did, but nobody got mad or argued even heatedly...that was amazing to me.

Jerry got really blessed, He somehow wooed Carol-Her charm, and candor, and humor was the perfect fit for this family. Jean and Randy are blessed with a wonderful family and many friends. Johnny was an educator and a coach and into real estate now-He has been blessed -with Bonnie and together they have three super kids and lots of love...Oh one other time Joan came over and I went upstairs and hid under the bed-Jerry came hunting me and that was sorta embarrassing-She intimidated me what with the kissing and all-

What can I say about Boyd and Rena-I love them both so much-though I really have never figured out why Rena waited on him hand and foot...I have so many wonderful memories of the old farm house-Jerry playing brother Dave and Elvis on the record player-and the house alive with friends and Mary's sweet tea, and Johnny's grin when we teased him—I miss the old farmhouse and Uncle Bud and Aunt Mary and I am thankful that I could get in my truck tonight

Jack Burris

and go stay awhile—that is something worth holding on to......

A Boy And His Dog

Well the leaves are full-grown now and the grass is in the grown up stage and tough--like me I guess. The sunsets and sunrises are daily shows of breathtaking splendor. And in between those are moonlit nights of magic and days that reflect our own moods-both stormy and serene. It's hard to stay in bed these mornings. If you can beat the sun up there is a brief time between night and day, when it is both morning and night.... Behind the trees to the East, morning awaits in the wings; clothed in robes of pink and red and gold ready to make her entrance.... To the West, the moon hangs on, reluctant to leave, clothed in silver light—this is a day the Lord has made—I will—I am—always—thankful—whether stormy or benign. A dark shadow on the way to the outhouse was scary to a little boy, but not to Butch...he would rush to challenge, to bark at it and run it away...old Butch, man he had it made...freedom—the catch wasn't important, the hunt, that was it. The smells, running through the fields and up the hills, and finally showing up at home with a silly grin—to play with a little boy—and wait for night once more.

Sometimes I stand now looking out the backdoor in the morning watching the sun come up and the moon go down, with a sense of regret and loss.... A speeding car (to me) got my pal at the school bus stop one morning but I still can feel that cold nose pushing on me saying —come on, let's go run and play, nights on the way and I must be gone—I got a feeling the rabbits and coons and possums and dogs hugged one another and said 'see you tonight boys'. Listen close tonight, I bet you can hear them off in the distance-running free in a time gone by—

Pennies From Heaven

I was reminded about the value of pennies a minute ago. I read an article about how this fella, every time he found a penny he stopped and read "In God We Trust. It calmed him down and helped him to put things into perspective. A penny found, meant an entirely different thing to me 17 and a half years ago. The death of my wife had left an empty place and a feeling of being alone —really alone. It was a new experience, different from other loved ones somehow. And I know lots of you have experienced the feelings...

Like being in a room and having the radio going and maybe the TV too but the silence is deafening. One day I got out of my truck at the gas station and was running low both in my truck and me, when I looked down and there was a new shiny penny. Something clicked inside— That represents her somehow. A new beginning, no more pain. A new body and heart...shiny new. I clutched that penny so hard and I cried. I put it deep into my pocket and thanked the Lord. Now I know, some would think that is crazy, boy ole Jack you've lost it... But it did something.

From that day on, children, I found a penny here and there in the most odd places, and I am thoroughly convinced angels placed them for me. I mean when I needed a pick me up or just needed to be brought down a notch, there would be a penny. And it is interesting also that I didn't find any shiny new ones during that time. I went on a date and there was a penny under the catsup bottle. Now I don't know what that meant yet but there it was. After a time I would say hello darling, nice to see you and jam it deep into my pocket. The incidents gradually disappeared. I can't remember when I found the last one. When I'm on one of my canoe rides I find myself looking every once in a while....

I know, I've had some "doozies" happen to me...But He said I will go before you and make the crooked paths straight. I'm convinced He sent angels with pennies to steer me and help me along. Whether it makes sense to you or not, doesn't really matter—I know...Someone out there will "get" this because I have never shared this with anyone, but I felt the need...You be blessed this 4th and every day, you hear me???? And look down every once in a while, no telling what you will find...

Check Yes or No

Just a dream, just a dream, all my plans and all my schemes—You all remember that song from the fabulous 50s??? Wake up little Susie, Wake up—I dreamed that experience would happen to me—It didn't have to be Susie either, anyone of the beautiful girls I went to school with would do. I always felt like it would be worth it to get my goose cooked.... No shotguns by mad dads though. I fell in love so many times and most of the girls I loved never knew it. I was bashful and would turn red as 'a pickled beet'. It was so much fun getting in a fight with some boy over some girl who never knew we were fighting over her. Paul Capps and me fought numerous times over different girls to bad they usually didn't know it.

You remember the notes I'm sure. 'Will you be my girlfriend?' check yes or no. No's were devastating. Then along came Elvis and 'Don't be Cruel' and the Platters "Its Twilight Time", Jerry Lee and Roy Orbison. I fell in love with a red head in Tennessee one year and 'Only the Lonely' was playing on the radio. Boy that was a heart breaker; but when I went to Tennessee on a greyhound to visit, she had to chase me down in the backfield where I went to get away. I kissed her and she had a fever blister and I suspect that started the downward slide of that love affair.

Don't you all remember all that good stuff with a warm feeling?? I fell for Virginia Freeman at Erwin the first time I saw her. She wasn't aware or interested. I sat beside her in English and after a time she let me copy some stuff. It wasn't that I couldn't do the work; it was a way to communicate with her. And after many, many years when I found out that she had passed away not to long after graduation, I was really saddened, because she was such a sweet girl. Any of you fall in love and the other person didn't even know it??? I think boys are good at that. Kicking the dirt or talking about cars and looking sideways at you ladies was a special gift we all had. Love doesn't change does it??

Even now I think back on those times at Pisgah and Enka and Erwin High and sometimes it feels like something swells up inside —And its good—I understand a whole lot of folk don't even think of those times and probably think its foolishness and that's okay. People I thought were life long friends have no need to 'keep in touch'. I just don't forget folk like that; I love to think about them and those good days of growing up. I've never seen or heard about Connie Davis and we played every day for a few years and had so many fights and so much fun in the creek and marbles and all that. But I still think about him and wonder where life took him, and I hope life was kind to him.

I fell in love in the tenth grade at Erwin for good. I slicked my hair down and put on quite a show (my opinion) and she fell for it. I think I told you this, in my senior year at Erwin, Outside in the hall at the typing 2 classroom just below the office, I kissed her, maybe more than once, and the principle tapped me on the shoulder and said Jack, don't do that right here beside my office'. I turned red; he smiled and walked off. How could I forget that??? I guess that was my "Wake up Little Susie" episode. She died at 56 so young, 39 years of marriage--so many good memories as well as troublesome times--part of life But you know what??

Love is a gift from God because It originates from Him. And I have loved again; I think I'm gifted at 'falling in love'. One difference now though. I'm getting older every day and I've long sense quit slicking my hair down (a lack of and gray is the main two reasons). I can't run anymore, I've never won the lottery; My rich uncle has gone on already and we sold his trailer, and, well, you get where I'm going with this—I might not be able to cause another one to fall in love with me, so I'm earnestly praying I go first. I love these little forays in my old canoe down the rivers of my memories, especially when all you good-looking girls come to mind—Will you be my girl-friend?? Check yes or no.

Mixed Emotions

I have some very mixed emotions this night. I took the day and went to Pisgah and Hominy Valley (Pisgah is where the Lord went to pray). I really wanted to meet Chet Hill and talk to him face to face; but he wasn't home, and I don't have enough sense to call first. I met two outstanding ladies, one named Lorri who lives where I did in 1948 thru about 1953—somewhere in there.

They are from New Jersey and New York and bought 30 plus acres from the Robertson family. Her and her husband grow organic everything. The other lady grew up in Hominy Valley and moved away. She is back settling the property of Charles Davis, who owned and operated the store just before Stony Fork School. Me and Walker Hinson were regulars there for RC's and Moon Pies. I took a picture today and I swear I could see my feet hanging down off the porch and a grin on my face. Her name is Ann McElrath Isbell. She is across the road from the store if any of you want to see her or the store. She will welcome you. Such a very nice lady.

Some of the dirt roads are paved now and the old oak bridge over the creek has been replaced with concrete (ugh). And I see a lot of run down homes piled up with trash, etc. Which is usually indicative of addictions and such. I wanted to tell them that this was hallowed ground, a wonderful place for kids, good mountain folk with a firm handshake and whose word was a bond. God-fearing, hard working people who would give you anything but who would take nothing—I hate to see things rundown and neglected... when everything was clean and beautiful in times past...

This was mostly one road that was like that, so I really enjoyed the other roads and stops just looking and stopping and taking some pictures (again and again)—1 love that valley and majestic Pisgah shrouded in fog always the same. I visited the old shelter Chet talked about and remembered picnicking there at times. I found two ginseng plants just a short walk up an old logging road...Course I left them there to see again. But I don't know, kinda a sad feeling seeing some places all growed up and roads paved and houses up on the mountains-

O I know I'm just old fashioned and resist change, but I reckon everything has changed. Some of you I bet don't look like you did when I knew you in school, but that's the way I remember you...Like I said times change so don't put off going back too long-winters still coming like a runaway freight train—some of us may get run over so we need to be more loving to people, and not hold grudges, and for goodness sake some of us need to forgive and forget. Seems like we get the feeling we are going to live here forever, and so we put off things...

I hope we don't end up saying 'oh I wish I had gone back to the old home place and put some flowers on Ma and Pa's graves; and I wish I had talked to my brother and told him I loved him. Me? I gotta go see my kinfolk and my two sisters-I hope I don't put it off too long and find the road tore out and rerouted and paved, and the old landmarks growed up and un-recognizable—like the two wonderful June apple trees with the old limey horse apple tree beside them—I could not find them today. No trace that they were ever there. But they were because I can dose my eyes and see them and I can taste them too—one sour one sweet—I'm glad I went to look—So—Go—

Jack Burris

While we can—

Ways To Starve

I have done figured it out. Why is life so difficult now? In the 50s and 60s no e-mail, Internet, voice mail, or texting. When on vacation no one could reach you. So you rested. No coming home to 500 emails. No computer, laptop, tablet or iphone 6, 5,4,3,2,1.... Ask granny if you needed to know something. If she didnt know the answer she would just make something up

Now if you want a box of cheerios you cant just run and grab one...there are now plain, honey nut, honey nut medley, crunch, multigrain, multigrain peanut butter, multigrain dark chocolate crunch, apple cinnamon, cinnamon burst, protein cinnamon almond, frosted, fruity, banana nut and 4 kinds of berry variety. It will soon be suppertime while making up our minds which one is 'right for us'....

It gives me diarrhea; I best get some toilet paper. Do I want the strong, ultra strong, soft, ultra soft, basic, chamomile, or sensitive....??? Hmmmmm—ultra strong feels like--4? 6? 8, 9 10, 18, 30, 36 or 48 pack...hmmm 18 pack ultra strong feels like O Lordy—mega, mega plus, double, double plus, or triple roll??? Hmmm 50 choices on ways to wipe your azz... No wonder we are stressed out.... Too many choices.... And that makes our vacations our work. We check in every little bit—we take pics and post on FB. 95 percent what we do is practically worthless...2 percent is useful.

We go somewhere and Google in directions, that is a real problem for us men. We can't pretend we know where we are and we know where we are going. We miss out on seeing that satisfied look on our wives faces when we finally ask directions at the filling station. We seldom get to hear South Hominy or Madison county directions like--Wal you know where Isrials barn burned summer fore last, wal jist pass that take a left at the old oak that was lightin struck and not to fur, heck, son you cant miss it....

Technology is killing us...Life is too complicated. I just wanted to try out one of them 700 HP Mustangs, but I had to look at Fusions, Crown Vics, Focus, Taurus, Thunderbird, F150, 250, 350, 550, Vans, Super Duallys, diesels, gas, 4 by 4s--I gave up went to Chevy to see the hot Camaro—first the Impala, Cruz, Silverado—well you get my point. Too many choices for old people. I go shopping I know what I want, where it is and I race the clock to grab it and check out ASAP-- A woman goes shopping and may spend a entire day and never buy one item, and say they have had a good day—true story —Amazon is my friend now—one click and I sit and wait and think about Pisgah, and Enka High and my Alma mater Erwin High...

Uh-oh that's technology, right? Well guess I best close this laptop and check my voicemail on my smart phone and then see if the Revenant is downloaded on my tablet yet. Just to dang complicated, that's all--too many dang choices. Didn't get the toilet paper in time either, dang it.... O well guess I'll go see about washing powders—that has to be simple, huh????

Hunting Avids

I used to be a hunter. In my youth I was after squirrel and rabbits with great enthusiasm. I was also an avid hunter. Now I never actually killed any avids though I did try. Everyone said I was a very good avid hunter. I looked everywhere for the elusive avids and was never fortunate enough to get one in my gun sights. I didn't tell anyone but I really didn't know exactly what they looked like. I just figured I would recognize one when I saw one. I don't know for sure if they were dangerous or if they were big or little creatures. I was still a determined avid hunter.

I think they come in all shapes and sizes. Even to being adaptable to water. Cause I heard my friend Jock was an avid fisherman. I wouldn't even know what bait to use or how big a hook to use. Kinda threw me for a loop to find out they were in the water too. But that ain't all. They can also fly I think. Cause my friend Frank is an avid golfer. It must be true cause he is all the time hitting into the woods trying to get one I think. And another friend has spent years trying to get a photo of one... I heard he was an avid photographer and I went to him to see a picture but he didn't have any.

The avids are so elusive. I thought snipes were hard to catch but these avids are something else. I had no idea that so many hunted them. Oh well, there goes the phone and it's my avid golfer buddies—I became an avid golfer awhile back, because so many of my friends were one. I can hit some beautiful hooking, slicing shots deep into the woods but so far no avids have been found... O well better get a few extra balls, today might be the day. Stay tuned for more updates on being an avid hunter...

Mouse Hunt

I took a part time job at Rock Barn Golf club a few years ago for free golf and extra income. This is a true story with a great message; that seems to happen to me occasionally-and I am grateful. I got a phone call at 2 am from a lady, and she was hysterical-she said a rat had run under her recliner and she was terrified, could come and kill it. I said 'I'll be right there'. I got some gloves and a broom handle and went to war. She met me at the door and she was all to pieces, she was sobbing and loud. She said he is under the recliner.

So I attacked the recliner and he wasn't there. She panicked and said well we have to find him; I can't stay here. She had a Louisville slugger in her hands and she was literally crying. I was flabbergasted though I didn't laugh or anything-she said it was big as a guinea pig. There was a wash room there that led to the carport and I said maybe he went in there, she backed up to a wall and slid down it and put her head in her hands and wailed and kept ahold of the baseball bat... I went into the room and shut the door and looked in the obvious places and slid the dryer out a bit and then the washer machine.

This rat ran out from under the washer machine and under the door and out where she was. She screamed and you could of heard her, I thought for miles. Which way did he go-and she pointed toward the kitchen. I looked under and everywhere-no rat. She was bat ready, with tears and wails. I called my boss about some traps and he said could I run to Wal-Mart and get some. I told her I had to go and she got hysterical. Finally I got her to go downstairs into a bedroom with a low door and I assured her the rat could not get under the door. I said I'll get a trap--she said get a lot of traps she couldn't stay there--So I came back with 8 traps and took 4 in the house with some cheese--she said is that all you got? I said no, she said get them all—

So I set 8 traps, and finally got her calmed down and agree to go in the bedroom and if she heard a trap to call me. Wasn't 15 minutes she called ecstatic, I think you got him." It was a little woods mouse and she stood over me with the slugger while I cleaned up the blood and such. I was at a loss for what to say really, I had never seen such a reaction to a mouse-- I had seen the little fellow when he ran out the washer room and so knew he wasn't a man-eater. I sat down at the bar and was cleaning up the cheese wrappers and she told me the rest of the story--She said I have a potentially terminal illness. Any germs could land me in the hospital, and could trigger reactions that would kill me. That's why I reacted that way.

My mouth was open I'm sure--and the thought came to me--Aren't you glad you didn't laugh or make lightly of her actions or the size of the 'rat'? Lesson learned--never judge others merely by what you see on the surface--we became real friends and she still had the bat- The Louisville Slugger was autographed by Derek Jeter of the Yankees. --And her husband, who was traveling told me when he came home, that he thanked me so much for helping her and that lucky she didn't remember the 45 in the desk drawer. I was lucky. But not because of that. I was blessed that the Lord taught me a real life lesson that I can share. You be blessed this day you hear? And if you see a 'rat' pick up the phone, I know how to deal with them

Marriage and Cornbread

Boys how many can still remember when you were young and trying to impress the girls??? Get excited when they would walk by and pretend not to notice. The shimmer of her hair, the shape of her legs, the way she walked made us want to follow. The red lips and the flash of a smile, —my, my it made a young man turn red and gasp for breath; and daydream.

Then you meet the one and you hold hands the first time. Feels like you got your hand in a furnace and it's your hand all the time that is melting. And that first kiss? Lordy. Is anything ever been sweeter? Your hair stands up and you break out in the stutters and kick the ground and for a bit you forget about cars and trucks...And you can't dance but you will and you pull her in close and almost pass out.

Love till death do us part...and you hold doors open, and you help her sit at the table, and you hate to go to work, and you can't wait to get home What happened? Age is what. Now you will be halfway up the drive and she is still trying to get her legs in and the door shut. Share an apple? Ha, no more.... and then we settle in and we forget sometimes...And they still love us for some reason—All of a sudden corn bread and bisquits are more important than sex, and that secret thought, I wish she cooked like my mom....

Sometimes I think we should be killed, but then again I really like my truck. So maybe there is a lesson here, at least we can walk down the street with our bellies sticking out and hair gone or uncombed and still think we are sexy...with no make-up and chocolate stains on our t-shirts. Another lesson I've learned—Heat and sex and love will get you wed, but maybe for a long haul, boys need to make double sure she can cook cornbread...close to how mama used to. I agree with Jeremiah Johnson movie—I loves the wimmens, I shorley do." And that's all I'm gonna say about that...

Jock Fender, Mountain Man

Jock Fender and I met at Enka when I worked there for a year after the Air Force. He was from Foster Creek on Big Laurel. You turned up Little Foster to his childhood home. His dad farmed those hillsides with a team or with one mule. They were mountain folk. They canned in the summer and put up apples and potatoes and sweet potatoes in the root cellar. They had a milk cow. Later on there wasn't enough money so Chauncy went to public work. They were workers.

Jock and I are close to the same age. He and I trout fished, ginseng hunted, rabbit hunted, went to church together, spent lots of family time together. We also drank together for awhile. I'm not proud of that but we were young and full of mud. He handled it better than me and when I finally quit that was an example that I leaned on. We almost had a free for all once when he came to my house and jumped me about not being in church and drinking. I got mad and run him off. But I didnt want to cause he was right and I knew it.

Pride, will get you hurt or cause you to hurt those you love. But what he did was what friends do. Real friends don't walk out when you get in a bad place. Real friends are coming in when everyone else is leaving.... I have been there for him and his family and he has been there for me. It might be 6 months or more now when we talk but when we do it's like it ant been but a day or two. Him and Linda came down when I had the heart spell and it was good. We can sit without talking. We have been to Canada fishing a few times and it pains me to admit it but he is a better fisherman than me. I can fish awhile and lay back awhile or even take a nap but not Jock. He loves it and he goes after it.

We rebuilt a ford van together to go to Canada in. I came up from Georgia once and my car tore up and Jock gave me a '54 Mercury. I loved that car. And it was his brother in laws car. But he worked it out. Jock has a mountaineer's sense of humor and so do I, so we get along real well. Jock, like his dad was uncommonly strong and I've always been mad cause I could never beat him arm wrestling. I finally quit trying....

I guess I've written this little note to somehow say how grateful and blessed I have been to have had so many friends in this walk of life. Jock is a special one. And I am grateful. I would remind each of us no matter where you are in life, whether sick unto death or full of life on the go, take time to reflect on those folk who have helped and encouraged you—those who would come when you call, those that show up and say I just had a feeling about you today. I learned a long time ago when I get someone on my mind I'm going to try to get in touch with them. It's a wonderful thing what a neck hug can do or a phone call. After all that's why we are here isn't it?? Thanks to all you old friends here on FB. After all these years we can touch each other and relive some great times in our lives.

Autumn's coming on now, seems like at a high rate of speed; and I don't want to leave here without saying to those that have made a difference—I love you and I appreciate you —If there is anything I can do for you—you have to tell me —I think that's why I'm still here-to say or do something to help someone else on this journey...You be blessed this day and every day, you hear me???

Barlowe, Boker and the Case

There was a Barlowe, and there was a Baker, and then there was the Cadillac of knives 'the Case'. Just in case. I had various knives as a boy, and where all but one of them came from I haven't a clue. Lane Watts gave me a Barlowe one time. I think I was around 7 years old. One of the black 'bone' handles was missing, and I remember the other one came off too. But it was a knife-a real honest to goodness knife. I cut fishing poles with it, I made arrows with it, scraped the bark off of them with it, I picked creasy greens for mom with it, and on rare occasions I probably cleaned my fingernails with it. It was very difficult to keep it really sharp because of constant use. But those old Barlowe's and Bakers were prized possessions to a mountain boy, pin hook fisherman, cowboy, Indian, lawman and outlaw.

I had to be the outlaw when the older boys came around or at recess cause they always got to be the good guys... or you would have to fight them. And that was a losing matter for sure. And you know what, I carried the Barlowe to school lots of times. But I kept it in my pocket cause there were some older boys who would take it away from me. I lost one to a Sharpe boy once and was scared to tackle him or tell cause I wasn't a tattletale. But I hated him from then on. Sorry. You carry a knife to school today and there would be a lockdown. I would say 90 percent of men had pocketknives back then. Walker Hinson had a Case. And Milton Price had a Case. Both had yellow handles that made me drool. Walker used his constantly on hay bales and around the house and barns. Milton pulled his out several times a day to cut string or something. I have a couple of Cases today—one a canoe and one yellow handle.

I don't carry a knife but once in a while. If I think I might run up on that perfect slingshot, I want one to cut that hard dogwood. I force traded a Barlowe with no handles to Connie Davis, my neighbor in mischief, for his birthday Boker. His mom came marching up the hill and nullified the trade. O well, I was older and thought that was the way to do things. Mom didn't agree either.

When I had to go cut Mom a switch I couldn't find my knife usually. There was something about cutting a switch with my trusty old Barlowe that didn't set well with me. So I usually took a kitchen knife. Switches grew scarce around my house and I had to travel farther and farther to find a good one. I got to where I would cut a little place about halfway up the switch and when mom would give me usually about 2 or 3 licks the switch would break. I thought I was a smart cat for that little trick. But you know I think she knew all my 'tricks'. I was a mama's boy and loved every minute of it. I was 'the' baby...Wonderful.

Shirley reminded me yesterday about Valentines Day and love. Mom would fix me bisquits and homemade syrup and butter—that was love. She would take her thumb and wet it and clean my face in various places, and not be easy either—that was love. She would iron my clothes, even my blue jeans and overalls and wet and comb my hair and make sure I had on 'clean underwear', that was love too.... Thanks Shirley for reminding me what real love is, the sacrifices our folks made for us, the sacrifices we now in turn make for ours.

Everyday is Sunday and Valentines Day when we take time to reflect on those slow, warm hazy days of a time slipping away. Tell your grandkids all you can or write it down for them. I wished I had asked more questions... You all have a wonderful Valentines Day and don't send your kids or grandkids to school with a Barlowe. The Law will come after you—Think I'll carry my Case today, Just in case—

Funerals

    I have a question.. How important are funerals to you? Expensive funerals with fancy caskets and 2 or three preachers and all that? Is that important to you? My mom said she didn't want water to get in her vault. I got to thinking, and that's always dangerous. What difference does it make?? Dust-to-Dust–the rotten old body ain't going nowhere. We start dying at birth and we have to buy tons of deodorant and perfume and wash about every day to keep from stinking. Then we wear out and die... and get embalmed to keep from stinking and lay around in a open casket while folk say how good we look. Dead is dead–and it isn't pretty. We might get powdered up and 'look' nice dead but we ain't pretty...Are we??

    Do you want a big funeral?? Lots of crying? I'm sure there will be tears from some-for all of us. But I think the funeral business has gotten out of hand. Families face huge debt along with being heartbroken. Now some plan and pay and that's good if you can–pick that perfect spot with no water seepage and a good view and go for it. I would not be surprised if our loved ones don't look down at us and laugh out loud–screaming 'I ain't there sonny, I'm up here'—or on the downside-get it? Down side? I would be perfectly happy like my ancestors-build me a pine box or just dig a hole, and don't wrap me in mama's good quilt-I'll haunt you. A piece of burlap or an old sheet if you must and kick me off in the hole...

Predicated on a decision God made before the foundation of the world, I wont be in the hole; so I won't feel the dirt or be mad at you. And for goodness sake don't buy no flowers–I can't smell no more. What are they for anyway? To impress or maybe just to show some respect to the family I guess–and that's okay. Hug me and tell me something now -good or bad–If you are mad at me tell me and I'll try to fix it–and if you love me tell me now so I can cry-I am a crybaby and love it–And for goodness sake don't say 'Old Jack was a pretty good fellow, but you remember when he done messed up?

Death will let me forget some of those things I wish I could forget–don't bring them up for goodness sake. Well enough ranting I reckon–I do hope you have a beautiful funeral if you want one, and that it ain't anytime soon. I hope to see you at the house. You be blessed this day and this New Year, you hear?

A Summer Place

I have been listening to music—A Summer Place, Elvis "Now and Then There's A Fool Such As I" Sinatra, "Summertime", Louis Armstrong, What A Wonderful World" Celine Dion, 'Titanic Theme" Dell McCurry bluegrass, Vincent Black Lightning, 1952" "Sherry", The Shirrells, Man of Constant Sorrow, Soldier Boy and Bill Gaither, "Old Friends" Merle Haggard, Natural High" Will You Still Love Me Tomorrow" "Just a Dream", This is Just What Heaven Means to Me, Vestal, I can listen to this CD over and over and over.

If music doesn't lift you up and help you to "get by", then you may need hearing aides. I say Thank God for music...All Music...Ray Charles, "Georgia" There is thousands of good songs that are good for the soul...Oh don't get self righteous on me and tell me I need to listen to just gospel...I have a lot of really good gospel, but I don't listen to it all the time...why should I?? I could pretend I do and listen to country when I'm in my truck...How about "I'm so Lonesome I could cry" Hank Williams. Get you an I-Pod, load it up, get some earphones, kick back and relax—you will be glad and blessed...

Warm Rain

The Rain is softly falling here in NC. There is a soft patter of rain that brings good feelings. I guess it's a holdover from when we were kids and played in the barn or sheds that were covered with tin roofs. I can't remember another sound other than a good hound on a trail or treeing that causes me to just relax and maybe even take a nap... The sound of rain falling through some old growth timber and falling on the forest floor has always been one of my favorite things in this world.

I love music and have been blessed to love all kinds...Where would we be without good music??? It soothes the soul and spirit, it calms and excites, it makes us sing in the shower, or in our trucks and on our tractors and lawn mowers... We may not can carry a tune but we got a bucket anyway to try and carry one.... That's how these early spring and summer rains do me. They make me want to sit down against an old, old oak tree and just travel back in time to those 50s and 60s—when I was young and full of vinegar and quick to fall in love with all the girls...

One thing I fell in love with in the early 50s was hunting the most beautiful plant in the world... Ginseng, or sang as we knew it.... Invariably, every time it comes one of these soft rains and I get quiet and still, at some point I go back to Pisgah and climb those slopes and hollers once again. And I always have some memories that recur.... A five prong I found waist high. 13 four prongs in one small patch and small stuff all over with 3s and 2s. That drink of ice-cold water out of the branch and looking up and Red berries all around.... Things like that are worth saving in your memory....

That soft rain and just you and maybe just you and her—or you and your dad or your best friend. I liked being alone in those woods with the patter of a soft rain. I felt small and I felt blessed...That's why I think it is spiritual being out in His wonderful creation and listening to the falling rain and hearing music—fit for kings--you be blessed you hear me??? Good hunting.

Donkeys

Big heads, huge ears, loud hee-haws from the female, Polly Ann, and loud brays from the Boss, John Henry–not pictured here–this is Polly's big baby Jake... I wanted to put Polly over in the other pasture and got a halter and a rope and tried. She dug her heels in and I wrapped the rope around her rump and pulled, begged, pushed, sweated, wanted to cuss, inch by contested inch. It became a battle of wills. Across the field and through the woods. I was wringing wet with sweat. She did not yield a inch.

When we got to the barn, I had some feed already in the bucket She acted like nothing had happened, just as calm as could be, dipped her head in the bucket and turned and looked at me while chewing contentedly. The look said, "Why didn't you say there was feed here to start with". I was sitting on a stump trying to breathe. Free advice-never try to take a donkey anywhere–lead them–a bit of feed and a scratch behind the ears will keep you from sweating; I have had donkeys ever since. They are "good for nothing but eating"–is a statement far from the truth.

Any animal that gives you pleasure and laughter is worth their weight in gold...These little donkeys, with the cross on their backs are loyal, social, sweet to a fault. I've carried them to Christmas services and they will interact with both grownups and especially kids for hours...Polly would let me know distinctly when she had had enough attention. She would nip at my clothes; and I would take her home and give her a hug and a treat. John was the boss but had the same disposition. He was passionate and gave Polly fits sometimes. She would kick him anywhere and everywhere with bad intentions but he was stubborn too....

I put John over into another pasture so as not to breed Polly and of course he broke down the 4-strand barbed wire to fulfill his passion. There is a tremendous lesson here–sometimes we let fences and barriers keep us from fulfilling our own dreams and passions—I say break down those barriers and go back to school, take a chance on love again, start that business, do some painting, go out west or somewhere–Like old John; life will be rewarding.

These wonderful little donkeys walk the same trails from one place to another. Very distinct and well defined. Another lesson here–Make it a habit to go to those places that satisfy you. A prayer room, church, school, the gym, shopping...wear out the paths with consistency. Rewards are there–John and Polly have distinct paths to water, to the barn and to the gate where I or we show up. It is longer than a straight line but they don't cut corners–another lesson.... These donkeys will line up for scratching, brushing and petting–the babies will climb up in your lap and bite at you if you don't pet them They know their names and they answer...Their love makes them gorgeous, and worthwhile.... Just like God's love makes us worth something valuable to Him.

At the end of our "roads" is provisions for our needs, He gives us more than we can ask or even think...The place of rest is dry and safe from the storms of life. The trail to the Water of the Word is life cleansing and life giving...And at the gate, "Enter child, I know you", I know your determination, your stubbornness to travel the good paths, and I know your love. Polly didn't get mad and run from me at all over the struggles to move her. She held no grudge...In fact she seemed amused so

I wasn't mad either; why should I have been, I just got taught a lesson from a unlikely source Polly and I didn't have to make things right with each other, but there was a lesson there too —Make things right with others if needed—

Well I guess you know I love these little friends—They have been abused and in bred when the price was high...greedy folk will do anything for a dollar. Be careful when shopping to question bloodlines...I've got John loaned out to Steve for a spell—Steve has several Jennies and he needed a new line. I am going to let them keep John and I will keep Jake and Polly for a while longer. It's hard to let go of things that make you laugh, cry and cuss—besides I need more lessons on life... I will tell Steve one thing–he best have his fences pig tight—John will tear down barriers to fulfill his passions I can hear him braying right now–enough to wake the dead...O well—

PS I was reminded of some of these blessings from "Flash" a donkey.

Recess and Ginseng

I'm an old man now. "Only" 72 but that is old. The want to and the dreams are very much alive. But the body is like an old car, pieces wear out. Knees need greasing. Back needs WD-40. Eyes automatically droop upon sitting down in a recliner. The Y is hard to get to every day. Things are heavier. If there are two screws to take out one is very difficult. Opinionated and stubborn to a fault, are usable adjectives. I started out poor and still have most of it. I refuse to be hateful, mean or rude to anyone...even though I may want to...I'm a sinner saved by grace. Only reason I'm not a bigger one is lack of opportunity.

I've always loved recess, dessert, old paths, music, good preaching, pretty girls, good men, fishing, sports, and ginseng hunting... I am so fortunate to have had two really good ladies in my life. Unfortunate that one passed away after 38 good years of marriage. Fortunate that I found another to love. I took both of them fishing and ginseng hunting. I'll be getting into the woods along about September. No really steep or hard to get to places anymore, maybe up some logging roads where climbing ain't too difficult. I hope I find some 4 prongs but if I don't find any at all, I will be blessed.

Age makes the reward not in the 'finding' but in the journey. And one thing I know for sure, the journey produces great memories; but it also produces hurts and disappointments and tragedies. So make all the good memories you can, be nice to everyone, smile and laugh often, be patient and kind, encourage and help others achieve their dreams, then your own will come true. Take a kid to church then take them fishing, arrowhead hunting, and ginseng hunting. Now that's some memories worth thinking about. Think I'll get in my old wore out canoe and take a ride down the rivers of my memories right now...No telling where I'll wind up today.... You be blessed...

Curtis Creek

Well here I go off on the river again. Today I'm living on Curtis Creek again, across from Walker and Lois Hinson. My sister Laura and Bill West lived directly across the road. On our left was JC Hinson. Jennings lived on our right side, a bit up the road. Jennings, JC, and Bill all moved to Douglas, GA. Jennings became very successful with a burial vault business and block plant. I worked for him in GA a couple times. I helped run the block plant and did funerals on Sat and Sun. I remember me and this black gentleman were digging a grave by hand; it was mostly sandy soil and relatively easy to dig, when I dug up a skull. This guy, his name was Omey, never touched the side of the hole, but went straight up and out. I had to finish the job with no help. He wouldn't even help cover it up. We laughed about Omey many times.

Anyway I had a wonderful time there on Curtis Creek. We had a pigpen down below the house and just past the outdoor toilet. We had running water in the house for the first time. It's funny, I don't remember washing in a tub so maybe we had a sink to wash in or something. I set 2 muskrat traps in the creek for 2 months and never even got a look I don't think. Course I was hoping for a mink. I had heard they were worth 25 dollars-a small fortune to me. I do have a nudge in my memory about a part of a foot in one of the traps, and I'm pretty sure that was when I quit trapping. 25 cents for a hide wasn't worth that to me after that; but I was really into squirrel hunting and it was a wonderful place for that. Tall hickories and oaks was squirrel heaven. There was a few grouse on the mountain too, and although I shot at one occasionally I never was quick enough. They had an uncanny way of putting a tree or bush between them and me and being stubborn I would shoot anyway.

It was fun at that point of time in my life... I was in a different time of life at this place. Cowboys and Indians were for little kids then, though I probably wanted to play some with them. Girls became the ones to impress. No more valentine notes and such. No more 'will you be my girl' check yes or no. Note writing was for little kids. Heck I was 12 or thereabouts. And I had been in love since the first grade at one time or another. Dreams were being born in my mind. Play baseball for a living. Make lots of money. Build Mom and Dad a new house. Dreams—ain't nothing wrong with dreaming. And it is true—if you help enough people achieve their dreams, then your own dreams will come true—

I didn't get to play baseball-threw my arm away at Pisgah playing for the Junior Deputy League. Wasn't that strong to begin with, but I had a dream...Still do occasionally. I think I loved about every girl in our class and most of the 'older ones too. Trouble was they didn't know it. One thing for sure-wasn't any finer folk to go to school with than those that were at Pisgah Elementary. They make memories worth remembering. Oh we had fistfights for alpha male reasons or for a girlfriend who had no clue. But we were mountain folk. Independent, honest, Christian, caring, strong—Oh at that age we didn't show all those traits but we had been taught, sometimes with nary a word said.

Funny I used to detest water and soap, now I'm in a voluntary mode. Mama used to fuss at me most every day to wash your hands, take a bath, wash your rusty feet...and I resisted, but now??? Something had ahold of me. A girl could look at me and smile and my legs would get weak, I'de blush, my mind would go blank, and if I spoke at all they thought I was speaking in tongues. Well I was. Tongue-tied tongues. I didnt get to go out with, must less marry one of the gorgeous creatures of South Hominy. The Lord had another plan for me; but I can still picture a bunch of you as you looked way back there. You ain't changed a bit. At that time if a girl let her dress slip up over her knees, she would be the center of all who could look. And now? Go to school and see what's up with dress codes.

I loved that house on Curtis Creek, the wrap around porch where we broke thousands (seemed like) of bushels of green beans. My Schwinn bike dad sacrificed for, silver, red and black-with a horn to. High cotton for sure. I haven't forgot. Dad in his work clothes, Mom with an apron on–seems like always.... Family time—I wasn't a child anymore but I wasn't a man yet either. Kinda somewhere in between. You all remember that feeling don't you? Acne, insecure, wondering what's next, high school coming up—Well seems we made that transition–well at least some of you did–I'm still dreaming and growing up at 72. Thinking about the good old days—you be blessed today—you hear??

Lazy Or Just Old?

Everything seems to be getting more difficult. Like getting out of my truck after driving for a ways. Or climbing a ladder. Or taking a screw out of something. Or keeping up with where things are. Seems I spend half my time hunting stuff. Taking a lid off a pickle jar requires Herculean strength seems like. What's up with all this junk going on anyway? I used to 'jump up there' and 'jump down there', Now I have to 'climb up and climb down'.

My mind seems to be pretty good its just my body has gotten lazy or something. Wonder if a facelift would help? I guess I'm slowly dying cause I have to use deodorant and 'Old Spice' to keep from stinking. Oh well. Least I wont have to put up with this stuff in Heaven. But my mind is okay I think. Some says it is and some say I'm crazy. One thing I have no trouble doing is riding the rivers of my memories in my old canoe; Surely you have a memory lane you can travel for a little rest from the journey, or a dream that you still hold on to.

Well yesterday I musta rode and paddled a thousand miles. And some of you all were with me on the river. We went up to Wytheville Va. to the Waufenhaus dinner theatre. You are served a wonderful dinner which begins 2 hours prior to showtime. In the theatre. And the performers are the servers etc. Then you are treated to an excellent show of some kind. Yesterday and the month of April has been 'Back to the Fifties They did 71 songs. Of course not every verse but some part of 71 total songs. It was a fantastic trip down memory lane. Wake up little Susie.

I could see the drive in there on the left before you get to the old Enka plant site. I could see me in a white t shirt and a rolled up in the sleeve a pack of Luckies telling her Dad with a shotgun that we 'fell asleep and our goose is cooked', and him believing it--like he wasn't a teenager at once was on Blueberry Hill and I was the Leader of the Pack doing the twist with Peggy Sue. At the prom all dressed up trying to dance with 3 left feet and a red face. Seeing all you all, all cleaned up looking gorgeous and handsome, ready to graduate and conquer the world. You girls with your low cut gowns and heels on and us boys talking about '57 Chevy's and stealing peeks at them bare shoulders and legs. And dreaming.

They woke me up with Chain Gang and Jailhouse Rock and Elvis. Orbison showed up and The Everly brothers... Corina and Will You still Love me Tomorrow, Who put the rah in rah ma rah ma ding dong, or something like that. I never could keep up with that song. When A Man Loves a Woman, and Do you Wanna Dance seems to always bring good feeling with them. And on and on for a couple hours.

Taken to so many old scenes and places in my mind...To South Hominy and Pisgah and on to Enka High and on to the prom at Erwin. And singing Elvis in Medford's old pulpwood truck with Steve and Larry and Asheville's former sheriff Bobby all crowded in that rickety old dodge truck.

Music and Song. Boy what would we have without a song? A song to make us cry, a song to make us laugh, a song to take us back someplace warm and friendly, 'Our song' Where you 'Lay your head on My Shoulder', and the two of you take on the world. And its because of 'Just a Dream. Just a Dream'. Boy, I couldn't make it without a song. My truck or car gets serenaded to every time I get in them. Especially in the morning. Just like a daily devotion, a song gets the day started off right... Gaither's 'He Touched Me' is one favorite Gospel and of course Elvis's Gospel. You all do realize old time southern Gospel is fading away. Seems only us old folk keep it going.

Now that's sad, but yesterday was no different than that. Saw one couple in their 20's. Everybody else had gray or colored hair-my wife said as long as they made color I wouldn't see no gray in hers- But our old time rock and roll is rocking on out--so put on a CD or find an oldies station and take a trip down memory lane it will do you really good. The theatre is doing Beach Music next month—I'll shag some at least I call it that.

Baseball and the Yankees

Well I took a ride in the old canoe again and floated down the rivers of my memories-and as usual I smiled some and was saddened some--The junior deputies came to Pisgah School and started a club--Man, real sheriffs with guns, and blackjacks and stories, and cars with long antennas and sirens. Of course I joined up. They tried to teach us that crime doesn't pay.

Well, I took that in somewhat but I was really interested in playing baseball on the team they started. One of my favorite dreams was to play centerfield for the Yankees. Mickey Mantle and the Yankees were my dream outlet. I would imagine showing up at Yankee stadium from out of nowhere and becoming the greatest Yankee ever. That's one reason I loved the movie 'The Natural' with Robert Redford.

We would go to the Asheville tourist's games, Larry Medford, Bobby Medford (sheriff until) and me with his uncle in the back of a pickup truck. We would get behind home plate and down the left field line and fight the black boys for foul balls. We had 13 one time. Now that was a big deal to us then. Funny, I don't know what happened to those balls. Any way we played ball down below the school and other teams would come and it was marvelous.

I distinctly remember when my baseball dreams got busted. I was playing center field, Robert Hinson was in left and I think his brother Larry was pitching. Anyway we got behind and the sheriff-coach called me to come pitch...no warm up and you can guess the result--I threw my 'arm out' I had to hold it up it throbbed so bad--I could never throw hard again without pain...oh I knew in my heart I wasn't a Mickey or a Whitey Ford anyway, but I had a dream.

Anyway I played all summer with a sore arm...should I have quit dreaming?? Lord no. We need to dream and have wants and goals. I still have dreams-- "I've dreamed many a dream that never came true, but enough of my dreams have come true to make me keep dreaming on—I'm 70 now and I wouldn't trade those times of dreaming as a barefoot tousled headed little boy for nothing. Zig Zigler said If you help enough people achieve their dreams, then your own dreams will come true' So find out what your kids and grandkids are dreaming about---who knows, you just might help some of them come true.

Squirrel Hunting

I woke up this morning and the frost is on the ground. It always brings back a flood of memories. And always some I had sorta forgotten. Squirrel season opened way back in the 50s on October 15th. Rabbit season usually on Nov 1st. When I was 9 or so poppa let me take his 12-gauge hunting. I still have the gun, and usually shoot it at New Years, though it seems to kick harder now than when I was a boy.

When I first got to go hunting he would give me one shell. No. 5 shot, 12-gauge. So you can bet I didn't shoot until I was pretty sure of hitting something. I used to take an old broom over in the woods and sweep me out a trail up the ridge. Then I could go creeping along thinking I was as quiet as and Indian. You could hear Mr. Squirrel cutting a hickory nut a long way off. When he was eating I was sneaking. If they saw you they would get on the backside of the tree. So I learned somewhere than you could throw a stick on the other side and they would run around to your side. Kaboom. Squirrel and gravy. Not for me but dad liked it. After awhile of responsibility with one shell, got two, then three etc. I became more selective too.

I hated to kill one as soon as I got in the woods, when I only had one shell. You see, it wasn't just the hunt and the kill; it was being in the woods. The leaves turning and crackling under your feet gave Mr. Squirrel a pretty good chance. Though with a 12-gauge, not much of one. I finally got me a 22

Remington bolt-action single shot. This may be some kind of record, because one season I got 82 Squirrels. Now you do that with a 22 and you can say you are a woodsman and a hunter. I thought I was equivalent to Daniel Boone. I think it was in my 'blood'.

I haven't been hunting in 45 years or so. But these first frosts bring a smile to my face and I think on it. Back then I contributed to the family. We didn't waste anything.

Walker, Me and the Bull

Davis Store just before Stony Fork School. I sat on that porch with my bare feet hanging down many time with my friend Walker Hinson. Walker had grandchildren but for some reason they didn't like to go with him to cut, rake and bale hay. Walker took a liking to me. He always stopped here whenever we went that way— always a moon pie and an ice cold RC. That was the best times. I chased rabbits and helped him fix the twine and such. I could catch the small rabbits, and I turned them loose of course. It was great fun for a little boy. I did small chores for Lois, Walkers wife. She was a good cook who made cookies on a regular basis. So I went up there on a regular basis.

One time he had a huge whiteface bull. He was so gentle and Walker led him to water or different pasture on occasion. And I rode on his back—to me it seemed like his back was an ax handle wide. A little scary but I didn't let on. I remember holding or helping hold calves for him when they were sick or had the 'scours'. He would pour coffee down their throat and they usually got better. I don't remember why but he had a bag of arsenic and I was playing in the barn and knocked it off the shelf and one of his calves got into it and died. I won't tell you whether I confessed or not. But, really I think he probably knew. Lesson learned.

He had a show bull, I guess for 4 H and I led him to the

creek for water every evening, or most of the time,.. That was scary to but I never let on. It's good to take a ride in that old canoe on the river of so many good memories this morning. I wish I could run up to Walker's, barefooted, and get a saucer with 2 cookies and a glass of milk this morning. Or hear that old Ford truck's horn blow and Walker say 'come on boy, let's go to the store'. You be blessed this day for sure, you hear me???

Bluejeans from Sears-Roebuck

Man I woke up so excited this morning, just like it was Christmas time. I was 7 years old and we were living on Davis Creek in South Hominy. near Mt Pisgah where the Lord went to pray. I was so excited and it wasn't even daylight yet. I remember going out in the yard but not all the way to the outdoor outhouse cause it was in the woods; there wasn't enough light even though my dog was there too. I had heard all about the 'painters' in them woods—and my dad had seen a bear in the woods above our house.

Also I remember reading at those stories about 'Lil Red Riding Hood, and the Phantom. And there was a radio program called something like 'the inner sanctum'...spooky stuff. So I closed my windows most of the night during that time. But it was August the 3rd and school was starting next week, and today was the day. We were going to Sears in downtown Asheville. Sears was on the right going into town, back this side of Woolworth's and all those stores. It was magic. There was stuff there that I didn't know existed. Tricycles, tires, clothes, toys, paint and on and on. I know my eyes were big as saucers.

But today mama was going to buy me new school clothes. Two or three pairs of blue jeans and I don't remember the shirts except they buttoned. New socks and a pair of shoes dad bought at or through the Enka plant called brogans. These britches was dark blue and stiff but it was so much fun to dress up and feel 'special'. You just knew you was going to impress the girls and the boys would eye your new clothes with envy. Truth is, most everyone had on new stiff jeans and the girls were dresses to the hilt with bobby sox and new shoes and dresses. Some of the classmates you hadn't seen all summer. Some I had played baseball with or met at the creek.

What an exciting time. Get all dressed up and mom pack a lunch in a brown paper poke and off to school. Now children, if there was a marble game going on, you know what happened to the knees and toes of my jeans and brogans. It ain't no wonder mom sent me to the woods to cut switches so much. Man I wish I could go back to that sears store and feel that excitement again and see all them toys, especially that daisy red rider and that other gun that smoked when you shot it. Connie Davis got one and we fought over it and it was his gun. Oh well another switch.

You all remember the end of summer, sad that summer was ending and excited to see everybody again—in your new sears and roebuck clothes? Wasn't long though till you noticed some didn't have new stuff, just hand me downs or homemade. That always bothered me and took some shine off my happy Well it wasn't even plumb daylight and I was in the yard ready to go to Sears...and they didn't open till 10 And dad wouldn't let me wait in the '35 ford, so I fiddled around I reckon till finally we loaded up and were off to Sears and Roebuck...what a memory—

This is my dog (silver) Butch. The cat was Boots. The chickens were eventually Sunday dinner; and I got something besides the back when that dratted 'ole preacher didn't come for Sunday dinner. I never did like him. This was at Hollis Robertson's rental house across the creek at the foot of the mountain, just across the ridge from Con Davis's. I was Jack (alias: The Lone Ranger, or Lash Larue, or Johnny Mack Brown, or the Cisco Kid, Hopalong Cassidy maybe—but never Roy Rogers or Gene Autry—they sang to much for me. Old Butch would play those games until I wore him out, then he would crawl under the smokehouse and pretend he didn't know me. He was my pal. He followed me to the road one morning to catch the school bus and tragedy struck a little boys heart.

Laura knows what happened from her river of memories; but seems like I tried to carry him home, and there was blood and dirt all over. He was too big. I couldn't get him home. I have this memory of mom showing up (could of been Laura) and hugging me and I was bawling. You all know what bawling is; don't you? It's when your insides are shaking and you can't get a hold of it. Then the snubbing begins. You do know about snubbing don't you? Anyway dad buried my friend, and the playtimes were difficult for a spell. He's still around--In fact he just took a ride in my old canoe on the rivers of my good memories.

Some say if you have one good dog and one good friend you are and have been truly blessed. I've been blessed for sure. Con Davis's had a son named Connie Gene. He was one year younger than me, so I bossed him around. We played together a lot. He had two cocker spaniels that I despised, so I aggravated them. And the red one bit me. But honey child I carried two bean shooters most days and I was deadly with them things. I shot more rocks at them dogs but they still chased me. I think looking back that they enjoyed the game; same with his whiteface bull. The fence ran right beside the road and I would take a red rag and run up and down the fence yelling in my cowboy outfit and homemade wooden pistol-See it in the photo. That bull would paw the ground and come to the fence and walk up and down the fence--usually by that point I was moving on sonny.

I don't think I was 'mean' through and through, just a little mean streak. It was a quarter mile to the road and a few times I come across there at dusk—and walking beside that fence made the hair stand up on my neck, especially when the old bull was close and I could hear him paw the ground. 100-yard dash?? I set many records. I went back there awhile back and laid down in the hay field and looked up at the wide blue sky and wished the old bull or Butch was still around. The old wooden bridge made out of oak logs was where I spent many, many days with a pin hook and sapling and string and a can of worms in a prince albert can, was gone.

Replaced with a concrete bridge. I couldn't hardly look at that cold thing and I've been in the concrete business 50 years, seems like. The outhouse was almost gone and the smokehouse where we cured the hog or hogs, was gone and the well not used. But the house looked about the same out-side and memories flooded in and I just sat down in the woods there and laughed and cried some. Connie Gene got a toy rifle that puffed smoke when you shot it, so I took it away from him. I laughed at that memory because I had to make 3 trips to the woods before I came back with a switch worthy enough for the crime.

I guess I cried because I miss those long hazy days of summer, a good dog, a good friend to play with and fight with, sisters to aggravate and I guess just family, when things seemed simple and folk were kind. Life is fast isn't it? And we have accumulated all this stuff to take care of and its gotten even faster. Yes sir, winter is on the way in more ways than one. But, I reckon, I'll keep riding my old canoe on the rivers of my memories, until it freezes over. After all, I'm still dreaming —hope you are too-now you be blessed this day you hear me?

Decisions! Decisions! My bare feet hit the wood floor and I have major decisions to make. I won't wear shoes again but to church and such till school starts back, in August. It's summer time; around 1951, 52, 53. What to do first?? Maybe I'll go pin hook fishing from the old oak bridge, or maybe I'll go get Connie Gene and play Cowboys and Indians, or I could run through the woods riding saplings down and having great fun, or probably the creek needs damming up first, or I could go out and lay down in the tall hay field and look at the Carolina blue sky and dream of playing for the Yankees, or maybe go over to the Shooks house and trade for her funny books (I hardly ever had any new ones but she always did and never mentioned it was mostly a one way deal), then I could sit on the high front porch and read every page including the ads over and over, The Lone Ranger, Silver , his horse stories, Lash Larue, Jughead, Archie and Veronica, Superman, able to leap over tall buildings in a single bound—and Hopalong, Roy, Cisco and Pancho and on and on...

Which will I do first? Maybe go tease Con's bull again till I get scared. Uh oh, gotta do chores first. Cut some kindling out of the chestnut we got off the mountain behind the house, split some stove wood and fill the wood box. Feed the chickens and get any eggs, and at times do damage to the occasional black snake in the hen house; carry slop to the hog or hogs— now that was a chore, the hog pen was in the woods and to get the slop bucket there was work...I would get me a stick and scratch their backs and I believe they loved me–they would grunt and squeal, and I guess that was why It was sad when the 22 went off at hog killing time–but those tenderloins and bis- quits for dinner soon erased my anxiety.

Oh, Lordy, it's washday. Gotta pump the tubs and washer full. I'd pump with both hands and it was a chore...Then wash the clothesline-twice-not washing it one time got me a switching for the ages, so now I had to wash it twice. Crime does not pay–Then help carry and hang out and take in. Lordy I can hear the creek gurgling my name. I guarantee you it was a prettier sound than a phone or tablet or some game starting up...

Finally, we finish up or so I thought. Now got to go in the garden and pull weeds and be so careful not to step on anything... I can't remember my two sisters ever doing anything...but I know they swept, and cleaned and helped with the washing. They learned to sew and to cook. My Lordy they washed their hair and combed and brushed all the time...And they were always looking in the minors... Enough to make a little boy sick. And they even kept their shoes polished and shined up, and white socks rolled down-disgusting stuff, all that primping...Finally I'm flying down the hill to the creek and let the adventure begin. I've decided to shoot water snakes laying on those limbs with my bean shooter–I can't ever remember killing any but I knocked--scared a lot off those limbs....

I figure I'll stay down here as long as possible, I heard mom say to leave the tub on the porch. That meant her baby boy Jack was gonna have to wash his "rusty feet" sometime in the late evening. Mom would come to the back porch and yell 'Its supper time' or time to come in'...We would sit at the old wooden table and perhaps dad would talk about him and George Suttles getting behind an AC unit at the Enka plant and eating lunch; and having a prayer meeting right there. Mom might mention quitting with some neighbor ladies, and commenting the beans were almost ready to pick. Or she might need some more mason jars this year...my sisters might talk about boys and school. They said they couldn't wait for school to start back–how disgusting is that?–Especially at the dinner table–Then I might tell dad about the crayfish I caught or the hogsucker, or about the snake in the hen house.

It was family time–no phones, tablets, I-pads or TV.... We had each other and didn't realize how important that was. I rode around some last Saturday and began to notice and look for kids outside playing. You know how many I saw? One little girl on a bicycle. No baseball or basketball, no horseshoes, no tag, or hide and seek, no hopscotch–nothing. Technology has come a long way and we have seen tremendous things since the 40's. I'm just not sure its all that great for families....

Oh well, I can still dream. Think I'll stay in my old canoe on the rivers of my memories and go out on the porch and dream once more of throwing a 100 MPH fastball and playing for the Yankees with Mantle, Ford, Martin and the rest.... You be blessed this day and every day, you hear me?????

I've had 6 hospice patients over the last 5 years...all had lung cancer....only one had never smoked....my very first one was a multi millionaire and scared of dying... me and the chaplain tried to help him find peace.... all the money and prestige he would have given up gladly for peace with God—we can have both you know—the redtail hawk that died hung up in my fence brought back this sad reminder—some struggle for success and get hung up on that and never make peace with the Giver of peace—and die like the hawk—struggling—

The other five patients? Some had quit smoking for awhile ...two had struggled with it up till sickness came—but all were at ease and at peace with Him...It's the first one that I can't get off mind at times...I'm convinced death bed repentance is possible— but I am equally convinced that it is very rare—make peace now friends—and for family sake quit smoking and dipping....lung and mouth cancer is terrible

This here hernia business is taking its toll on old Jack. I'm so sore I can't even think above a whisper.... He said I may get home tomorrow or Sunday...I walked to and fro like an old man in the hall...Slow and easy.... I think this hospital stuff has gotten out of hand the last two years...I never thought I'd say that I can't wait to get 73.... Go from never been sick to 3 surgeries is outta hand, I'd say.. I'm afraid to cough...Oh well, don't get me wrong, I'm still blessed way over and above all that I can ask or think.... So I guess I better quit whining and man up...But if Mom was just here for a few minutes she could kiss it and make it all better...My sweet lady is so good to me... I am so thankful for the doctors and nurses, and I make double sure that they know that......

Every time I go up to South Hominy, a place where, if our Lord had visited He would have went up on Pisgah to pray. I always stop on Davis Creek and look over at the house we lived in beside Con Davis, and rented for 25 dollars a month from Hollis Robertson. The very best 25 dollars ever spent in my opinion. The mountain overshadowing the house and the hay field and the creek —what more could a boy want? And Connie Davis to play and fight with---

There is a popular tree on the right side of the house that brings back a twinge of sorrow even to this day, 60 something years later. I had made many bows and arrows from hickory saplings, carefully shaved and whittled and placed behind the cook stove, bent in a curve, to dry out. While they lasted for a while, they never made the long haul; and I'd be back in the woods hunting that perfect sapling.

Well we had little money for Christmas and the brown poke of goodies at church was one highlight of Christmas. But Mom and Dad bought me a real bow and arrow set. Three arrows that had a point and feathers not from a chickens butt. Of course it was just a small fiberglass bow made for youngans, but it was more than that. I would shoot it straight up and seemed like the arrows went a mile high. Well I stood the bow against the popular tree and proceeded to climb the tree, just because it was there and I could. I was a tree climber in good standing. Well I put my foot against the end of the bow, and when I jumped for the lower limb, I missed and my weight broke my bow.

So now you know the rest of the story. And perhaps understand why that old popular tree causes me to pause and reflect on doing such a dumb thing. Now I've did lots of dumb things and I have many 'twinges of regret and sorrow at times'. But one thing I do—In the quietness of my mind I can go up on Pisgah and meet the Lord there, and I always find rest and peace. I sometimes wish I could just go in the woods and not always be looking for that perfect bean shooter or hickory sapling to put behind Mama's cook stove.

While sitting here in Novia Scotia, Canada, looking out over His magnificent creation, the old canoe came floating down the rivers of my memory and of course I took a ride —my thoughts turned to Davis Creek that I waded in, spent hours damming up, fished for hog suckers and hornyheads in, skipped rocks on and sometimes just laid on the bridge and looked down into the clear cold water and dreamed- and dreamed-and dreamed—This ocean and beautiful scenery here in this picture?? Doesn't hold a candle to that creek and what pleasure it gave a little boy such a long time ago.---Lordy me

The 50's, Those Golden Years

I used to chase and catch rabbits when Walker mowed the hayfields. The rocks and stubble were no match for my bare feet. I have been so blessed to have known so many men and women who 'took a liking to me' and helped me on my way. I just wish I had asked more questions, especially my Dad and folk like Walker, who had their own story to tell. I can't tell you how good it was to get to go with him to the fields. And the RC's and moon pies??? You cant forget those-kinda like when we used to put peanuts in Cokes, and the girls played hop-scotch and we shot marbles and played Cowboys and Indians, and jacks and sticks....

Don't tell me those weren't the golden years—You helped each other and prayed and went to church together. We sat down and ate together—I really liked that except when that dratted Berry Watts came for Sunday dinner... He always got the prime pieces of chicken and I was usually stuck with the back and such. I guess I wasn't very religious on those Sundays.

After this heart business I find myself asking myself—what are you doing for others?? How can I make a difference in someone's life?? So that's my prayer these days–Lord let me help someone along this journey—A little honey for the journey—like I had.

If I look closely down the road a bit I can see a man and a boy on the porch of the old country store having a RC cola and a Moon Pie–Me, sitting on the edge of the porch Walker Hinson took a liking to me and I went with him to cut, rake and bale hay. We would always stop at the store for an RC cola and a Moon Pie–I see my stubble and gravel toughened bare feet dangling from the porch– I mostly chased rabbits and carried tools for Walker when the bright red New Holland baler acted up.

That old country stores front porch was and is a place of great enjoyment. Walker was good people and I will always be grateful that he helped a little boy along the way—a little honey for the journey—I rode the back of his huge whiteface bull and fed his calves and led his show bull to water in the evening.... I took this hill for granted then, but I soon realized how blessed I was to have Mt. Pisgah always in the background —What a wonderful place, this valley in the magnificent Smokies.... I've been blessed man; I wish I was barefooted with a RC and a Moon Pie.

Did anyone besides me read Burgesses Books on Old Mother West Wind- and Jimmy the Skunk, and Reddy the Fox and all those wonderful stones he wrote??? What about Jim Kjelgaards Big Red, Outlaw Red, Haunt Fox and so many more?? Lad- a dog? I think I read all they ever published many times along with Jack London —

The book mobile came to London's store on Saturday— I do not remember if it was every Saturday or not-but I would walk, bike, crawl or run to get there-Do you believe I can still catch that smell once in a while and it will remind me of that old yellow van type truck—they got to know what I liked and would try to have something for me-If they didn't I read some stuff over and over and tried all kinds—

Man I wouldn't take anything for those books-Did I

mention Walter Farley and the Black Stallion?? A whole series of those...I have ridden the Black Stallion many times—I
cannot remember who lived in the brown house beside Hollis Robinson, bur we traded comic books-she always had new
ones and I mostly just took hers back but she never let on
or seemed disappointed-I devoured those comics-I read every
word on every page-advertisements and all-remember selling
grits??? I couldn't give them away-Thank God for writer and
books and good words—we will talk about music later—there
has to be a book and a song-

I Am A Mountain Man

I am the whisper of the wind in the pines and oaks and dogwoods. I am the dear, cold water in the spring. I am the smoke of the Smokies; and the blue in the Blue Ridges. I am the rainbow of colors in the leaves. I am the butterfly on the rose. I am the red tail, soaring high and free over Pisgah; and I am the music of the Carolina wren...I am the logs in the old home-place.

I am the grandma sewing the flower sacks into beautiful quilts. I am the smell of the old tobacco barns. I am the ginseng hunter; and I am the silence and solitude of the mountain coves...I am the melody of the music; I am the shape notes in the Hymnal. I am the fog on the mountaintop that lies like a quilt over the valley. I am the sweet smell of honeysuckle; I am the yellow of the Carolina jasmine on the fence. I am the raindrops on the old barns tin roof; and I am the squirrel hunter with the single shot 22.

I am the gentle snowfall in the pines; I am the old, old man plowing with the mule. I am the corn shucks in the field, and I am the haystacks by the barn. I am the smoke from the chimney at the old log house in the holler. I am the wildflowers in the meadow; and I am the old woman as she hums amazing grace as she sweeps off her porch in Hominy Valley, I am in the fresh plowed field barefooted; I am the warmth behind the cook stove. I am the ghost of chestnut trees, long gone. I am the overalls on the clothesline, and the bleakness of winter. I am the warmth of summer; and I am the newness of spring, and the color of fall.

I am the lonesome bark of the coonhound. I am the peace in the valley, and I am the grief in death. I am the kiss of a grandchild, and the hug of a mom. I am the footprints of dad; and I am the church bell on Sunday morning. I am a mountain man. I am a believer. I am the result of love, tragedy, and sorrow; but I am a believer, and I am the South... And I am blessed because He is the real I AM—

Fishing and A Pinhook

I was around 8 years old and I remember going out to the chicken house with a Prince Albert can and digging red worms. Sometimes I dug up a wriggler-which was not good bait. The intense joy and anticipation of going fishing is a feeling I miss these days. I have a bass boat and I bass fish some but I really like to catch crappie. They are delicious fresh, and rolled, and fried ....I like to go when I can at certain times of the year more than others. Crappie lay their eggs in the spring and also move back into the shallows in the fall. I love to see those ultra light bobbers go under—either with jigs or minnows. It's fun. But I've lost something along the way somehow. The joy and excitement have abated. I find myself talking to myself with words like this—now watch your step, old man its wet and you might slip; or don't go jumping down out of the truck anymore; make sure the life jacket is out and put it on.

Somehow this careful stuff is depressing. I want to jump up there and I want to run over there and so what if I fall in; but that old enemy of mine—time—has taken a toll. These knees won't climb a ladder like they used to and the ankles hurt a bit when I jump down; and this old metal shoulder ain't what it used to be. My heart is strong, and my will is good, and I am strong and my mind works well at times—It's just this old body—It feels like a '50 Ford and not a 2014 Cadillac....I don't do well on low octane, though gas is no problem. And sometimes after a trip, and sometimes after a short ride I kinda have to roll out and get my bearings and legs headed in the right direction....

But you know; this is the emotion known to man. Late mortgage payments, car wont run, child is sick, parents need us, letters from school, doctors with bad news, doctors with good news, funerals and vacations mark our calendars permanently. Tragedies and Victories write their messages on our hearts and they are part of the reasons we cry at weddings and laugh at some things that aren't even very funny. I am glad to be here, and gray and tired at times. I don't intentionally try to be depressing but this is life isn't it?? The autumn years when we can say I'm sorry or I love you and really mean it—because most of us don't put on anymore—what's the use?

But I want to experience that wonderful anticipation and excitement like I did way back yonder. Bill West was coming and we were going to Enka Lake, brim fishing. I went around the house and smokehouse and outhouse and chicken house and found a couple wasp nests and knocked them down without getting stung—I want to run like that again—here he comes and really he is in love or something like that with Laura, my sister. And I probably begged and groveled to get him to take me, but he did. We sneaked out on the pier and caught brim and crappie until we got run off...Then we went to the other end and fished from the bank; seems like hours. Now that my friend, was worth the excitement. I wish I could hear that old '46 Ford coming again—shoot, I can—just closed my eyes and listened..Like I said I am grateful to be here-I don't deserve the Grace that has been shown to me. Just to work and paint some and listen to good music and see my kin folk and see a baby's little foot and dream about the hills, and have love in my life, and the truck still runs today and to still pour a little concrete and to catch a crappie should be enough for me, shouldn't it? It's not. It's not enough. It all is wonderful, but it ain't near enough. This right here is.

I reckon I'll just trust him to get me there—after all, He got me here, beat up and scarred by my side tracks, but He, not the babe in the manger, but the Lord who walked out of that tomb, took care of me. You be blessed this day—you hear? And take a child fishing so you can at least see that joy and antici-pation that has faded in some of us—Take them to Church first, then take them fishing——

I wrote this before heart bypass, but most of it really hits the nail on the head—I thought my heart was strong—then I was probably 2 minutes away from staying dead—no warning or chance to hug somebody or tell Gerri I love her —I don't think I'll pour any more concrete, I think I'm going fishing or to play golf...and I know I'm going to be more thank-ful....you be blessed and hug someone this day.

Well its nearing Christmas time, and I'm sure you know by now the real 7 wonders of this world. It's been on FB before lots of times. To see, to hear, to feel, to laugh, to touch, to taste, one extra one to me is to be able to talk and sing, but of course the greatest of these is love. Not just an emotion but also a feeling so wonderful, it's hard to really put in focus. It's sorta like when your insides swell up seems like and your throat gets full and tears are near and feelings are laid bare. Its a difficult thing to lose or have that one you love not return that love. Life can get mighty lonesome especially at Christmas season. But time and our Lord has a way of easing that broken feeling so we remember the good times and be-come thankful for what we had.

Life is very brief in a way and it can be wonderful and it can be cruel at times. We lose a lot of things as the years slip away. We can't run anymore, jogging was stupid cause our knees hurt now; we can't play basketball or soft pitch softball. Oh we can play some golf from the senior tees and have a ball. And some mornings that costs us when we have to take ibu-profen to ease the joint pain. Cry wrinkles down our cheeks, laugh wrinkles around our mouth, stress wrinkles around our forehead–all these wrinkles add up and we see somebody in the mirror who has went over the hill and don't remember climbing to the top.

Love Unmatched

But I tell you friends, Christmas has a way, with the music, and the old, old story of the new kid in town- (He's lying in a manger just down the road) helps us to put the joy of life and love in the right place. What amazed me about love is the fact that it was and is the same no matter the age. I fell in love so many times after I started grade school at Glady that I lost count. I just wish some of the girls woulda fell in love with me. I could really write some memories then.

There is so many kinds of love. I love the mountains. I love driving up South Hominy. I love all those interesting characters who I have met. I love small brooks running down the side of Pisgah and getting a drink or catching a lizard out of the ice-cold water. I love tobacco barns. I love warm spring rains. I love flowers and birds. I love volunteering. I'm certain each of us could go on and on about all the things that we love and take for granted...Maybe this Christmas we should just think bad (and realize how much love we have been given and how much we have given love to others.

The greatest gift was given at the stable a very long time ago. Love was put into action. Listen it's not about giving gifts and cooking and having family and friends over; or candlelight service at our church, or caroling and special enactments of the Birth of the Christ child. Listen it's really not about those things; but they are a by-product of receiving the Gift God gave so many years ago. Oh sure, lost folk who don't know Him have special times at Christmas. They laugh and they cry and they love. But I say there is a difference. Somehow there is a kindness, a deeper kind of love, a love that comes from a heart that only God Himself can give...

There is a feeling of; I guess security, when you know, that you know, where that place of rest and peace is. I love this season and I love the peace I have. I could not have survived with all the sad times without Him. So, I am, and I know you are thankful for the wonders of this life. Some will see their grandchildren and hear them and laugh and feel their love this season... All I say is this, love them hard and tell them about the old, old story.... They will remember it, and you, maybe for eternity—Merry Christmas

The Silence and Grief

I recall sitting on the back steps torn by grief. So sad it seems because of the things both done, and things not done. So, so sad because of the words spoken, and the words not spoken that should have been said out loud. It is difficult to lose a spouse, a partner, lover, and friend...But burying children is another kind of grief.

A friend, a real friend who had come in when everyone else was leaving came and stood on the bottom step and leaned back on the rating and said things like—It was Gods timing to take away, and he spoke of Hope beyond the grave, Of no illness or addictions, no blindness or pain, and of folks being 'free' in Heaven with God. He talked for awhile and I was unmoved. Except I wished he would go away. I knew he spoke the truth and I knew he loved me and was trying to give comfort and hope, but I was unmoved by any of it... I wished he would go away. Finally, finally we embraced and he went away.

I did not see where another friend from Weaverville came in a few minutes later and sat down beside me. He just sat beside me for about an hour. He listened when I said something, answered briefly when I asked a question. After an hour or so, he asked may I pray...Of course you can pray....He prayed simply and briefly, and he left...I was so comforted. I hated to see him go......

Later Than You Think

It's later than you think. Everything is farther away now, and there's a hill to climb now. I've quit running stairs and am taking the elevator. Steps are steeper than they used to be. Have you noticed the smaller print they use in the newspaper now? Nobody can read them anymore without glasses. No sense asking anyone to read aloud. Everyone talks in such a low voice I can hardly hear them.

People are changing, people look so much younger. On the other hand, people my age look much older than I. I ran into an old classmate the other day and she had aged so much she didn't remember me. I got to thinking about the poor girl this morning while combing my hair. I glanced in the mirror at my reflection, and confound it, they don't make mirrors like they used to either.

This chill in the air takes me back to another time this morning. Especially after traveling through the Smokies yesterday. The early morning fog rising off the creek and seeing folk with jackets on said winters coming. I can hear my dad say to me along about 6 pm, 'Jack go slop the hogs.' We had two on one particular winter morning. When we first got them they were so cute and I used to get over in the pen and play with them. But the bigger they got the less I did that, because I was told they would bite you and wouldn't let go. Kinda like the tale that a 'mud puppy, alias water dog wouldn't let go till it thundered. I'de see one of them in the creek and dodge it for sure.

Anyway, when pop said go slop the hogs, it meant picking up the bucket that had left overs, and what ever else had gotten accumulated for them to eat that day. And most folk poured warm dish water in the bucket. Sound good? The hogs loved the stuff. It was a real chore to lug that bucket across the yard and through the woods to the hog pen. They would be squealing and hungry. Sometimes I cut and pulled weeds and grass for them. And of course dad bought feed and corn for them.

It led to one thing; Bacon, ham, tenderloin, lard, livermush and such. On a cold frosty morning we would build a fire under a barrel and fill the barrel with water. We had running water. It ran after you pumped it up and into a bucket. Many trips later the barrel would be filled about 3/4 of the way up. Dad made a tri-pod with a chain hoist in the middle to lift the hogs. We borrowed a horse, I think from Con Davis, to drag the hog to the barrel. First, of course dad would take a 22 and shoot the first one between the eyes.

I remember watching that process and getting a little sick at my stomach. We dragged the hog to the fire and hoisted him up with a chain horse and dipped him into the barrel! We usually had to turn him and dip them twice. Then you scrapped the hair off. Smelly and hard work for a little boy. Then the process of raising the hog up off the ground and washing him off and then butchering it. You always took a piece of tenderloin to mom and usually the feet to cook for dinner. Despite the process that was the best dinner you ever ate. Hot bisquits and fresh tenderloin.

Well we and everyone else had a smoke house so the meat was taken into the smokehouse and put on tables. Dad would salt and salt the meat down for curing purposes, and then it was ready to hang up in burlap sacks (the feed came in them). Later in the winter dad would take a knife and go out and cut off whatever he wanted to eat. Lane Watts helped us two times I know for sure and of course you either helped them or shared the meat.

You may wonder why I choose to think about this bloody process. Well for one it was a way of surviving winters from the beginning of time. No gardens until way up towards summer so you had to can and can stuff, and the root cellars best be stuffed with potatoes, apples, sweet potatoes etc. Mom and Dad would process all of the hog. Everything.

We were blessed in that dad had a job at the Enka Plant so we had cash money. Lots of folk struggled through the winters. So it was a mountain way of life. I wouldn't take anything for those memories of family time, for feeding the hogs, the labor of helping contribute to the family. No wonder Dad always said grace at the table. You were thankful. We throw away more than we eat these days... I don't want to go kill no hog this morning, but when there is a chill and the first heavy frost hits the ground, I think about it.

I can see Dad, in his 40's, (I thought he was old then), Black hair combed back with his sleeves rolled up, with a knife in his bloody hands laughing at something Lane said. Now Chats worth something to me I wouldn't mind a tenderloin bisquit this morning, one without steroids and antibiotics, one from a 'slop' bucket and feed from the grist mill. You think that was an easy chore? You try dragging a bucket across your yard and up a little hill and through the woods to a couple of squealing hogs It might just make you glad when you see your dad get the 22 out. Wish I could ask dad what the joke was that Lane told that this morning—I shoulda listened and asked more question back in that other time, for sure....

Moving Time

Well when we moved to Woodfin and left South Hominy it was devastating at first for me. I was in the ninth grade and knew no one. But Eddie Bartlett lived next door and he quickly became a friend. My dad had some block to lay in our basement and through church he found someone to lay them. His name was Milton Price. He belonged to Lessie, and one son named Ted. Somehow or other Ted and I met and became friends. We had some terrific ballgames in the pasture across from his house. A lot of the fellows came and played ball with us, so I got to know a few more.... But Milton sorta took a liking to me and became someone that I admired and looked up to. He took both Ted and I to work in his concrete company. He taught us how to form and pour and finish concrete. Ted was more meticulous than me, and a better finisher though he was younger...But man it was fun going on those jobsites and producing something that you could be proud of—And I loved it. The first job Milton left me and Ted to finish was just above their house and we musta troweled that thing 10 times, and it was slick as glass.

Ted and I both loved music and we lifted some weights and we boxed some and had some fun growing up. Well, I went off to the service and when I came back I worked at Enka for about a year and hated it...So I looked

Milton up and went back to work with him. I was drinking too much and he didn't like that. Ted had gotten married and built him a house and I was envious. But man, could we pour and finish some concrete. Well anyway we eventually parted ways; and at some point Ted went to work for the railroad, and retired there. He was smarter than me. I finally got settled down and tried contracting around Asheville and about starved. But after an Easter Sunday morning meeting, I really settled down...especially when the Lord said 'son there's a better way'.

So I moved to Statesville and worked for the flour mill for a while and started pouring concrete on the side —I hauled forms out the window of a 70 Plymouth fury. Then I started contracting and have been at it every since until this heart failure mess...Racing was really getting going here and I poured concrete for about all the NASCAR drivers including Dale Sr., Buddy Baker, Wallace, and on and on—but one individual that really helped me through the years was Butch Stevens...probably one of the smartest men in auto racing, I worked for him off and on for 30 years He called me 'no crack Jack'...

I have loved this trade and have taught it to several others who are contracting themselves. But it all boils down to Milton Price—He helped me along and showed me things I never realized until I was older. Milton's been gone awhile but I still think about him now and then, and I smile. And Ted? He's around Asheville and he finally got on Facebook and that has brought a lot of memories back. Hay, Ted, lets call Eddie and Gene and Jeff and the Chandler boy and George and the Medford's and some of the others and lets go crawl through the barbed wire fence and play a little tackle...What you think??? I loved your mom, Lessie, and I loved your dad—

We had a good run for awhile—you be blessed, you hear me???

I'm in my old worn out canoe that leaks a bit this morning, floating down the rivers of my memories. Dang, I didn't expect this ride. It's taking me to some of the old outhouses I have visited. If I'da knowed this I would have used some of dad's Old Spice or Vitalis. Sometimes the smell is peculiar in these things. My first stop was at my grandfather's in Marshall. His was down the hill from the house and a kinda rickety looking out-house, but it had one of my main attractions. There was a Sears-Roebuck catalogue on the wooden shelf and inside that huge book was semi-soft paper that was suit-able somewhat to use for cleaning purposes. But over about halfway was the toys; beautiful red tricycles and wagons and guns and trucks and such. I would endure smell, flies, mosquitoes for long spells and drool over them toys.

My next stop is the outhouse in South Hominy. It was out in the woods, a fair distance from the house. I had no prob-lem going there in the daytime, but I never did make it all the way at nighttime. It was scary out in them woods. I got more switchings from running out in the night barefooted and run-ning back in with dirty feet and piling back up in the bed. Not for not making it all the way, but for messing up a perfectly clean bed. Mama had a thing about cleanliness and I attracted dirt...

I built two outhouses over in the woods where I used to live. I dug holes and they were usable, fully functional, and complete with Sears-Roebuck replicas. Built in wasper nests and some black widows. Now really how many folk do you know that ever got bit by a spider sitting in a relaxed pos-ition?? Yesterday the pool was full of kids and I saw boys and girls run over behind he bushes. Now that's natural, right there. And they don't even care that here is an outhouse in the house. My bride spent 15000 dollars on one bathroom. I'm afraid to use it. I tried to build a good one here but she wont let me. That bathroom is gorgeous, tile and cabinets and super soft paper—I'm afraid of it. Shoot for 15000 I could of built 10000 real bathrooms.

I am now floating in East Tennessee. One of my all time favorite people is my Uncle, Bud Chandley. He had on top of the hill above his house, an outhouse. I do not know for sure where he got it, because I don't remember it being here in my youth. Anyway we went up there just to visit and pretend we had to go. We like the old paths. Now what has floored me about this one is, it is a three seater. And it has vent pipes out the roof. And I ask you, who in the world is going to go into an occupied outhouse and pull their pants down or skirt up and sit down beside somebody else???? The holes are so close together you would probably touch. And what if you had gas?? Or the catalogue was empty? Or maybe extra offensive odor??? Who would do such a thing??? Why build a three seater?? Or a two seater??? Now I know girls don't have any problem sharing a bed to sleep. But boys??? Never. I take 20 men to play golf at Myrtle Beach and separate beds are the only option. The bed could be 40 feet wide and two men ain't gonna share it. And if they did try it and just almost touched, one would go sleep in his car. An outhouse??? Never.

Looks to me like a wanna be carpenter got carried away. Maybe advertise Bed and Breakfast with a Three Seater with built in Vents. No extra charge. As you can see by the pics Bud and I took turns just getting our picture made. And the vents, like the odor is going to run right out the vents and be pleasant and smell like Old Spice and Vitalis. Oh and by the way, if three of you were in there what would you talk about between grunts and moans? "Billy's doing good in, ugh, school." Or "Excuse me, we had corn for supper last, ohhh, last night." Or simply " pass me the catalogue, I wanna see, oops, that latest tricycle."

Well I gotta get out of this old canoe, It's getting deep in here. You all be good and where two or more are gathered together, somebody will probably stink things up...You all be blessed this day and every day, you hear me? And don't be so serious, lighten up, you know its the truth...Unusual ride today, hee hee.

Made in the USA
Las Vegas, NV
15 February 2022